BATTLEGROUND
IRAQ

JOURNAL OF A COMPANY COMMANDER

By Todd S. Brown

DEPARTMENT OF THE ARMY
WASHINGTON, D.C., 2008

Library of Congress Cataloging-in-Publication Data

Brown, Todd S. (Todd Sloan), 1974–
  Battleground Iraq : journal of a company commander / by Todd S. Brown.
     p. cm.
  Includes index.
  1. Brown, Todd S. (Todd Sloan), 1974– 2. Iraq War, 2003—Personal
narratives, American. 3. United States. Army. Infantry Division
(Mechanized), 4th. I. Title.
  DS79.76.B774 2007
  956.7044'342092—dc22
  [B]
                                                              2007018112

First Printed 2007—CMH Pub 70–107–1

For sale by the Superintendent of Documents, U.S. Government Printing Office
Internet: bookstore.gpo.gov Phone: toll free (866) 512-1800; DC area (202) 512-1800
Fax: (202) 512-2104 Mail: Stop IDCC, Washington, DC 20402-0001

ISBN 978-0-16-078706-5

... To the Soldiers of Bravo Company, 1-8 Infantry, and the Family and Friends Who Support Them

FOREWORD

The Army's 4th Infantry Division (Mechanized) spent a long and demanding year of successful combat operations in Iraq. As its commander, I daily witnessed the phenomenal courage, competence, compassion, and sacrifice of our soldiers. We experienced high points such as the capture of Saddam Hussein but also endured the rigors of extended operations against a dogged opponent in a complex and often hostile environment. Soldiers en route to such a theater should be not only properly trained and equipped but also psychologically prepared.

Capt. Robert ("Todd") Sloan Brown was among the best of our company commanders. He and the soldiers he led performed magnificently in some of the division's toughest and most critical operations. Indeed, some of the materials he wrote or briefed received wide currency within the division when preparing others to follow him into rough neighborhoods. I believe his journal can serve a similar purpose for those on their way to Iraq—or someplace like it. His narrative is not thoroughly analytical nor is it always fair; but it is gripping. It provides useful discussion of tactics, techniques, and procedures as they evolved in Iraq. It also touches on the conflict between combat operations and nation building. More important, it captures the stresses of combat and corresponding emotions as they accumulate over time in a combat outfit. Understanding these could prove invaluable to those who courageously serve our nation and will continue to endure them in the long war. However, this work should also be taken in context. The timeframe was 2003 to early 2004—tactics and the environment have changed over time.

The U.S. Army Center of Military History has provided helpful prefacing and contextual materials to sustain the perspective of the reader. Appendixes reproduce materials Captain Brown authored in Iraq to assist his comrades and provide insight into the command and control process at Brown's level. Taken together, this collection should prove constructive and useful to deploying soldiers and remarkable to those who appreciate what our soldiers do to protect our way of life.

Baghdad, Iraq
22 March 2007

Raymond T. Odierno
Lieutenant General, U.S. Army
Commander, Multinational Corps–Iraq

Maj. Todd Brown commanded an infantry company in the 4th Infantry Division (Mechanized) during Operation IRAQI FREEDOM and has served with the 1-508 Airborne Battalion Combat Team in Italy and 2-75 Rangers at Fort Lewis, Washington. Brown is a 1996 graduate of the U.S. Military Academy, where he served as First Captain—the highest ranking cadet. He is currently assigned as an associate professor at the U.S. Military Academy and has an MBA from Stanford University. He is married, an avid Ironman Triathlete, and an Eagle Scout.

PREFACE

This book originated in the small green notepads ubiquitous among U.S. Army soldiers. As time wore on in Iraq, computers and printers became more accessible and I transferred my thoughts onto an external jump drive. When I had printer access, I would print these thoughts as portions of letters to my wife and parents, in part answering the inevitable question: What are you doing now? I thought the more thorough the descriptions I sent home, the more robust the care packages of Cajun-flavor beef jerky, Gatorade, and Gold Bond powder I would receive. My father, ever the careful historian and on the Army Staff at the time, organized these letters and tied them to the headline news and the Pentagon's contemporary appreciation of events. My wife, mother, and Aunts Margy and Nancy sent me more than my body weight in beef jerky, Gatorade mix, and other delectables.

The idea of transferring these letters and thoughts into a book proved almost as daunting a task as fighting insurgents. I received a lot of encouragement to publish, but the one thing that always stuck with me was the idea that writing a book may help someone deploying to combat. It became my goal—in my own mind, my duty—to write an honest account of my experiences, thoughts, and feelings to help deploying combat leaders. As I reread this book with the luxury of hindsight, I am always amazed at some of the tactical mistakes we made. I often debated taking out sections of the book so as to not look foolish, "cherry," or "junior varsity." Each time, wise counsel reminded me that descriptions of evolutionary tactics are far more instructive than revisionist history … we learn so much more from our mistakes.

I learned an incredible amount tactically, emotionally, and psychologically during my time in Iraq. I consider the level of combat and danger I personally faced there as pretty standard for an infantryman in the Sunni Triangle. This book is not a collection of one hair-raising RPG ambush after the next, though they exist. Instead, it reflects the boredom, camaraderie, and moments of terror I experienced throughout my tour. It also discusses many of the leadership challenges, frustrations, and personal squabbles that affect units. I always strove to lead an organization that could rapidly adjust to the changing threat; hopefully, this book conveys the lessons we learned. The views expressed are my own and not those of the U.S. government, Department of Defense, or U.S. Army.

This book is the product of so many people's hard work and sacrifice that I feel guilty putting my name on the cover. The first person I have to thank is my wife Kris, who has sustained me through eight years of marriage and countless deployments. I can never thank her enough for her love, care, support, and understanding while both living and writing this book. Our Army asks so much of our loved ones—they are the true patriots. Special thanks to my mother and father: their love, leadership, and sacrifices are awe inspiring. They are my heroes. Thanks go to Oscar and Meyer, amiable Dachshunds who provided great late-night-writing companionship—although their grammatical contributions were dubious at best. Thanks go to the platoon sergeants and commanders I have had through the years; I carry invaluable leadership lessons from each of them. To the Byers, Faunce, Panchot, and Paliwoda families, thank you for raising and nurturing such wonderful sons; I am a better man for having known each of them.

Thanks go to the Center of Military History. Jeff Clarke pushed this project along and read the manuscript in the early days. In particular, I must thank Diane Donovan, my editor, who taught me that communication without expletives was in fact possible. I will miss seeing her e-mails in the mornings with their words of encouragement. Thanks also go to John Shortal, Richard Stewart, Keith Tidman, Beth MacKenzie, S. L. Dowdy, Michael R. Gill, Diane Arms, Dale Andrade, and Bill Epley for all their hard work in making this manuscript into a book.

West Point, New York   TODD S. BROWN
23 June 2007   Major, U.S. Army

CONTENTS

APPENDIXES

MAPS

ILLUSTRATIONS

Photos courtesy of Maj. Todd S. Brown. Other illustrations from Department of the Army files.

BATTLEGROUND
IRAQ

JOURNAL OF A COMPANY COMMANDER

INTRODUCTION

No two memories of war are ever the same. Soldiers serving side by side can give very different accounts of their battlefield experience. Eyewitness testimony must be understood for what it is, the opinion of an eyewitness. Such testimony does, however, remain one of the most important ingredients of the historian's craft. Only participants can communicate the emotional and physical feel of events that the official record chronicles. Due attention to the "little picture" can offset too grand a sweep in the big one. The confusion, points of friction, and general messiness of war are more apparent in history as remembered than in history as reconstructed. In unconventional warfare and operations other than war, so many of the meaningful measures of success are local that the little picture becomes even more important.

Historians at the Army's Center of Military History have been no stranger to the big picture of the campaign in Iraq as reconstructed day by day in the operations centers of the Army and Joint Staffs. Indeed, the Center ultimately inherits service responsibility for culling all of those briefings, information papers, interviews, memoranda, and the like as they pass from fiery currency into fading memory. The Army History Program also attempts to track the little picture, with Military History Detachments (MHDs) deployed well forward to collect interviews, documents, and artifacts as the action progresses. In perhaps a generation some capable historian in the Center's employ will fuse together all that has been gathered at every level with materials from other sources to write a definitive official history that will stand the test of time. Meanwhile, the Center of Military History will publish selected monographs, interviews, and accounts—many written by veterans of the events described—as interim products until the time for such a definitive official history has come. In sifting through potential candidates for publication, I was pleasantly surprised by a journal kept by Capt. Robert "Todd" Brown, then a Bradley company commander in the 4th Infantry Division (Mechanized).

There is a lot that Todd Brown's journal is not. It is not an official account, nor does it purport to be. It is not consistent. Todd experiments with his writing style—he was a civil engineering major at the U.S. Military Academy—and bounces around with respect to structure, organization, and delivery. He also bounces through mood swings reflecting good days and bad days. Reading a paragraph in isolation might cause one to believe the war was winnable or hopeless depending upon the exigencies of the moment rather than upon some overarching theory of campaign progression. Sometimes he speaks casually of breathtaking courage, and other times he seems almost whiny.

His mood swings are the most dramatic when it comes to the Iraqis. He can effervesce when he has had a pleasant experience with locals, such as the sheik in Balad who celebrated his birthday, fussed over his glacially improving Arabic, and offered him a daughter in marriage if only he would convert to Islam. He can evince dark hostility when grinding away through recurring insurgent ambuscades. Indeed, he personally created a bit of a flap in a number of newspapers when he made some not particularly flattering comments when enforcing a cordon after one of his sergeants was killed. We do not expect homicide detectives to rhapsodize about the virtues of human nature nor do we expect embattled company commanders to glad-hand the press. Brown's journal is not objective. It is a captain's eye view of the world from which one might surmise most units other than his own were half-stepping, those in branches and services other than infantry are hardly soldiers at all, and everyone above the rank of major is a geriatric case.

All the above having been said, Captain Brown's journal is worth publishing because it is the best continuous narrative that we have yet seen concerning what it was like to endure a year in Iraq. From a historiographical point of view, it may gain value because his experiences were wholly contained in the so-called Phase IV, after major combat operations were purported to have ceased. It amply features the frenzy of combat, the boredom of intermissions, the thrill of operations gone well, the frustration of operations gone awry, the little joys of personal affection, and the grief of personal loss. It provides a medium for explaining and depicting the everyday life and vocabulary of the contemporary soldier. Brads, TACs, T-rats, UMCPs, groundhog days, and the like come alive in his narrative. His story also provides the experiential underpinnings of papers Captain Brown has written that were widely circulated at the time amongst units in or going to Iraq, such as his accounts of fighting in Samarra and countermortar operations around Balad, both of which are included as appendixes. Altogether, this work represents the memories that one man accumulated during the course of one tough year. Hopefully, it will be of use to those about to deploy into similar circumstances and to historians who must make some sense of it all upon its conclusion.

JEFFREY J. CLARKE
Chief of Military History
23 March 2007

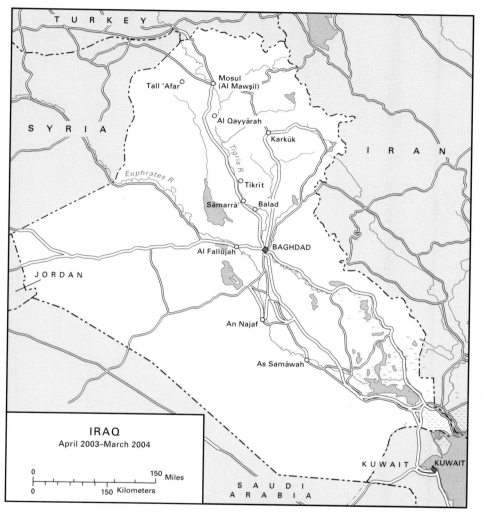

Map 1

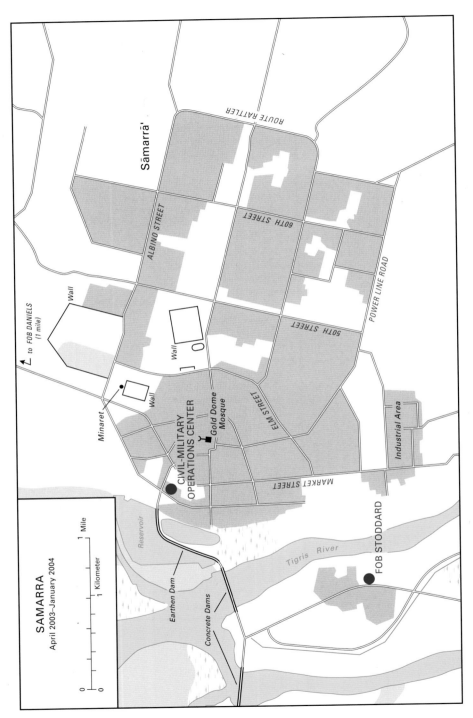

SAMARRA
April 2003–January 2004

0 — 1 Mile
0 — 1 Kilometer

Sāmarrā'

to FOB DANIELS
(1 mile)

ROUTE RATTLER

ALBINO STREET

60TH STREET

50TH STREET

POWER LINE ROAD

Wall

Wall

Wall

Minaret

CIVIL-MILITARY
OPERATIONS CENTER

Gold Dome
Mosque

ELM STREET

MARKET STREET

Industrial Area

Reservoir

Earthen Dam

Concrete Dams

Tigris River

FOB STODDARD

Map 2

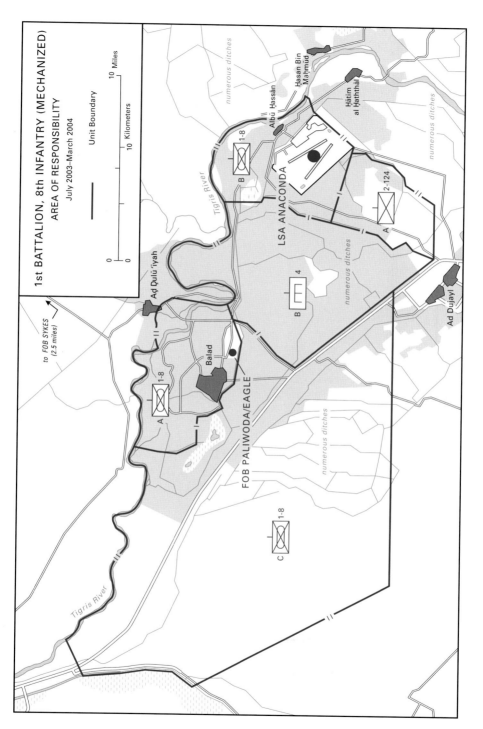

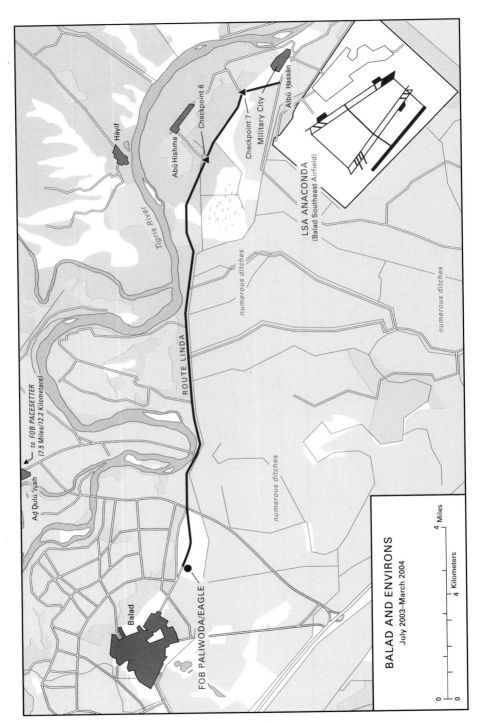

BALAD AND ENVIRONS
July 2003–March 2004

Balad

FOB PALIWODA/EAGLE

Ad Duluʻiyah

to FOB PACESETTER
(7.5 Miles/12.2 Kilometers)

Tigris River

ROUTE LINDA

Hāyif

Abū Hishma

Checkpoint 6

Checkpoint 7
Military City

Albū Hassān

LSA ANACONDA
(Balad Southeast Airfield)

numerous ditches

numerous ditches

numerous ditches

0   4 Miles

0   4 Kilometers

Map 4

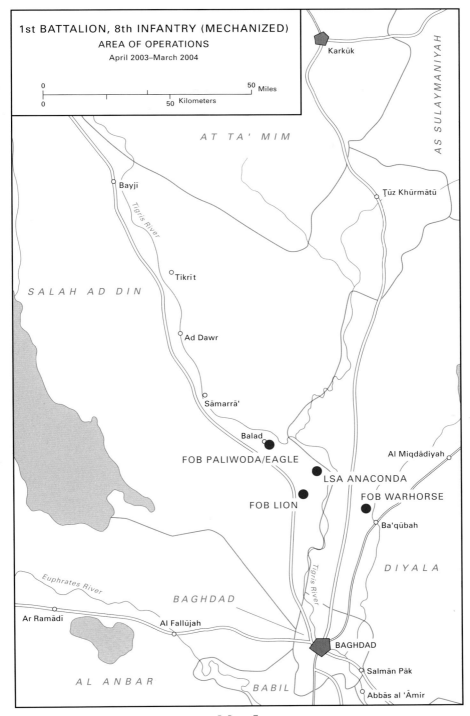

1st BATTALION, 8th INFANTRY (MECHANIZED)
AREA OF OPERATIONS
April 2003–March 2004

0 _____ 50 Miles
0 _____ 50 Kilometers

Karkūk

AS SULAYMANIYAH

AT TA' MIM

Bayjī

Ṭūz Khūrmātū

Tigris River

Tikrīt

SALAH AD DIN

Ad Dawr

Sāmarrā'

Balad

FOB PALIWODA/EAGLE

Al Miqdādiyah

LSA ANACONDA

FOB WARHORSE

FOB LION

Ba'qūbah

Tigris River

DIYALA

Euphrates River

BAGHDAD

Ar Ramādī

Al Fallūjah

BAGHDAD

Salmān Pāk

AL ANBAR

BABIL

Abbās al 'Āmir

Map 5

APRIL

April 2003 was the month of America's apparent triumph in Iraq. The mechanized blitzkrieg up the Tigris and Euphrates Valleys had come to an end with the fall of Baghdad, and the news media feasted on graphic imagery of Saddam Hussein's statue being pulled off its pedestal amid ebullient crowds. Embedded reporters carried the soldiers' experiences live into living rooms and offices around the world, and public support of embattled soldiers was never greater. The destruction of Saddam Hussein's supposed caches of hidden weapons of mass destruction (WMDs) seemed imminent, as did the rooting out of terrorist cells he was alleged to have hosted. Survey teams were on the ground in Iraq to pull together accounts and analyses of the great victory—and of the lessons to be learned from it.

For all the euphoria, the triumph had not quite achieved perfection. Outside Kurdistan, coalition soldiers were seldom greeted as liberators, and a highly visible frenzy of looting and lawlessness accompanied the collapse of the Ba'athist regime. Critics who had deplored the paucity of ground forces committed to the initial attacks returned to their theme of insufficiency: if we had won the war, could we keep the peace?

Capt. Robert ("Todd") Sloan Brown's journal begins as the 4th Infantry Division (Mechanized) to which he is assigned rushes forward from Kuwait to reinforce divisions already in the heart of Iraq. Initial operational plans had the 4th Infantry Division invading Iraq through Turkey; its equipment had been shipped from Fort Hood, Texas, and Fort Carson, Colorado, to stand off of Iskenderun and other southern Turkish ports. At the eleventh hour the Turkish parliament refused passage, and the division belatedly redeployed through Kuwait. Although it missed the dramatic march on Baghdad, it was on time for reflexive efforts to secure the country when law and order collapsed. Dozens of convoys rolled forward bearing the division's troops and equipment.

In the minds of Brown and his colleagues, the focus was on the residual regime elements, a view that corresponded with the generally accepted big picture that American forces were entering a mop-up phase. This mindset presumed that those resisting or defying American authority were diehard Ba'athists and that Iraqis intimidated by them would welcome the coalition after this residue had been swept away. A few hard knocks should be enough to collapse the local Ba'athist infrastructure, city by city and village by village. American soldiers were ready and willing to deliver these hard knocks. They also knew that some kind of national reconstruction and rehabilitation phase was to follow, and the best informed among them knew it was labeled Phase IV. None of Brown's peers knew how this was actually supposed to work, however. Prewar planning and the hasty efforts of recently appointed Lt. Gen. (Ret.) Jay Garner and his Office of Reconstruction and Humanitarian Assistance (ORHA) to bring order from the postwar chaos had not yet translated themselves into details that brigade staff officers understood.

At the time, Captain Brown was in the queue to assume company command but was still assigned to the 3d Brigade staff of the 4th Infantry Division as an assistant S–3 (operations officer). His specific responsibility was to serve as the officer in charge of the brigade Tactical Actions Center (TAC), a small contingent of tactical vehicles and communications equipment that allowed the brigade commander to position himself well forward on the battlefield and to sustain communications while moving quickly from one position to another. Brown had come to this assignment after two years as a platoon leader in an airborne battalion and two years as a platoon leader in a Ranger battalion, so he had appreciable light infantry experience that proved of use to the mechanized brigade staff as operations progressed.

---

21 April: Just crossed into Iraq … what a sh—hole! They are so poor here that the kids are running in front of the vehicles trying to get us to stop so they can hijack all our gear. It is a mugging, but they have nothing. I'm sitting in the back of the Bradley with the door open pulling security. It's hot. The people are cheerful and waving, but they are simply a suppressed nation. They are skinny with all smiles. Roads aren't too bad; the countryside is desolate, though. Houses are made out of mud, and it looks like they are desperately trying to farm.

This is my second convoy; the first time we broke down. These guys are slow as sh—. Luckily I got decent sleep last night on the bench seats. There are all kinds of tank-fighting positions abandoned. Looked like they had plans to defend well south but left the AO [area of operations]. They are dug in right off of the highway on the desert floor. Saw "el donkey" running from his herder. It was funny to watch.

The crazy aspect thus far is the unknown nature of this for the soldier. You don't know when the next hot meal is, the next shower, the next good night's rest … or the next rest for that matter. We don't know where we will be twenty-four hours from now or what mission we will have. We aren't suffering like in Ranger School, but we don't have a "next" phase, etc., to look forward to—physical training is out the window, but we are becoming better soldiers each day. A lot of the training and exposure I had as a platoon leader rings true here. PowerPoint and the planners are proving ineffective; not their fault—just the fast-paced and unknown nature of the next mission is not streamlined to their process. It's up to the operators, as I have always believed it to be. You can take a garrison [lock-step] style to the National Training Center [NTC] but not to Iraq. It just won't work.

Just pulled into CSC [Corps Support Command] CEDAR. It is a wreck. There are well over 1,000 vehicles waiting for fuel. D-Main [Division Main Headquarters] is in front of us clogging the line. There needs to be a prioritization of refueling. The problem right now is with the HETs [heavy equipment transporters]. They need to do everything possible to keep them rolling. Instead we have a giant [i.e., 3d Brigade] cluster. Someone please take charge of this place! The HET drivers are all flying American flags— despite the Frago [fragmentary order, a brief attack order] not to. I say good for them. They are the real workhorses of the war. The two guys driving the vehicle with thirty-seven flags on it are hilarious. Reservists called up from Florida and North Carolina: They wear cut off T-shirts and tell funny stories. I asked them what they did back in the world and they replied with a litany of different jobs: Taekwondo instructor, Miller Lite truck driver (paid in beer), shelves stocker, barber, tattoo parlor guy, etc. They were definitely "America." They had an American flag that everyone they took north had to sign. They actually had a lot of signatures. They had all the prerequisite interesting stories of their travels along the "Baghdad Express." Total patriots and representatives of what is good in America. The longer I am in the Army, the more I realize that we have it all backwards. Everything is logistics based … everything. The tactical-type stuff is all preordained by logistics; planners are faced with a fait accompli. Now if we would distribute our focus that way we would probably be much better off.

The wind and dust here are absolutely horrible. They are everywhere. My Mohawk haircut was awesome, but now it has given way to the buzz cut. So much of this deployment has been lying around in the back of the track sweating it out with the master gunner, "Jonny Fogle." Carlson, "the porn star," is just chilling up in the driver's hatch, not really all that fun. Your lips get so dried out, and your body just absorbs more and more dust. Eyepro is a necessity in this place. I really would like to write an eloquent description, but I don't know if I could capture the magnitude of vehicles, trash, crap, and the acrid smell of diesel. It is just a massive collection of the aforementioned products … mixed with omnipresent gritty dust. I so want to find a body of water and jump into it, wearing everything, for both the cooling effect and cleansing. Weapons maintenance is difficult here: my stuff is already filthy again. Hopefully, my smallpox heals rapidly, and I don't relapse into the whole-arm cellulitis incident—scary. It is tough staying clean. I think it has gone away, though. Can't believe McDermott took shrapnel at the airfield; hopefully he wasn't being stupid—the verdict is still out. Also can't believe that I did all the legwork for that first march unit and then my vehicle broke down; it was/is probably still painful for those guys as well. Maybe it was a blessing in disguise. Poor Major Dan, the colonel is probably hammering him.

22 April: Just got mobbed by a bunch of kids at 0600, after a full night in the back of the Bradley. They were trading Saddam dinars for dollars … that's a good sign since it wasn't for food. Staff Sergeant Fogle bought a Lawrence of Arabia head wrap. Last night blew—but not that bad—we are just moving so slowly. This company is about the slowest unit I've ever seen. They move forward about twenty kilometers and then sit for hours on end. I've been on a HET now for two days, counting our little rest halt at the ALOC [Administrative and Logistical Operations Center] for about four hours. I guess it is a mixed blessing because the TAC is probably pretty nutty right about now. All we do is lay in the back or chill in the turret. Well, I need to go clean my weapon. The weather and scenery are much nicer up north. Hopefully, it will continue to improve. Kinda funny, but we have no clue what is going on in the world, particularly in Iraq. I guess if you don't have CNN and the Internet you are isolated. I don't know if the war still holds the sensational journalism it once did, but we still feel it is a dangerous place to be. You don't want to get shot, but at the same time you don't want to be the cleanup crew. I guess you really just want to go home safely with all your friends.

Got off the HET—I think we set a record: fifty-five hours on the back of that truck. Waiting right now at a Military Police checkpoint to road-march through Baghdad. We already uploaded the TOWs [Tube-launched Optically tracked Wire-guided missiles] and everything else. The flies are driving me crazy. This checkpoint is a dive; everywhere we stop is a dump. We have zero trash-hauling capability so we just pitch it. Everyone is pretty motivated—even the dirtbags. I guess people shape up when it's for real. Excitement level is still pretty high, especially road-marching through Baghdad. Here come more kids. Feels so good to be out of Kuwait. This part of Iraq actually looks like Florida. Airing out my small smallpox scab right now. Hopefully, it heals soon.

Got the word to roll with that same company of M1s [Abrams main battle tanks] through Baghdad. Of course the vehicle right in front of us breaks down; unbeknown to us, he calls a Brad up to his side and guess what ... traffic jam. They ended up sending us forward alone for the first five miles. We were cruising down the highway with everyone zipping in and out. It was crazy; you just don't drive these vehicles on highways in America. We finally caught the convoy. I was starting to get a little nervous after seeing a burnt-out M1 under one of the underpasses. It looked like a pretty good firefight went down south of the airport. It certainly inspired me to always keep flak vest and Kevlar on. The people were all out giving the thumbs up and waving. They pretty much just wanted food. We ended up at Taji Airfield and saw lots of abandoned Iraqi equipment. I finally linked up with the rest of the TAC after that crazy truck-riding ordeal. We had a mission right away to seize Samarra Airfield East and then move to secure Ba'ath Party HQ in Samarra. Pretty fast paced. Fuel is going to be a huge issue. They are turning this ammo dump into another CSC, it looks like. Push north, push north. Saw a lot of tracer fire north last night. I think it was mostly friendly; we saw only a few green tracers. I saw lots of equipment, though. I pulled into the plans bunker—it looks pretty much like Auschwitz. They found tons of munitions here. I don't really dig this place too much. I hope we keep on moving—stagnation equals demotivation. I do need to run.

23 April: Rolling down the road right now to Samarra Airfield East. I'm in the back, watching the rear. [Col. Frederick] Rudesheim is up top. My feet are totally asleep due to the vibration of the track. Another tank just fell apart ... looks like we are waiting. No excitement at the airfield. We heard lots of reports of tanks and technical vehicles. Just a bunch of bunkers and burnt hulks. I got in and set up the TAC and then coordinated with the 571st Helicopter Medical Evacuation Company for coverage during the morning operation. We got the 1-12 IN [1st Battalion, 12th Infantry] brief for the takedown of the Ba'ath Party HQ—very liberal ROE [rules of engagement]. That is good. We roll at 0500.

24 April: Call to prayer is going on right now—it is really kinda freaky. Reminds you of *Blackhawk Down*. Very eerie feeling. Well, today was a bit crazy. Rolled out of Samarra Airfield East to Warriors [1-12 IN] attack position. Got out and pulled security for the colonel. I wish he wouldn't stand up on the back of the track. From there, we rolled on Ba'ath Party HQ. One of the Brads couldn't fit through the archway and just leveled the building ... crazy. Well, we got into the compound and dropped ramp. There were twenty guys stacked on Building 10, so I yelled for them to get into the building for cover. We then moved over to the police headquarters. [Lt. Col. Timothy] Parks threw me an AK–47 as the ramp dropped on our Bradley. I thought he was carrying a firing-port weapon. Kinda freaked me out since the scene that greeted me as the ramp dropped involved six EPWs [enemy prisoners of war] flex-cuffed in the water fountain, a guy with a broken ankle screaming next to my track, and a tossing of an AK–47 (not to mention two asleep club feet on my person) ... surreal feeling. We moved up to the police HQ and began interrogating the "police" guys; they had uniforms and a sticky that said "Police." I had them bring in the boss to talk to the colonel through our FIF [Free Iraqi Forces] translator; they were all standing around outside ... we need more MOUT [military operations on urban terrain] training.

We got established and then I went upstairs with Eric Koenig to set up the TACSAT [tactical satellite] since we couldn't get a shot on the bottom floor. I ended up demolishing a door to get out. It was pretty funny. I fell out the bottom of it as I was kicking it, and then ripped the top half all to shreds ... Comedy Central breaking down a plywood door. We found some .50-cal. ammo and a bunch of trenches to defend the police station. Pat Stobbe then had a Bradley knock down another wall, and we moved over to the Ba'ath Party headquarters building. We found a bunker full of 82-mm. mortars and shells for recoilless rifles. Everything looked old and rusted. About this time, an ex-general Samarii [General Wafik Samarii, former chief of Military Intelligence] showed up and told us the police were good and invited us to a meeting of the town's important people. We then released the police and set up shop in the police station.

A reporter from England showed up and tried to describe the whole situation— the blood feuds and tribal alliances. He basically said the "London General" Samarii was full of sh— and tied in with some bad dudes responsible for some ethnic cleansing of Kuwaiti women and children. I knew I smelled a rat. He also said Chemical Ali [General Ali Hassan al-Majid] was still alive running around to the north. I guess we'll find out soon enough. We decided to get these guys up to division for some clarification; I guess we'll be chasing "clues" for a long time. The reporter had a friend that he wanted us to talk to, so

I had just "battled" my way to the roof of the police headquarters so we could get better tactical satellite reception. Behind me at ground level is a cemetery.

Pat Stobbe's company, B/1-12 Infantry, in front of police headquarters. To the right behind a stone fence is the cemetery.

Lieutenant Colonel Parks sent me and Nick Fuller to go get this guy out of the crowd and search him. We found him and brought him in no problems—just a little crazy with the crowds, but they move away from you when you look serious. Heard his story for a little while and then went searching around the compound. Found a water-hose shower and got a razor shave. The people here are definite characters. Our FIF guy ran into his cousin; he was security for the ex-general director of intelligence. Had a good talk with Parks once things settled, then got on BFT [Blue Force Tracker] for the commander's update. We are continuing to hear small-arms fire throughout the city. Patrols will be taking off soon. Would be more nervous if it weren't for the Bradleys. The combo of infantry and Bradleys really works.

25 April: Got the word early this morning that we would grab the "general" and disarm the forty Peshmergas [Kurdish fighters] for processing as EPWs—turns out this guy must have been bad. I guess you don't serve as the Iraqi intelligence director and not have blood on your hands. Very thought provoking on the dealings with the Peshmerga guys—it has the potential to go south rapidly.

Started the day out in the Bradley commander's slot. Looks like the colonel has switched to the Humvee [High Mobility Multipurpose Wheeled Vehicle, or HMMWV]. We had the engineer battalion commander and field artillery battalion commander going with us. Gave the little convoy lineup brief, and they all just jumped in wherever and screwed the whole thing up ... figures. Anyway, we got rolling pretty good and then wham, all of a sudden we broke track. The thing came right off. Fogle worked it pretty good. While we were working, a soldier from A/1-12 IN [Company A, 1st Battalion, 12th Infantry] got shot in the arm. Initial reports were that it was a drive-by on a motorcycle.

The FIF translator, Koenig, and I (background middle) removed the skirt to give Fogle (foreground) access to the track.

We finally got back on the road. Once we got to the compound, we heard the plan for the Peshmerga operation, and I watched it go down from the roof. Our security in MOUT is pretty lax. After the operation, we set up shop in the police station—that place blows. The air quality and dirtiness are horrible. I really don't want to spend too much time in here; I don't want to catch some biblical disease. Small-arms fire continues. Will probably really heat up at nightfall.

The BRT [Brigade Reconnaissance Team] took some small-arms fire during one of their recons. It seems that people are getting braver. I got a good nude "hose" shower today—it felt awesome. The shower was filthy, but I got somewhat cleaner. This place is a pigsty. The whole country is not up to code. I went through the prison-cell area of the building. Scary to say the least. All kinds of ampoules of bromide and horrible living conditions. Makes you wonder how many people were tortured and killed here—if these walls could talk. Pulling my radio watch … all is quiet. I actually read for a little bit. Listened to the Victory Corps BUB [battle update briefing] via TACSAT. There are lots of random adventures going on. I think that 1-12 IN is going to move out of here to the pharmaceutical plant up the street. Should be better—it certainly is bigger. The Civil Affairs teams are going to the hospital tomorrow. They went to the radio station and found it inoperable but manned. This place is shady.

We are supposed to launch on a "chicken farm" outside Ad Dawr twenty-four hours from now. This is supposedly something pretty important—a two-battalion operation. Tanks isolate, and infantry clears. There is a building offset and guarded with triple-strand wire. I wonder what was there. They say no one has been there—looters or military. I guess 1-10 CAV [1st Battalion, 10th Cavalry] found a missile-storage facility. They are trying to figure out the chemical status of the weapons. Wonder what is the status of General Samarii. Hopefully, he is a real bad dude and that way I can say I was the first to search him. He seemed a real Slick Willy. I talked with our interpreter, Sergeant Ali, this afternoon. He was pretty upset about the Peshmerga deal. I guess we all have our orders. Hopefully, they all get to go home. The longer we sit here, the braver the populace becomes. We have gotten some good information but no real actionable leads. Hopefully, we will find Chemical Ali. Well, I'm almost off shift; this blows—I'm tired.

A good way to find weapons is the floating checkpoint. Roll around the city, set up for an hour, and move on. Don't establish anything permanent. Hop and pop. Had a soldier killed in a vehicular accident; we have got to watch the driving. Apparently they were in pursuit of some technical vehicles. MPs just showed up with the forty Peshmergas that they took to Baghdad … not good. We disarmed them and now wish to release them back into an Arab town weaponless. They are requesting transportation to Irbil. We need to get them north fast before they get pissed at us. Their boss just went to look for a car. I hope "car" does not equal RPG [rocket-propelled grenade]. The XO doesn't want to help these guys out—big mistake. They are our allies and have fully cooperated with what we have asked of them. We need to fix this. They sent me out there to talk to them, like I speak Kurdish. I basically punted on it and said I was working on the issue.

26 April: Well, the XO showed up and the Peshmergas left. They went back to the government building. The XO then decided to run over to the house alone in the middle of some town meeting—great idea. He then got two Peshmergas to go with us on a recon of the pharmaceutical plant. He wanted them to drive home in five dump trucks … yeah right. They obviously didn't like the idea, so back to square one. I checked out the SDI building [pharmaceutical plant] to set up the TAC—pretty nice. I went through the building: running water, AC, rugs, and a bunch of drugs. Need to keep the soldiers away from there. Of course, we aren't staying here tonight; we are moving north to the chicken farm. It's a pretty large objective—two battalions. Drug company is pretty nice; we should set up here for awhile—good comms and good facilities.

I found a bunch of blood in the second floor bathroom and the packaging from a GI bandage. Turns out it was Jones' blood, the XO's driver. Got hurt during the XO's "mission." Well, the story improves. He decides to go downtown with the JAG [Judge Advocate General] vehicle and no escort, just injured Jones, T.K., Vivian, and Donaldson. Well, we knew this was a bad area with lots of arms deals going on; so he gets stuck down there and wants to organize some huge rescue operation. Huge expenditure of staff energy to get these guys back. He throws down wire and starts signaling with yellow smoke, talking about being cavalry and maintaining contact with the enemy. Lieutenant Colonel Parks gets on the radio and tells him, "Striker 5, leave. Get in your car and drive." Of course, he won't. T.K. wanted to kill him since it was five Americans versus 200 weapons-dealing Iraqis. He finally left. They sent down a patrol and found nothing.

Finally got back to the SDI building, and some soldiers proceeded to pillage it. Connely decided he should take some drugs for later use—turns out they were anti-epilepsy pills. Major Martinez ordered him searched and his weapon secured—good idea. Well, the drug lab didn't last much longer. We moved out to the walled city of Samarra, a 3,000-year-old ruins. We go to pull into the city and whacked the Bradley on the wall, ripping our bags off. How ironic. The wall stands for 3,000 years and we whack it with a Brad. No damage to the wall, just Eric's rucksack. Anyway, we found a bombed scud inside the AO. We couldn't get comms, so we moved back to the pharmaceutical plant and re-set up. We got back to the plant, got the brief for the operation, and racked out.

27 April: We LDed [left the line of departure] for the chicken farm at 0200 Zulu [Greenwich Mean Time]. We had some initial contact. Tough to figure out what is going on in the back of a Bradley. TF [Task Force] 20 was supposed to do a takedown in the vicinity of our objective last night. Don't know how it went, but everyone on brigade staff was boo-boo lipped that TF 20 wouldn't talk to them about it. The BRT reported a guy being taken out with a bag over his head. Now everyone thinks it wasn't TF 20 but an American prisoner of war. That kinda makes you wonder. Well, the chicken farm operation went off and it was just that, a farm for chickens. 1-68 AR [1st Battalion, 68th Armor] scouts shot and killed a fourteen-year-old boy—sad scene. They fired warning shots at the bus, but it sped up. They just didn't know; they were scared. No weapons were found, and they engaged them from about 500 meters. I guess it is covered by the ROE, but they jumped the gun, in my opinion. I guess you just never can tell. Well, we are sitting at the "hospital." It is camouflaged and has a MIG flight simulator and lots of munitions. The colonel just returned. I guess we'll set up here for the night.

The BRT got launched south to grab Blacklist #47. (This was the forty-seventh name in the infamous deck of cards—the three of hearts, I think.) No real guidance. A soldier in the BRT apparently tried to commit suicide—shot himself in the abdomen. What a nightmare. Spent a lot of time on the radio net trying to get the medevac [medical evacuation helicopter]—painful process. I was calling the 9 Line [standard medical evacuation request] on the radio all the way until the bird landed and couldn't get any confirmation from the pilots. Thank God they got the message the first time. We did pretty good other than the commo difficulties. I was pretty nervous about it—being someone's life and all. We need to work that piece hard since the BSA

[Brigade Support Area] and standard procedures aren't applicable right now due to huge distances. It turned out fine, but it was a nut roll.

The TOC [Tactical Operations Center] rolled in. Good to see some of those guys, but it sucks being collocated with them; they are a pain in the ass to say the least. The XO comes through the place casing the joint for the best stuff and nicest places to sleep. Unreal. We are all sleeping outside; it's much more comfortable. Well, time to rack out. What a day.

28 April: Slept in late this morning and really haven't gotten going again. I had a good talk with T.K. about the Army and life in general. He is a really good dude. After that I went and made some maps and the order for the Tikrit Airfield East operation. The 1-68 AR is the main effort, and I'm riding shotgun in the S–3's Humvee. I think we are getting used to running these kinds of operations. It actually got cold here last night. They said we were going to get T-rats [tray rations, precooked meals served hot] tomorrow. We will probably have jumped by then and miss the meal. We have run these vehicles hard. I had the guys do a little maintenance, but it is going to get harder and harder the farther north we go. We had a "riot" at the gate today—400–600 pax [people, derived from "passengers"]—no big deal. Also had a trailer catch fire. By the time reporting was complete, it seemed like the battle of Mogadishu. Well, it's about time to roll. They are having a pro-Saddam rally down at the traffic circle in Samarra. It sounds like it is total chaos.

The armor airfield seizure went fine. No issues. They caught some guy who said he knew where the mortar fire was coming from. The 1-68 AR is now working on it. Never thought I'd see the day that an armor battalion takes down an airfield, and I was riding on a Bradley. I got the S–3's Humvee stuck running around the airfield. We towed it out with the Bradley. It is starting to get dark now, so we need to get back to the factory to sleep. No telling what will go on tomorrow … Happy Birthday, Saddam!

29 April: Oh sh—, sitting in an abandoned hotel in Samarra planning this Delta Force–type mission. I didn't really want this, but Lieutenant Colonel Parks asked for me. I got back from the airfield at 1730Z, and we left at 1800Z. We are working through all the contingencies right now. We got a BRT platoon going in with a backup platoon of Brads. Parks will be the command and control, with a group of what they are calling the shooters if things go south (Nick Fuller, Pat Stobbe, Chad Christman, Sergeant Major

Bond, Staff Sergeant Brown, and me). We are in three Humvees. BRT will be going in while we isolate and reinforce, if necessary, on a star cluster [a star-cluster pyrotechnic will be the signal to execute]. The composition of senior guys is pretty crazy. It wouldn't be so nerve-racking if it wasn't for the ad hoc nature of this event. All the guys are super competent; we just haven't worked together—ever.

The mission dynamic changed several times as the target building floated around the city. We finally got the recon done (Bill and Nick in the informant's car) and then we went to the [former] Iraqi terrorist-training camp for final precombat inspections and vehicle loads. I ended up riding with 1-12 IN in a scout Humvee with all the reinforcing shooters. The mission went well, and the BRT sped by with the target back to the camp. We offloaded him there and unsandbagged his head, and he started chanting, "Death to America! Saddam! Saddam!" Needless to say, he was our guy and got placed into the EPW vehicle rapidly. The other two guys were freaked out, and one passed out. Don't know what we did with them as we were next in the order of movement, so we sped off back to the TAA [Tactical Assembly Area]. Good call by Lieutenant Colonel Parks to take only one target building and to roll the Brads—seeing as how we didn't have any aircraft support. I would have recommended the same, seeing the ad hoc nature of the operation. Glad it went so well, but it was nerve-racking and adrenaline-pumping to say the least. It seemed like a great Ranger company mission. Too bad we didn't have one of them.

30 April: Slept in late today. There is nothing going on after the late night last night … 0400. Just sat around all day BSing. They had a little church service, and I went to that. The big issue today was the mail. Turns out we have three trailers of it in the rear with the S–1 [personnel officer]/S–4 [supply officer]. I truly wonder what they are doing back in Kuwait, seeing that we left weeks ago. Different lives. We are just wasting people back there. It gets cold here at night, so I am pretty happy about that.

Well, Victory 6 [the V Corps commander, Lt. Gen. William S. Wallace] came to a meeting yesterday. He said we would be here for a year or until the job is done. Sad face for everyone after that meeting. Morale kinda sunk. It's been pretty boring since we got back from the raid last night. We actually haven't moved from this compound. That makes things go much slower. We still haven't gotten the water turned back on. We are dirty and getting dirtier. They say we are on a two-liter water bottle ration. No water for personal hygiene, so we are going to get filthy if we don't get this fixed. Everyone is working but not really accomplishing anything—just sustaining. Now the CG is coming for a visit, so we are going to spend an inordinate amount of time preparing a briefing and sitting in a briefing. I have to go fix the colonel's map, but he took off somewhere with it. I sat in a meeting with the XO last night. He briefed us that we came to this country to take risks. We have RBA [Ranger body armor] (without plates) and ammunition and must go after the bad guys whenever we see them, regardless of the security we possess. Well, everyone pretty much ignored him; he thinks he can just go all around the country in a soft-skin Humvee. He is hazardous to everyone around him. It's one thing to risk your own life, completely different to risk the lives of others—especially your eighteen-year-old driver's. I just don't see eye to eye with that guy at all. Well, it looks like we are going to have company changes of command in May.

MAY

On 1 May 2003, the United States officially declared an end to major combat operations in Iraq. President George W. Bush's dramatic announcement to this effect on the deck of the aircraft carrier USS Abraham Lincoln—after landing in an S–3 Viking—underscored the transition from Phase III (decisive combat operations) to Phase IV (postcombat operations). Emphasis would shift to stabilizing and reconstructing Iraq, if it had not already.

Phase IV altered the geographic scope of operations. To this point, combat power had been fairly concentrated to deal with a similarly concentrated adversary, and civil-military affairs progressed in the relatively modest areas in the wake of the advancing forces. On 9 May the United States and Great Britain presented the United Nations with a draft plan for postwar Iraq that gave them control of its oil revenues and acknowledged their responsibility as occupying powers. This obligated them to fan out quickly to secure and service the entire country, disarm residual resistance, and initiate a return to local governance.

No one had more ground to cover than the 4th Infantry Division (Mechanized) as the transition to Phase IV progressed. Original planning had apportioned it postcombat responsibilities for a broad swath of northern Iraq, and this assignment remained even though the division had entered the country from the south. In Captain Brown's narrative we find the itinerant companies and platoons of his brigade operating ever deeper into Iraq and ever farther from each other. We also find them heavily involved in the disarmament and the destruction of munitions caches large and small, the total volume of which was astonishing. Wags say that before the war Iraq was an ammunition dump with a government and after it was an ammunition dump without a government. At least one of the disarmament efforts involving the 4th Infantry Division proved dramatic and externally visible. The Mujahedin-e Khalq (MEK) was an exiled, anticlerical Iranian organization that had operated against Tehran out of Baghdad with the blessing of Saddam Hussein and had also cooperated with him against the Patriotic Union of Kurdistan (PUK), now an American ally. Disarming this formidable organization required posturing overwhelming force in difficult terrain while reassuring the MEK that they would not be turned over to the Kurds or their own countrymen for massacre. In the end the MEK was neatly handled and complied with requirements without the term surrender being used.

During this month Captain Brown's brigade got some exposure to the profound ethnic tensions bedeviling Iraq, but the soldiers' dealings with the locals seem to have been friendly—or at least manageable. In part this was because of the northern, largely Kurdish, area of operations to which the unit was initially assigned during Phase IV. The men had already had a taste of Sunni hostility in the towns immediately north of Baghdad to which they would soon return. Well to their south, the Shia, long the victims of Saddam Hussein's brutal repression, were evolving their own internal leadership in the newly permissive climate. Supreme Council of the Islamic Revolution in Iraq (SCIRI) leader Ayatollah Mohammed Baqir al-Hakim returned from years of exile in Iran to promote the cause of Shia unity. The revered Ayatollah Ali al-Sistani called for a meeting of Shia clerics in Najaf for the same purpose. Key players include al-Sistani, al-Hakim, Baghdad-based Dawa Party leader Abu Malik, and Muqtada al-Sadr, the fiery young son of an ayatollah martyred by Saddam Hussein. As Captain Brown's men sorted out issues in northeastern Iraq, the future implications of Sunni unrest and Shia empowerment were not particularly clear to them.

Another major issue only marginally visible to Captain Brown's brigade was the search for weapons of mass destruction and the associated political furor. He and his colleagues had a few scares with respect to chemical munitions but no actual finds. They would have had to have been watching television regularly, which they were not, to appreciate the media interest in this issue. By 30 May both Secretary of State Colin Powell and British Prime Minister Tony Blair felt pressured enough by allegations to deny that they had distorted or exaggerated prewar intelligence concerning WMDs.

The high-level decisions that arguably would most affect the duration of Captain Brown's duty in Iraq are not visible in his narrative but were announced to the Iraqi people during 13–15 May. General Garner, head of the Office of Reconstruction and Humanitarian Assistance, had planned a "gentle de-Ba'athification" of Iraq. Borrowing from precedents of denazification in Germany and recognizing that many Ba'athists with key administrative skills had become party members merely to secure employment without becoming involved in war crimes, Garner proposed to skim off the top layer of the party and put the rest back to work. He also agreed with existing military plans to coopt selected units of the Iraqi Army for security, vetting their leadership over time to deal with war criminals and other undesirables. He envisioned expenditures of up to $1.6 billion in monies seized from Saddam Hussein to employ up to 300,000 soldiers and a not-yet-determined number of civil servants. Twenty of twenty-two ministries (excepting Intelligence and Propaganda) were to reopen with about the same staff as before.

Several major contingencies that had consumed the lion's share of Garner's planning time were already overcome by events. The oilfields had been secured with minimal destruction or sabotage; fighting had been precise enough to avoid major refugee movements; food was adequately available; there were no casualties from weapons of mass destruction; and prospective epidemics had been avoided. With these worst-case scenarios out of the way, ORHA planners scrambled to deal with the crises actually developing on a lower tier of severity. Garner had the counsel of Iraqi advisers to put an Iraqi face on the reconstruction, had conducted at least one major meeting with countrywide representation, and bore witness to numerous local elections in cities and villages under coalition control.

For reasons beyond the scope of the book, Jay Garner's ORHA was abruptly superseded by Ambassador L. Paul Bremer's Coalition Provisional Authority. The CPA would make no deals with the devil. Rather than the gentle de-Ba'athification ORHA had recommended, Bremer directed the dismissal of all Ba'athists down through the sixth level of the Ba'athist hierarchy. Rather than co-opting the Iraqi Army units that existed, Bremer disbanded the entire Iraqi Army at once, intending to build a new one from scratch. Bremer similarly dismissed Garner's council of Iraqi advisers, preferring to develop one of his own, and served notice that all governments elected locally remained subject to the review of the CPA for validation. It is too early to tell whether this attempt at a radical top-to-bottom reconstruction of the Iraqi social order will achieve its intended purposes. The immediate result was to alienate perhaps a half-dozen key political figures, an estimated 30,000–50,000 Ba'athists, and perhaps 300,000 Iraqi soldiers. Captain Brown and his colleagues would cross paths with too many of these people in due course.

---

1 May: CSM Johnson told us last night that we could do PT, so I went for my first run in a long time. Running around the compound, I thought I had asthma. I was sucking. Yesterday was pretty boring. Just BSed, took a shower, and read some of *Gulliver's Travels*. We are set here right now for an indefinite amount of time. If the Iraqis did not have that Saddam rally, we would have moved out of the AO. Our enemy is cunning but not smart. He needs to just lay low until we move on and then resurface—follow the principles of guerrilla warfare. Again, he is cunning but not smart.

There were lots of explosions yesterday. We blew all kinds of caches. They still have the ever-elusive mortar team running around dropping rounds— but totally ineffective. The Apaches [helicopters] went up last night and destroyed something in our AO. The colonel was pissed that no one went up to look for BDA [battle damage assessment]. They wrote an article about our operation the other night. It was pretty funny. The *Newsweek* reporter with 1-8 IN wrote a pretty disparaging article about the men getting to the war late and creating their own action. I guess he wasn't briefed on the small fraction of people that actually see ground combat in any war. Needless to say, he wouldn't go with us on the downtown raid in Samarra. I guess everyone has a personal agenda, but reporters shouldn't bash soldiers' contributions to their country to get a story. I think people will be fighting and dying here for awhile yet to come, whether it is sensational or just plain ugly. It's May Day.

2 May: Well, morale is a sine curve around here. We are still in the same place, so I am below the mean. Found out that my change of command [COC] might not happen until October. This staff stuff is for the birds. I am not using the skills that I want to use, and it's driving me crazy. The TOC was a million degrees today—all those computers running and people zinging around; actually, it is only about four people doing all the work and getting beat up by the XO. I guess Matt wanted to quit today after the XO stopped his doing the BDA from an AH–64 [Apache helicopter] strike. Basically, the XO told them not to send 1-68 AR out to assess the damage but didn't tell the colonel. Well, in the morning the colonel comes in with quite a mood and staples Matt's lips to the desk for not sending those guys to assess the damage, and the XO didn't back him up. Go team!

Much of the rest of the day I spent reading *Gulliver* and doing a little PT. I had the TAC organize some classes for the morning to try to keep them out of trouble. I guess they were playing cards today. The S–3 told me to figure out something for them to do, but no one had anything for us to do. Now I will have to start being creative. The command thing hurt me today. It is taking so long. Oh well. Time keeps on marching. Supposedly we are getting mail tomorrow. You always hear about how soldiers look forward to mail in wartime—now I know why. It breaks the monotony.

Got another run in this morning—it felt better. We did a little weight training last night before dinner. It makes you feel a little better especially if you can then take a shower. I got to call home this morning. Everything is going good on the home front, and everyone is there. It would have been nice to be there for the graduation [of Kris, his wife, from dental hygiene school in Pueblo, Colorado]. I am sure they are having fun. The satellite phone works pretty good, but you have to limit your calls. Talking to home makes the time go by slower, but it's nice to hear how everyone is doing. The groundhog-day effect [a reference to the motion picture *Groundhog Day*, wherein the protagonist keeps reliving the same day] here really brings you down. Major Wright told me that I would change out command next week. I don't believe that; he's always screwing with us. It is all a conspiracy to keep you hopeful, so that hope does not become forlorn ... sine curve. Had hot chow last night—T-rat rice and beans with corn. Wowsers! Apparently it was such a success that they are going to serve the same thing again tomorrow night. That with our water ration—two liters per day—should really help our cause. Looking out the tent at the EPW cage ... that sucks. Both being in there and having to guard them in the hot sun. I wonder when we will start moving again. The TOC is crushing dudes. HQ63, the S–3's Brad, had my old mountain bike mounted on the front. The Bradley broke down, so they sent it to 64th FSB [Forward Support Battalion] for repairs. Well, Dena saw the bike on the front and stole it. What an Indian giver. One year ago today, I flew home from the Middle East. I was much happier last year at this time.

3 May: Got another shower last night and lived the camp life of eating T-rats on the Humvee while hanging out talking. It has definitely devolved into groundhog day. Saw the tentative command slate and it has me going in June. That would be great. Ran into Lieutenant Colonel Battaglia today and he was all ready for me to come down. Told me to get my stuff and throw it in his Humvee. I told him to go see the colonel and I would leave with him. We had a .50-cal. and a Blue Force Tracker class yesterday to keep the guys busy. The .50-cal. is tough for them to handle. I think we could develop a better weapon system of that caliber, but it works so well once it starts firing. Did a Combat Life Saver [CLS] class this morning—funny, I still hate needles even after seeing them so often. I had Private First Class Titus attempt the IV; but he missed, so we stuck him. Funny—he started squalling like a pig. He had never had one before. We were all cracking up.

I saw a briefing from division that showed us leaving Iraq in October. That made morale increase. Unfortunately, that will probably change about a million times. The TOC guys are still spinning even though nothing is going on. We are going to have massive turnovers here soon. I am curious to see how the change of command inventories go down. Hopefully, we'll just sign for major end items. Supposedly we are jumping to Jalula in the next twenty-four to forty-eight hours. That's good, but the movement will take forever. Looks like 100 kilometers on the map.

Finished *Gulliver's Travels* last night. Great book. I loved Swift's satire. The storyline itself proved entertaining enough without the added benefit of the parallel historical satire. So much of war is filling in the gaps between intense excitement. Started Voltaire's *Candide* this morning. Seems pretty good. Got another run in, but I woke late so it was hot. I sweated a lot and then found out that the shower water was off. Did the trickle shower. Our living conditions here are starting to deteriorate. They built wooden outhouses for us, but they immediately filled with product and flies. We need to move out of here soon or people will start getting sick. The stench from the burn barrels [55-gallon drums in which human waste is mixed with diesel fuel and burned] is asphyxiating. Mix that with the heat, and your body feels like decomposition has set in.

I feel guilty for the battle captains but am not sure how much of their pain is self-inflicted … or a function of being held responsible for everyone else's job in the TOC. You go in there and Martinez, Hancher, Beattie, and Kestian are running around crazily while all the other cells have privates in them. We also have four E–7s in the S–3 section, but no one lets them listen to the radio or holds them accountable for anything. They make the battle captains do everything. The solution isn't to put more captains in there but to make all the others work. Hopefully, Jalula will be nicer; however, I don't really see that happening … call me a pessimist.

4 May: Got another run and hose shower this morning. That is four days in a row. Very nice. Finished up *Candide* and would start another book but it is way too hot to go rooting around in the back of the trailer. The heat and flies are starting to get really bad here. Went to the latrine yesterday and it had overfilled. They need to do a better job burning it. Someone is going to die. Fortunately, we are just eating MREs [meals, ready to eat], so that makes things a little bit more sterile. My smallpox scab fell off. Very happy about that. What a nightmare that thing proved. Had my malaria pill today, so I should have crazy dreams tonight. The anti-malaria pills cause us to have the most realistic psychedelic dreams.

Our AO is huge. We will be in the northeast portion of the country along the Iranian border. The weather should be better there. Still getting the word that I will take Bravo Company, 1-8 IN, in June. That's good. I need a change of pace and to get back to soldiering. I have so much idealism built up about all the things I want to accomplish, but I wonder if any of them will prove feasible. Today is the hottest day we have had in Iraq. The sun just beats down. You can actually feel the pressure of the sun on your head. It has physical force. It still gets decently cool at night. That makes life bearable. It's when you sweat while you try to sleep that things get out of control. Everyone just tries to move slow and stay still during the heat of the day. The groundhog-day effect continues. They did have the mission analysis brief this morning but said the earliest move date would be 6 May. The 1-12 IN shot a guy last night. Apparently, he opened up in their general direction with an AK–47, and they shot him in the arm—moron.

The MEK and Badr Corps are the hot topics in our briefings now. Best I can tell, the MEK are Iranians who fled Iran and oppose the Ayatollah somehow, and the Badr Corps are Iraqis supported by the Iranian government against the MEK. They keep on fighting one another, but supposedly the MEK wants to surrender to 2d Brigade. We'll see how that goes. We are also waiting on the repair of the bridge from Tikrit so 1-8 IN can rejoin us on the eastern side of the river. Once they get here, we'll be ready to move out. Heard that a kid from 3d ACR [Armored Cavalry Regiment] died in a vehicle accident the other night—drowned in one of these irrigation ditches. That makes you very cautious around these vehicles. I always rehearse actions like that in my mind.

I got a letter from my parents yesterday. Getting mail is so nice. Got a letter and picture of the PETCO Easter shindig from Kris today, complete with Oscar [his seventeen-year-old dachshund] wearing bunny ears.

5 May: Well, I thought I would have another groundhog day on this same compound. It started out easy enough. Got a little morning run along the north wall but twisted my ankle and totally fell down. I had to sit there for about five minutes before I could start running again. It worked itself out soon enough; running in flak vest is always fun. I knew that today would prove a hot one, so I grabbed a cold shower and shave from the "high shower." It is an actual shower in which the spout is about ten feet in the air. The water hits you with such force that it goes everywhere. Gravity works even in Iraq. I love this shower, but everyone else prefers the heated ones. It was 107 degrees in the TOC today; I don't need a hot shower, thank you.

After the shower, I collected up my dirty clothes and headed over to the cadmium battery building to do some bucket laundry. I had almost finished my second bucket load when Schwartz (the colonel's driver) ran in looking for me all in a panic. "Sir, you got to go on a mission right away" … great.

I ran over to the track with all my wet laundry in the crazy heat. Dropped it off with Carlson, the porn star, and got my kit together. It proved much easier assembling the necessary equipment after having gone on the previous missions. I went over to the TOC and got the brief from Major Martinez. The BRT had watched a house all night that supposedly belonged to Chemical Ali, and he was there. Needless to say, we got pretty pumped and everyone was scurrying around.

I would lead the ground convoy for the commanders who were going in the A2C2 [Air Assault Command and Control] bird; basically, I was pulling glorified taxi. They wanted me to go in the helicopter, but the XO prevailed with the guidance of having leadership on the ground. Good. I don't really like flying all that much in this country anyways. I got the quick brief and headed down to Samarra. It felt weird leaving the compound for the first time in a week. I tried to link up with the engineers, who were trying to get the informant back. Apparently, they let the informant go after questioning him … that ain't real smart. Of course, they were not monitoring the net and did not have the informant, so we just blew them off.

I crossed the bridge over the Tigris. It looks like they have a dam here in Samarra. I saw lots of kids playing in the water below the bluffs. It looks like a movie with the giant mosque in the background. We finally got to the linkup point with Charlie Company, 1-12 IN. I rolled up and immediately started sweating. It is crazy hot. We listened to the radio for a little while and then realized we were at a dry hole. They found a bunch of pistols, chemical protective gear, and helicopter equipment in a school but no Chemical Ali. We found no one of significance occupying the target buildings. The A2C2 bird flew back overhead and called us back to the compound. Driving around the countryside is pretty fun; it's the static sweating out in the sun that drives you bonkers.

Hung out with Nick Fuller at the linkup point and he was relaying some stories from the TF 20 guys. Turns out they had a firefight about a week ago where one of the guys got shot square in the chest into his body armor. He said it stopped the bullet cold and they just issued him a new ceramic plate. Of course, they "neutralized" the perpetrators. I guess the confidence boost is a double-edged sword—good that it stopped the bullet … bad that the bullet ever got there in the first place. The countryside seems so pacified, and we really haven't seen any action lately; but then you hear those stories that make you realize it is still a very dangerous place. Fortunately, we have figured out how to deal with them—I think.

I got back to the compound and checked in with Plans. Looks like we are going on the road again—177 kilometers of road. The movement is supposed to take fifty-five hours for the brigade. That should prove fun. We are heading up to Tuz and then southeast toward the Iranian border for the MEK capitulation ... in theory. Trying to keep the MEK and the Badr Corps straight in my mind is hard to do. Which one is Iranian again? I got the gist of the mission and then read some news articles Major Martinez gave me. Nothing shocking there, but read some soldier anecdotes that made me laugh. I am looking forward to getting out of here. I will miss the running water greatly, though. Hopefully, we get better facilities there. I ate an enchilada MRE to celebrate Cinco de Mayo. Very festive.

"May Day Parade" en route to the MEK capitulation. I believe this is the city of Tuz.

7 May: Right now in the midst of the 177-kilometer movement to the Tuz Airfield and then south to the Iranian border. We are in a cluster since 1-10 CAV [Cavalry] got interspersed with us on the east side of the Jabal Hamrin Ridge and 1-12 IN has a bunch of vehicles broken down. I don't really know if we have a vehicle recovery plan. Yesterday was a no good, very bad day. Everyone wanted to do everything except listen. These are the consequences of staying in one place too long. I was pissed off all day yesterday. Gave a little Op Order to the guys and staged them over in movement order; of course, no one that wanted us to stage bothered staging with us since they still had running water and the building. When asked what we are waiting on … it's always "them." It hasn't been too hot today since we got cloud cover. I got a run in yesterday and two showers to leave extra clean. I went over midway through the day and soaked myself to get the cooling effect.

We are at Tuz Airfield right now. It looks pretty nice, but I don't want to go south. This is a long movement for the tracked vehicles. We have logged 700 kilometers on the Bradley in 2.5 weeks. Our optempo for the year in the U.S. is 600 miles, and we actually struggle to make that. It should prove interesting if we keep this pace with no service scheduled. Supposedly disarming the MEK and protecting the region from the Badr Corps should take a month and then we jump north again. North is good. I didn't realize that 90 percent of the MEK leadership is women … weird since this society normally looks down on women as subservient.

Well, I need to go put my CVC [combat vehicle crewman's helmet] back on; it is crushing my head. Our track is just crammed full of water and MREs. Everyone has a load plan for these things, and if they get crammed full then the solution is "fix the load plan, but don't make it look gypsy." I don't know how many times I have heard that. The truth of the matter is they weren't designed to carry seven days of supply and soldiers in the back while not looking like a gypsy wagon. The infantry squads must be miserable. Just stopped at Attack Position Striker A. Pulled a little maintenance and got fuel. Track 37 looked like a pigsty with all the dirt and dust flying everywhere. It was pretty funny how dirty those guys got. The temperature feels a little better on this side of the pass.

I ran into Matt Cunningham. He is doing well. They were glad to get out of Tikrit. He said he is ready for a change of faces down in 1-8 IN. Well, it's coming soon enough. Matt already finished his change of command inventories. The eastern half of the country looks very much like NTC. The mountain range to our east looks like the north wall of the central corridor. Our vehicles are fueled, and we are just waiting for the artillery guys and 1-10 CAV to move out. I guess 1-10 hasn't crossed the river, so we are going to wait awhile. They are supposed to give the MEK the 48-hour ultimatum for capitulation tomorrow. They say they are very disciplined and will comply. I linked up with the guys from 10th Special Forces Group. I don't think they

With all the guys' gear on board, this Brad could not help but look like a gypsy wagon.

struggled hard to find us; it is very difficult to sneak a mech brigade around these open areas. They were glad to see us and very excited about leaving the area. I don't think they want to hang out for the big double cross that is going to go down. This surrender could still turn out poorly.

8 May: Well, I was just sitting in the hobbit hole of the 113 [M113 armored personnel carrier] listening to the commander's update brief while eating an MRE when Major Barnett decides that I need to go with him and the interpreter to Jalawa to help out Pacesetter [3-29 Field Artillery]. Turns out they had taken over some of the checkpoints the armed PUK was manning and basically told them to leave. Since they are our allies, we allow them to keep their weapons. Well, Jalawa is an Arab town currently controlled by the PUK. Once we cut the PUK off from controlling the town, the Arabs went into celebration/riot mode. I don't think these guys have ever seen a foreigner out here. So they had about twenty vehicles drive by our location chanting "Go home, America!" and some anti-PUK stuff. They then went into the city and started launching rounds off. The PUK guys locked and loaded and then headed out; we wisely decided to stay put. Then they played the game of coming up to us, each side rotating to tell us their story as the other one left. We basically sat there and listened. I told them to schedule a meeting tomorrow with our Civil Affairs guys and the town mayor.

It was getting dark and there was a lot of traffic on the road. I finally convinced them to break contact and move back to the TOC. As we drove to the TOC, one of the M88s [armored recovery vehicles] took small-arms fire, so everything ended up spinning and I got stuck at the TOC for way too long. Five minutes is way too long in that place. The TOC has shower points and bank hours, apparently. The XO got all in a huff because I had the electric razor look going on. So I pointed out to him that my day started at 0330 with an electric shave—since we are on water rations at the TAC—and it was now 2100. I also informed him that I looked worse since I had just come from a riot downtown. How out of touch can you be? Well, we finally left the TOC and got back to the TAC uneventfully. I linked up with the AH–64 pilots who will fly a screen mission along the border looking for Badr Corps guys. The next few days should prove interesting. The MEK is probably the best force in Iraq—better than the Republican Guard—but they are our terrorist allies in a way. Like the enemy of my enemy is my friend. Hopefully, we go north soon, although the weather today was quite nice.

9 May: Woke up late this morning. It got hot pretty quick after being quite chilly last night. Have not accomplished anything today. The division commander is delivering the ultimatum to the MEK right now; they all flew down there this morning. We have not heard anything from them. Apparently 3d ACR was en route to seize some of the MEK's equipment in the midst of these negotiations. That could have made things go badly. The reporters are here just hanging out with us. There is not much else going on. The planners went up to Kirkuk this morning—so that is a good sign. Division does not anticipate us remaining here much more than a week. That's good since we don't have any running water to bathe with or really anything for that matter—just a big dusty field. We have lots of wild dogs around here. They had a huge dogfight last night over by HQ63B. Everyone enjoyed listening to the dogs howl. We are very much ready for the 1500 hours heat respite to hit … one hour and twenty minutes away. I would read my book, but we sent the Bradleys over to the UMCP [Unit Maintenance Collection Point] for some maintenance. I had two strawberry MRE milkshakes today. What a big bonus.

10 May: Looks like the MEK didn't like the wording of the "surrender" documents. They have basically gone back to the drawing board on that one. The JAG folks are all spun up dealing with it. I think it went down bush-league style—no interpreted copy for them and no ability to negotiate. We continue to demonstrate our inability to understand these people. Not quite sure why we are still listing the MEK as terrorists seeing as how they haven't done anything of that nature during the lifetime of the current organization. They are an army fighting another army, bottom line. We'll see how the discussions go tomorrow. Basically, we proved quite Machiavellian in our dealings with them. I also don't think the State Department has done much in this arena; there just isn't any diplomacy going on here ... just brute force and ignorance. The fallout diplomatically from this war may prove more catastrophic than the actual gains realized and true threats eliminated. Only time will tell.

It's getting hot here, but we are supposed to leave this location by 15 May according to the division timeline. We'll see. I should have another boring day today as the colonel will have to fly south for negotiations. I think they just like talking to Americans. I heard over the TACSAT that a Black Hawk [UH–60 utility helicopter] went down in the vicinity of Samarra, which is a scary place to get shot down. I guess we will hear more in the morning.

I got some more rack and woke up to the dogs and the commo guy pulling security. He freaked out when Carlson popped the hatch on the driver's side. He started yelling "Someone's in there! Someone's in there! How did someone get in there?" Carlson looked at me and just started laughing. We did a little PT this morning—bungee cord lifting and plyometrics. The CSM showed up with mail call. I got two packages and a letter ... bingo. Mike Moon and Aunt Nancy sent me boxes, and I got a letter from Mom. Nancy's box proved a great success: beef jerky, Gold Bond, baby wipes, Gatorade, plus a bunch of additional personal hygiene essentials.

We had an unmanned aerial vehicle [UAV] go down, so that has gotten everyone's excitement going again. It went down right outside a MEK compound. Apparently, the max engine temperature is 75 degrees and they had it at 197 degrees. Not good. The colonel and JAG took off to the negotiation site. We are all taking bets on when they will return. Read the "Early Bird" [daily Department of Defense posting of selected commercial print media features] last night. I guess the Army news is still Iraqi-centric. We still do not have a great idea of what is happening in the world, but at least we know a little. The link we get through the SEN [small extension node] and Smart T communications equipment only has SIPR [Secure Internet Protocol Router] (secret e-mail), so no e-mails—just download. I got some good pictures downloaded from Major Martinez into some PowerPoint slides that I'll send out when I get the chance. I am just sitting here looking at the Buhayrat

Hamrin reservoir. Would love to drive down there and swim. I watched the sun go down. It moves so fast. The sunrises and sunsets in the desert are beautiful—big sky country with lots of stars. There are no cities out here, so lots of stars. Arabian nights. Looking through NODs [night observation devices] enhances the number you can see albeit in a green hue. I spent most of the day hanging out here BSing with the reporters (John Sullivan from the *Philadelphia Inquirer*). They are good guys. It's funny to hear their perspective on things.

Spc. Jason Boothby and 1st Lt. Jimmy Bevens enjoy a sunset in northern Iraq.

11 May: Well, the dream came true; we made it to the Buharyrat Hamrin reservoir. We rolled down there with a Bradley and three Humvees. We got out onto the causeway, established security, got naked, and did a little swim action. Saw lots of very white, skinny bodies out there in the mad torrent to get clean. It felt awesome. Between the care packages and the swim, this proved a much better day than I thought it would. I got some clothes cleaned as well. We hurried back as the sun set. Reminded me of *Band of Brothers* when they went swimming. It was very nice out on the lake. We got an information dump from the planners on Kirkuk. They gave us the rundown on the 173d [Airborne (ABN) Brigade] operations—it seems pretty quiet— and their standard of living is much better than ours currently. They ran into a lot of guys I know up there. Good to hear about them. Now I am just basking in the afterglow from the swim, beef jerky, and inundation of information on the home front ... even if it is three weeks old. *Newsweek* ran an article about all the archeological sites. Samarra was featured quite extensively. They showed many pictures of areas right next to where I slept. I am glad we didn't hurt the wall when we ran into it; that would have gone badly if they had featured HQ66 ruining the wall of Samarra.

Today proved long and boring with some spikes of excitement. I had the early morning guard shift, so it started at 0400. Very peaceful morning and a nice sunrise. Things zinged around with the colonel until about 1100. Then I did some personal hygiene and tried to avoid the sun. Recently, I have taken to drinking three-quarters of a water bottle then cutting it in half. I dunk my t-shirt in the water and wear it around. This probably cools me off about 5 degrees. The dogs are still roaming all around our area. They start howling in the middle of the night. I had one that wanted my beef jerky quite badly. The chaplain showed up to do Mother's Day services. It was pretty nice although we had it at high noon out in the sun—not very nice. I got a little nap action since the day moved so slowly and read a little.

Uploading MEK weapons for transport to a holding area

I woke up once the MEK started moving to cantonment areas. Everything went smoothly until 1-10 CAV aviation assets entered our zone. They saw some MEK in civilian clothes uploading ammunition to take to the cantonment areas. Obviously, they didn't possess the information that everyone else in the division did, because they started firing on them. Not real smooth ... like international incident not smooth. The MEK has proven very cooperative in all our dealings with them and then some Kiowa [helicopter] yahoos decide to fire them up in our zone with zero coordination during the division BUB. That didn't work out real well as one can imagine. The sun is dropping out of the sky again—literally. It moves so fast, like in the tropics. Amazing how fast it cools off as it dips down.

It's pretty scenic here, but I am ready to move north. I read all the city briefs for the northern cities. Much nicer up there. Jalula is still a little crazy. Hopefully, we can break contact and turn it over to the 2d BCT. The convoy movement sounded painful for the battalions in charge of moving the MEK. It went like one of our convoys except in Farsi. The tip of the orange globe just dipped below the horizon, and the sky turned pink. Very pretty. Our embedded media guys are all snapping photos. In twenty minutes we will have all the stars out. We don't complain about this place from 1930 to about 0830. From 0830 to 1930 it's just hot. I thought we might get to go on another water run tonight; however, 1-10 CAV got things way too spun up here. That is all right; we still have water left over from yesterday, and I have 200 baby wipes. The 1-10 CAV came by to conduct damage control. Apparently, their liaison officers gave them the wrong frequencies, and they could not contact us on the ground.

12 May: I couldn't sleep last night for some reason. I don't know why since I pulled a nineteen-hour shift. I just lay there thinking about how tired I was going to be in the morning. I also kept on going over company commander stuff in my head. Just trying to figure out what I wanted to say on day one. I still don't have a definitive date. The rumor mill started up again for redeployment. The latest from V Corps is an accelerated timeline for combat troops ... not really feasible but gave us a morale boost. I really cannot put that much stock in that rumor, though. The MEK forces have moved six march units' worth of equipment into the cantonment areas, so we shouldn't have to remain here much longer—provided we do not shoot at them again. The dogs are out howling once again. Sergeant Yeazal tried the red cayenne pepper trick on them. I think it made them worse.

It never fails. Whenever I have to wake up the colonel, a crisis immediately ensues. This morning we had an armored vehicle launched bridge leave the UMCP at 0230. No one knows why they decided to leave at that hour ... seeing how we don't need them at all. Anyways, they get down a ways and a MEK fueler is blocking their way. They decide to "push" it out of the way. That didn't work so well. The fueler flipped onto its side and leaked fuel everywhere. The colonel proved incredibly agitated seeing as how these guys have consistently struggled in the arena of asinine events.

We finally concluded that one at 0700. It gave way to the MEK movements. We had to coordinate some of the camp setups. Apparently, the female battalion of 800 soldiers with 200 male servants had special housing requirements. Makes you scratch your head. Funny—since that is the exact proportion Swift advocated in his modest proposal for a matriarchal society. Of course his satire dealt with controlling the population of Ireland, and he advocated eating the male infants before they could walk to ensure compliance. I wonder if the MEK does the same.

Still dealing with the PUK. They love us, but their obstinance proves trying at times. It reminds one of the trials of supporting dubious organizations. By utilizing them to destabilize the old regime, we provided them legitimacy. This legitimacy binds our hands when we wish to disarm them and enforce our will upon them since they are our allies. Daily we witness the double-edged sword of entangling alliances. Jalula actually has a CKP [Communist Kurdish Party]. There are just too many factions here, and they all vie to fill the power vacuum we created. We had small factions of clouds battling the sun today. We were grateful to them for their efforts, but it still got hot. Not quite as bad as yesterday. All the MEK forces have now left this sector; hopefully so shall we.

The sedentary TAC life has gotten old. Just sit inside the hot tent, read magazines, and answer frantic calls about random unanswerable questions. During this time, we discuss global politics and who stinks the most; both conversations prove equally enlightening. The TAC leadership has migrated to the TOC for future planning. That is doubly good since now we don't have to sit right next to the radio sticking to a folding chair and we will get on the move again. We are heading north, but not as far as anticipated. Hopefully, we can beat the weather. Seems that each time we jump the weather improves, however marginally. We get into the tolerable temperatures for a couple days prior to the heat wave coming up. We drive around the countryside on the fringes of the oven—just barely beating back the flames. Hopefully, we get well north before the nights get hot. I just can't bear sticking to the cot.

13 May: The clouds that fought so valiantly yesterday have since retreated. We have nothing between us and the sun. It has grown quite hot. Heated up an MRE this morning and broke out sweating. Not much going on today. The units are trying to blow their ammunition caches and preparing to move north. Not quite the exodus we wanted but going in the right direction. It looks like we will have the MEK zone for one more day prior to moving north twenty kilometers. In the process of washing some clothes—I just don't know how clean we actually get them. Seems like a never-ending cycle. The boss went on an aerial recon, so everything is quiet here. I am always amazed how things can start zinging so quickly around here. Hopefully, everyone chills out today, and we have no crisis. Got to read the "Early Bird" yesterday. Funny—getting the news from both ends—we hear it on the TACSAT updates and then read it in the paper. Not too much disparity, but it is funny to hear it in real time prior to reading it.

Just sitting down reading, listening to the radio, and trying to avoid the sun. Heard over the net that DIVARTY [Division Artillery] suffered a mass casualty chemical event. Apparently, they were moving large barrels across the warehouse when one broke open; approximately thirty people displayed nerve gas–type symptoms. They called all the medevac birds down to Taji Airfield to help with the evacuation. Crazy. I went through Taji Airfield when I first got here. The Fox [chemical detection vehicle] went up there and got a negative read on the site, and the 256 detection kits also turned back a negative result. Hopefully, nothing serious happened to all those guys. Chemical casualties are incredibly difficult to evacuate since you have to decontaminate everything they touch. The birds are lifting off right now to evacuate them to the 21st CASH [Corps Area Support Hospital]. I am sure we will hear more about this soon enough. Very scary the number of chemicals this country possesses.

14 May: Right now, it looks like the soldiers were exposed to a chemical not associated with chemical warfare. Hopefully, they will all recover in full. It gave everyone a scare, to say the least. I went for a little perimeter run. I have lost the aerobic edge. So depressing, but I will get it back once things settle down. We are jumping in the morning. I think they want us north even faster. That is even better. The guys have figured out how the DVD works on the computer. They watch *Band of Brothers* nightly. I think everyone strives to have similar blood-brother bonding experiences. It is part of human nature. The more miserable the experience, the greater the bonds we witness. Fortunately, we have the misery without the associated carnage.

I think that we get better incrementally each day. Things seem easier out here; I guess it stems from the knowledge and skills gained through repetition and sheer boredom. At NTC, each person had a stovepipe-type knowledge of his job, and we each performed a specific task—the driver drove and maintained the track, the commo guy did the TACSAT and filled the radios with the encryption codes, and the officers battle tracked. The countless days in the desert have enabled us to train on one another's tasks, so you don't have to wake up the commo guy when the fill fails or the TACSAT radar gets knocked over. You don't have to find the driver when you want the vehicle moved or the track tension adjusted. It makes life much easier and more efficient. It also enables us to operate at a higher level and not deal with all the nuisances experienced at NTC. The colonel yells at us about new things that we generally can't help, like another unit not answering the radio. It is a much better scenario, in my opinion. I now even know how the water heater works. Well, it is 0230, time for bed. The dogs are howling outside.

"Panama City," somewhere in northern Iraq

15 May: Woke up and packed up. We head to the TOC today to refit. That place sucks. Rolled through the town of Jalula. It is the typical Arab town of narrow streets, markets, and way too many people hustling about. Of course, the sanitation and housing leave much to be desired. They do have a very viable market with lots of TVs for sale??? I guess you know the color of said market. The children had all returned to school. We went by the little girls' school, and they were all outside playing. They have the most beautiful children. I have not seen a girl under thirteen years old who was not absolutely beautiful. On the flip side, I have not seen a girl over the age of seventeen who was not absolutely haggard. I guess that is the product of their lifestyle. The women all work in the fields while the men hang out in the town or drive the tractors. We got stuck downtown rolling through the marketplace for a little while. The PUK guys were still at it, armed to the teeth waiting for us to leave so they could harass the local Arab populace. We witness so much ethnic tension the farther north we go. Of course, the terrain and weather improve greatly. We finally reached the TOC after our Gulliver-type journey. Wow—the TOC is a drain on morale. They have hot showers and hot chow here, but they just sit out in the desert doing nothing except collecting dust.

The XO is beside himself at how limited a role they had in the last few missions. He is actively seeking ways to downgrade the TAC in order to increase the TOC's functionality, i.e., realigning communications equipment so that we have to relay reports through them instead of going straight to division and having them monitor. Can you say control freak? Wonder why everyone despises the TOC? I got some great sleep last night, and the TOC jumped in the morning. They started tearing down at 0600 and hit the road at 1215 ... model of efficiency. Just proof that bigger does not equal better. They went off the net at 0915 and came back up about 1700. Amazing. The TAC spent all day in the moon dust trying to hide from the sun and chasing stray goats in our perimeter.

As the TOC rolled, so did the local scavenger population. They just assembled themselves from the oven-baked air. We found it quite comical to watch. They moved like an army across the desert searching for remnants of anything usable. Of course, the TOC left all its concertina wire and the grand prize—the double-seated outhouse. We had tractors and search parties descending like locusts onto our trash piles and burn pits. I had the privates chase them back away from the wire and retrieve the pickets they stole. I called up the TOC to let them know if they did not dispatch someone soon all would be lost. I cannot cover my little perimeter and their grand perimeter with my small group. Especially since we located ourselves in such proximity to the grand-prize outhouse. The tractor brigade policed the whole area and then sat on the perimeter lurking, waiting to see if we would abandon the almighty tin-covered double outhouse. That is the Iraqi equivalent of adding a bay window to one's living room. Dave Brummet proved pretty callous in driving them back; however, he caved at the end right when he thought we would jump and motioned for two boys to come forward and claim their "west wing" addition.

An all-out onslaught ensued. We had tractors and shepherds maneuvering into position with all smiles and waving. They chanted and argued among themselves for awhile. I think they were trying to figure a few things out, namely what the two sawed-off 55-gallon drums contained (burnt byproducts of last night's dinner) and how they would lift and transport their bay window. Of course, at this time we got the call to hold fast in our location while they did a recon of the next site for us. Great. We have the moon dust blowing all over us as the great outhouse uprising ensues. By this time, the outhouse was on its side as one lucky farmer loaded up the 55-gallon drums. I don't think they had any idea as to the applicability of this thing.

We finally broke contact with these guys and moved out to the road so we didn't have to deal with trying to pull security in a mob-like environment — albeit a very grateful, friendly mob. We waited down on the hardball road and witnessed the TOC's outhouse stream by in various pieces of corrugated metal roofing and plywood. We had no way to transport the thing and no guard force to secure it from the onslaught of the farmers. I say "Good for them," seeing as how I haven't gone to the bathroom "inside" yet; I think that has become a personal goal of mine during my tenure in Iraq.

We left the moon dust TOC location about 1800. Just prior to leaving, we had two Chinooks [transport helicopters] fly overhead and blast us with the talcum powder–type dust. Just adding insult to injury — although I love watching Chinooks fly. They look so big and powerful with certain alien-like movements. I think seeing them fly is almost Pavlovian for me, as it signifies the end of a mission and return to home base. I always looked forward to getting onto them and flying back to the FOB… years ago.

We rolled north to the TOC, another moon dust location. The moon dust is not a naturally occurring phenomenon. It takes human intervention to create this effect. Basically, you take a field lying fallow for the season with a crunchy layer of hardened dirt and run tracked vehicles all over the place for five to six days. This grinds the top layer into a talcum-like powder. Once you have this powder, you mix constant twenty–thirty mph winds, vehicle/helicopter traffic, and dust devils (small mini-trash tornadoes) to achieve the proper TOC microclimate effect. Ingenious. Setup is not complete until one locates an infinitely better location 500 meters away. The TOC has that routine down to a T.

I guess we are going to collocate for a few days. The captain moves have commenced. Everyone is quite excited (everyone who is moving, that is). I should move within the month, but the massive exodus begins today. Mostly guys who will backfill battalion staff guys moving into command. It will provide them a little transition time. Looks like the pendulum of good guys will swing back in 1-8 IN's favor. I still hear B/1-8 IN has a change of command in mid-June. I will go down after Lt. Col. [Nathan] Sassaman takes command. I think that will work out better, so he won't hold me accountable for everything the day he shows up. You always need a little grace period. Hopefully, things settle down enough to conduct COC inventories with some degree of correctness.

16 May: I pulled the 0430–0600 shift this morning. It felt very peaceful and quiet. I thought the rest of the day would go the same. Everyone got up and started shaving while I pulled radio watch. I was just getting ready to shave and wash up when we had a frantic call from our commo section at 0750. The soldiers moving to replace our retrans [retransmission] site ran over a landmine. We tried to sort things out FM [by radio] and dispatched 1-68 AR to the site. Unfortunately, they were still moving up on HETs and couldn't get enough combat power and medical support there fast enough to clear the AO and set up a landing zone for the medevac. We couldn't land the birds in a minefield due to their rotor wash and susceptibility to mines. Major Barnett decided to roll down there with the Bradley and me playing medic. So I grabbed the CLS bag and a bunch of other field-expedient stuff to help us reach the patient and treat her (Specialist Espinoza, a twenty-year-old female soldier). I was praying that the double metal floorboards the Bradley has built into it would serve their role … if needed. I also prayed that we would miss the landmines and not need them.

We rolled up onto the site. It was very much a real-life minefield. The front right end of the Humvee was gone—disappeared. Fortunately, they had sandbags on the floorboards. That probably saved her life. It looked like a piece of shrapnel went through the floorboard and her leg. She was lying on the ground when I got there. Someone sent a doctor over, but he didn't have any medical equipment and was looking at me for guidance. I started rifling through my bag and retrieved some curlex gauze, and we began splinting the leg. I had Sergeant First Class Baker prep an IV, but no one wanted to fish around in her veins for the flash, least of all me. She is super skinny and was thrashing about ... and I hate the whole IV thing anyways. I told the doctor he was on that duty, and he did the fishing around while I stabilized the leg and got a sleeping bag to treat for shock. We pulled a Humvee up, and I jumped on the top with the IV bag as they loaded her onto the hood. We then moved down the farm trail ever so slowly due to her excruciating pain. It was very hard to watch the road and see her reaction as we hit each bump—knowing the bumps were coming. The doctor was trying to cut a hole in her boot to check the pulse in her toe—on a moving Humvee; it was not working real well. Espinoza was screaming for him to stop because every time he sawed it moved her leg. I told him the bandage wasn't too tight and to wait until we got some morphine into her. We couldn't do anything for her there anyways—the leg was shredded between the knee and top of the boot. I guess he agreed, since he gave me my leatherman back.

We finally got to the road and linked up with CSM Johnson and Sergeant First Class Barreto, who had the HLZ [helicopter landing zone] marked and birds inbound. They landed, and Staff Sergeant Belcher (the in-flight medic from 571st that I had coordinated with way back at Samarra East) came rolling off to do a face-to-face with us. He just told us to load and go. We ran her over and uploaded the helicopter. We shook hands, and I told him to give me my sleeping bag back; it still gets cold at night. All of this took place under the chaos of the whirling rotors. They took her to the 21st CASH.

We went back to the edge of the minefield; we still had another vehicle with a soldier who had passed through unscathed but was stuck in the minefield. By this time we had quite a crowd of local kids around us. They were guiding us through the field and pointing out all the mines. Major Barnett made the call for no one to move—Corporal Fread to us or us to him. Very wise call. We had an engineer element en route. I trust the local kids, but I think it would prove best if we had the experts in demolitions and the local pathfinders helping us together. There were mines everywhere.

Things calmed down enough once the bird took off that I decided to roll back with the CSM instead of on the back of the Bradley. We had a plethora of senior leadership already on the ground. We just don't have the expertise at the brigade level for the senior guys not to take charge in situations like this. Normally, I would tell a squad leader to move to the site, secure the casualty, and have the medic treat her, then set up the HLZ near the road and talk to the birds on this frequency. Much easier than having all the officers running around, but I guess that is what we sometimes have to do.

I witnessed the work of some pretty brave people from the first vehicle who moved back through the entire minefield to secure the casualty and help her initially. It didn't seem like it at the time, but it does now. Luckily, the treacherous mines had been identified by the time I showed up and Sergeant Barreto was able to point them out. It definitely gives you the uneasy "what-if," "what would I do," "is that thing real" feeling walking through a minefield. There wasn't much left for me to do. The engineers were going to clear a path to Fread using the locals as point men (they really want to help). I made it back to the TOC and went to see the XO to give him an update. He started berating me about one of my pant legs' not being bloused. He didn't ask me any questions about the whole ordeal—he just wanted to yell about something stupid. I guess you always have someone you can't get along with. About this time, the medevac birds landed near the TOC. I walked over there and got the sleeping bag back and refilled our CLS bag. I still haven't shaved yet today. I must be a terrible soldier.

17 May: I could go for more days like today. Woke up at 0500, read a little, and did circuit PT around the tracks with Major Barnett and Yeazal. We have a pull-up bar now, so it provides some mixing for the old PT program. I am so out of shape. Not much really happened today. I read a lot and listened to the command net on the radio. Whenever we collocate with the TOC our job becomes quite easy … just monitor the radios. That coupled with the plethora of excess officers in the S–3 shop makes the main enemy boredom and hygiene—namely keeping people from going to the bathroom right around the tracks. Thus far the training environment had proved much more strenuous than here. It is definitely more scary and interesting here, but the hours aren't quite as long. I am waiting for the Bradley to return, as it has all my gear on it. They took it to the 1-12 IN UMCP to get worked on. Hopefully, it will get up above twenty mph now. I think the transmission is shot. We will move north again tomorrow. We had much better weather here the past two days than we did down south with the MEK. I got a haircut today—very nice. Dave just got back from Kirkuk. He said it looked pretty nice. The 173d shot some guys today during a riot in that area. I guess they had a demonstration and told some guys toting AK–47s to put them down and they wouldn't—graduated response. No friendly injuries, so that is good. The nice thing about having tracked vehicles is that everyone listens.

Just drive over there, and suddenly they become fluent in pointy-talky ... and very cooperative. Not much else going on over here.

19 May: Had another boring day yesterday. We woke up at 0600 and did some decent PT. We now have a lot more people working on getting in shape: the small group has increased to five. After PT, I went and got a shower from First Sergeant Hodson's ingenious mobile shower facility. It is nice having an engineer as your first sergeant. He builds everything. Unfortunately, it is all for the TOC. After the shower, I went to "mass" at the MKT [mobile kitchen trailer]. We have just a Eucharistic minister; I think there is a shortage of Catholic chaplains over here. After mass, I ate some biscuits at the MKT and then went back to the TAC. We are jumping in the morning. Just hung out and read. We got ready for the move and then went to sleep. Got up this morning and headed north. Drove by the MEK/Badr Corps, Iran/Iraq, and Kurdistan/Iraq battlegrounds. It is difficult to determine how the defenses lay since they have three wars interposing one another. Every bridge/dry riverbed in the region had battle at it recently. Lots of supplementary and alternate fighting positions interspersed from both north to south and east to west. We drove through the city of Tuz. Very interesting. They had a huge line for gas and about seventy-five black-market gas sellers with five-gallon cans of gas ... black-market economy big time. I also saw the CKP headquarters building. I don't think they follow the same dogma as the Soviet Union, although they did have the hammer-and-sickle symbol out front. I think they exist in name only in order to oppose the KDP [Kurdish Democratic Party]. There is so much infighting in this country. I don't know how they will get everyone to coexist peacefully under one government; this is the Yugoslavia of the Middle East. We finally made it up to the "traffic circle." I did not have a grid to the new TAC location, so I just drove around the circle calling Warrior TOC for our new grid. They finally came up on the net, and I left the traffic circle. It proved quite funny. Our Bradley runs at twenty mph. Makes the long movements even longer. The mechanics can't figure out the problem. We keep on having them work on it but to no avail. Oh well. I don't have anywhere to go fast; if you're important, people will wait on you.

We had another weather break—a big one this time, at least 15 degrees cooler—and we have an abandoned building to work out of. We experienced a huge improvement in lifestyle. Right now, 1-12 IN is the only battalion up here. We linked up with 173d and are conducting operations just outside their perimeter. A lot of Arabization went on here, so bad blood exists throughout the area. Now that we moved in, all the Kurds want to de-Arabize the area—

therein lays the crux of our dilemma. The diplomatic entanglement occurred long ago; by supporting the KDP/PUK, we chose sides. Our best option for the region remains to maintain neutrality between the tribal factions; however, we can't do this now. We have to back the Kurds (our allies) and at the same time appease the Arabs. Someone needs to figure this out diplomatically … good luck. Took my malaria pill today—crazy dreams tonight.

20 May: Had a sleeping bag night last night (cold one). Yippee. Pulled the 0400 radio shift this morning. Very peaceful. I finished my book and read an article on Noam Chomsky. He seems like an idiot savant. Such a waste of brainpower. Went outside and watched the earth smoke cigarettes. All the oil derricks burn off their methane gas at night. It looks like huge cigarettes sticking out of the earth.

Nothing big happened last night, so I let everyone sleep in. We have a thirty-by-fifty-foot room we work out of, and it stays cool during the day. We also have a running hose 100 meters from us. It runs continuously, so we send guys down to fill up buckets, do laundry, and bathe. Morale jumps with running water. We did PT along the road right behind our building. Since we collocated with 1-12 IN, our perimeter has expanded significantly. Now we have a 300-meter stretch to run along. I ran about five miles along the stretch and did some dumbbell routines. Just trying to maintain.

After that I had a bucket shower and changed clothes. I also got to wash another set of DCUs [desert combat uniform] and my sleeping bag, the black monster. When it fills with water, it weighs about seventy-five pounds and proves quite ungainly. I wrestled with it for a good thirty minutes and came out soaked. The laundry process involves a 45-minute soak followed by three rinses—when you have running water. Therefore, I had to wrestle 300 pounds of water from the black monster. I got about seventeen pounds of water back into the bucket, so by my calculations I covered myself in a cumulative 283 pounds of water in order to liberate my sleeping bag of fifty days of dirt and grime. But liberate I did. Upon completion of the black monster liberation, I assumed battle-tracking responsibilities for 1-12 IN movement on Objectives WILTON and AUSTIN to the southwest. It proved pretty uneventful. No one messes with the tanks and Brads. The 1-12 IN apprehended twenty-seven looters down at Objective AUSTIN. I think they still loot here since this place went largely untouched by American forces and we just now liberated it. Now we have to detain the looters for twenty days. That could prove a monumental task—feeding and housing.

21 May: Woke up this morning right at sunrise. We've spent two nights in a row in a pretty decent place. That is a first. Pulled a little radio watch and then did PT. Just ran back and forth on the same road and did a little shoulder routine. Had another bucket bath post workout. Staff Sergeant Fogle found an extra bilge pump and has spent the day designing a "shower" with a little pressure. He tested it this afternoon, and it works pretty well. I think we'll have a trial run once it gets dark. I rearranged all my gear. I needed to do that as I have way too much unnecessary equipment due to our failed Turkey route. Found two more mosquito nets, so we are hiding from the bugs a little better. Everyone who has not slept with a net has bites all over; fortunately, I have utilized my net to advantage.

The CSM brought us hot chow this morning—pretty nasty, but they did bring salsa, which I ate on my MRE crackers. Tastes just like "Dos Hombres." I started a new book today: *Moby Dick*. We had just patrols moving through sector today, so not much militarily going on. We are just clearing all our original objectives albeit from the wrong direction—southeast to northwest. It feels like a staff ride/OPD [officer professional development] since we have planned so extensively on these objectives prior to our deployment and the Turkey denial. We have detained some individuals and looters but nothing crazy. I did a good job hiding from the sun today and just chilling out—reading, writing, and sleeping. I could get used to this sedentary lifestyle so long as we can do PT.

The division is trying to set up elections throughout the area. The screening and election-teaching processes prove quite comical at times. One of the towns wanted to have an election for the local grocery store. I guess democracy takes time to learn. Other than that, it has been a slow day… that's good.

22 May: We've struck water! Big time! Sergeant Fogle has rigged some old irrigation pipes to redirect water right next to my Bradley and into our pump shower. The water comes out with a little pressure to it, too. Bonus. Spent the day bathing and washing clothes. Our water supply and convenience are such that I now shower for enjoyment versus necessity. Did a little PT this morning, and I feel so sore all over. It takes a little while to rebuild the routine, I guess. We had high winds and low visibility today. I don't know if it was sand in the air or humidity; both are a common occurrence here. Regardless, the day passed quite nicely with no midday heat wave. The only element we battled today was the flies. I guess the high winds cause them to retreat indoors. I read a bunch of *Moby Dick* today—phenomenal book thus far. Best American author I have read. We had T-rat lasagna tonight—that is by far my favorite—and this was my first time having it here. Normally, you get lasagna every third night when you go on the T-rat cycle; this is my fifth T-rat—what's up?

Spent the afternoon walking the perimeter and going through some of the other buildings. We are trying to develop the argument to bring the TOC here instead of us moving to them. They chose a blacktop hardstand with no shade, lots of dust, farthest to the rear (behind the BSA!), and right next to the highway. Not smart. I guess the XO has visions of bringing AC trailers and such to the location; however, the mechanics still have to work at night due to the heat radiating off the ground. They say the tracks sink into the asphalt during the day. It does not get that hot where we are, and we have buildings. Since we are on a military compound, we have lots of space and it is also off the beaten path. It just makes sense. We have placed bets on when we will move. Of course, we have also developed a litany of excuses not to move. Hopefully, we can drag this out for another week. I know they will break. Got a letter and box from Aunt Nancy today. We always enjoy mail call around here. The Ross group out of Texas sent us sundry packs. We cross-leveled them all and now have a full supply. Unfortunately, the laundry detergent has yet again proven elusive to our search.

23 May: "Hey sir, wake up," Sergeant First Class Samples whispers.

"What time is it?" I groggily reply.

"0500."

"Anything going on?"

"Absolutely nothing."

"Good," I say as I stretch out and look at the waning moon from behind the mosquito net jerry-rigged to my Bradley with 550 cord and bungees. I lie there momentarily.

"Are you getting up?" he demands.

"Yeah, just a second." I stretch my body to its full length like a cat awakening from a long siesta. It's actually a little chilly this morning—good for PT. The dogs start howling at each other again. They fight constantly with everything. They are worse than our administration in that regard.

I throw my DCU pants on over my PT shorts, remove the belt with leatherman, Swiss Army knife, and Magellan GPS. I retrieve my weapon and Kevlar then walk to the clothesline and retrieve my white socks and running shoes. I view the battle update board through the dilapidated prison window and listen to the radio as I dress. Yep, there really is nothing going on.

"All right, I got the con," I announce while reaching for a Jolly Rancher from the free-for-all table. Sergeant Samples nods and walks back to his cot. I grab a lukewarm water and contemplate making some MRE mocha ... on second thought, it's too daunting a task this early in the morning.

The sun slowly breaks through the humidity on the horizon as another day begins. The deep azure predawn skies promise another scorcher of a day. I count myself among the fortunate ones to have a building to retreat into during the sun's midday onslaught.

I pull up a chair and read the log from last night while drinking lukewarm water. Nothing. I crawl through the hobbit-hole window into the M577 command track and sift through our BFT satellite messages ... nothing. I read through the daily Frago, thereby completing my early morning quest for knowledge to no avail. It's another boring day in Iraq.

The sky turns pink, and the darkness slowly retreats. We can spot the baying dogs well enough to launch rocks to chase them off. They keep their distance. The giant squirrel rat that lives in a hole by my cot finishes his final nocturnal meal and retreats into the cool darkness of his underground lair. I stretch and yawn. My back is a bit tight, so I hang from our "pull up bar." It is a marvel of engineering—six loops of 550 cord suspended from the ceiling with a camo pole net passed between. I have three fears of this trapeze-like contraption: 1) the 550 chord snaps and I crash to the floor on my knees; 2) the ceiling caves in and crashes on top of my head; or 3) the bar itself breaks in half, smacking me in the face and delivering two giant black eyes. Fortunately, I am not the heaviest guy to use this mechanism.

It's 0600 now. I must wake the PT criminals up. Their eagerness to face the day equals mine. They all roll back to sleep. The sun has broken the horizontal plane that separates the tolerable level of heat from the intolerable. If we are to run, we must leave now. The window in which you can see the gravel-strewn earth and not get scorched by the sun remains finite. It opens and shuts rapidly and assertively early in the morning and late in the evening. I walk outside and breath deep. The familiar scent of burning trash and sight of the broken obstacle course forces a juxtaposition of memories to the forefront of my mind. The burnt fields and campfire-like scents take me to Camp Freedom, a Boy Scout camp I knew so long ago. A very different experience with a dissimilar set of conditions, but the scent remains the same. In some regards, we remain the same, still chasing merit badges and adventures—albeit under much more hazardous circumstances. Burning cardboard and merit badges … I guess some things continue in a stream of time the world over.

We walk slowly down the road of our perimeter track; no one talks and no one runs. Our bodies are sore from the lack of true physical training lately. We stare at each other like members of the Polar Bear Club, cold-morning swimmers from summer camp that braved the cool morning air for a little fitness. However, like them, no one wants to break the ice. No one wants to jump in. No one wants to take the first step. We look around and shake our heads. I wonder if someone's legs will shatter with the first step we take attempting to run with such weak bodies.

I start out … slow. I feel old, but my body knows the motion. Rhythmically, I plod through the first mile. No one talks, but we start to feel better. Legs unfurl and blood migrates to the stiff joints. Things loosen up, and strides increase. The burnt-trash smell pervades the nostrils. Throats dry out as we round the burnt buildings and fields. Our breathing increases and sweat drips down. It's a cleansing sweat, one that liberates the body and purges the pores. The heart rate increases and the endorphins take over. The torrential sweat of hard work, I embrace it. The sweat I can get rid of, not the inescapable continuous damp sweat of the midday sun with flak vest and Kevlar helmet on. Our group stretches out as the pace increases. Soon we run alone but not in isolation. Alone with nothing but our private thoughts offset by our comrades sharing the same path. The sun begins its relentless climb. We finish running and wait for the string of comrades to once again coalesce. The sweat and steam rise off our bodies as our group rejoins. We are no longer alone. I guess we never truly are.

24 May: Finally starting to have a PT routine. I rotate a long run/easy run/tempo run/easy run. Unfortunately, my tempo runs aren't very fast and my long runs aren't very long; I will improve. Had a thirty-minute run and a little lift this morning. We ate some chow and then headed into Kirkuk to police up our PUK/KDP liaisons. Linked up with Colin Brooks at the division Assault CP [command post]. They set up in the middle of downtown Kirkuk. Funny seeing the woodland camouflage Bradleys of the 1st ID. They had good clean buildings, but I do not envy them at all. They have no room to move, and the locals are continuously on top of them ... "Mister! Mister!" they all chant. The Division G–3 [operations and plans officer] kept calling me Hackler (since I was wearing "Hackler's Molle Gear" with his name sewn on my shoulder and the G–3 had no idea who I was). Of course, we didn't make the correction and kept egging him on. It proved quite funny. He kept saying, "So Hackler, what do you think about this? Hackler, where are you from? Hackler, what did you do for your country today?" etc. We were dying. Half the group couldn't figure out who Hackler was.

Our liaisons didn't show, so we moved back to the TAC. Hung out there for awhile until things started zinging about one of the blacklist bad guys' occupying our area of operations. Of course, we did not vet the tip that led us down this road. We issued a two-battalion Frago and initiated movement to the town. We sent Beattie with the G–3, and I stayed at the TAC since they were not rolling the Brads ... and since the information was twenty-seven days old. I really did not feel like partaking in another all-night goose chase. Well, it seems to have unfolded precisely in that manner. We have UAVs flying around identifying dogs that we launch attack helicopters on. Everyone knows that we have unactionable information, but we face the fait accompli and the ever-present question: what if he is still there? It has become quite maddening. At least I was spared the associated pain of this madness. The engineers blew huge caches of weapons right next to our compound. We had dirt and dust falling all around us. It scared the locals out of their minds: 500 pounds of C4 and a cache of mortar rounds made for quite the shockwave.

25 May: Yesterday proved our last day of paradise freedom for awhile. We had our standard day away from the TOC with good PT, camp showers, and avoiding the heat of the day inside our building. We had to jump back to the TOC at 1700. The Bradley rolled pretty good today, and we made it back in no time. We had a briefing on the rules of the TOC ... namely, dealing with bodily waste. They set up on an asphalt pad—scorching hot with a perimeter in which we can't dig a slit trench. Of course, they don't have enough latrines for everyone ... two for 300 people, so they go in plastic bags and bottles and then throw it over the side of the wall into a giant fire ... that is probably the worst plan I have ever heard. Morale only improves since five miles away we have three unoccupied warehouse facilities that would prove twice as good, from both the quality-of-life and the tactical defensibility perspectives. I struggled all night to figure out why we came here until I went into the only building in our area. It is very nice. It has satellite TV and clean floors. It also has a sign on the front that says "Keep Out." It also has Internet connectivity. The soldiers are all out here baking on the asphalt, dodging these giant dust storms, while the XO observes from his nice cool building. The soldiers call it the plantation house. We had a giant dust/lightning/rain storm today. It blew all the equipment and tents everywhere. It was funny because everyone blamed it on the XO. I don't know why, but my natural reaction when it started was damn the XO. I can't stay next to the TOC—it drives me insane. The only good thing we did here was witness the UAV launch. Not real entertainment, but the little things amuse us now.

26 May: I broke away from the TOC at 1030 hours (the asphalt was cooking) and headed up to Kirkuk Airfield with Brummet. He had to attend a targeting meeting with the 173d ABN, and I had to not stay at the TOC. I ran into a bunch of guys I knew, including Danny Durbin, Fitzgerald, Major Petit, and Major Sanchez. Danny was hanging out at the front gate. Not sure what he was up to, but he looked good. They have contracted air-conditioning and live indoors. I can't begin to list all the amenities they have that we lack. We just aren't smart about things, especially in regard to our contracting. We don't contract for things the soldiers need. The 173d contracted barracks space and AC for their soldiers. We did the same for about five guys in the brigade. They had a dump truck out in front of their brigade headquarters. It had a single strand of concertina wire and some guards on it. Turns out, it had 999 20-kilogram gold bullion bars. The market value: $350 million. We will jump in a few days. I am not sure why we came back to the TOC. Clearly a case of misery loves company, but the TOC inflicts the misery upon themselves. Classic. We do still get to PT here, so we have a silver lining to our sand cloud. A soldier in 1-12 IN died today. Heard that he had a heart attack. He was twenty-five years old. That's crazy. I think we will jump here in a few days … until then.

27 May: Got a good 65-minute run in today. I am currently at twenty of forty-eight days in run days verse total days. We hung out doing PT and showering until about 0930. I really cannot account for the rest of the day. Went to the TOC for awhile and collected some awards information. I read a little bit, and then we had to jump the TAC twenty meters … we had some medevac helicopters stationing themselves here. Of course, we don't have any room here now, and we keep adding to the number of people in this area. Got to hold $10,000 in cash today. They confiscated it from some guy running cigarettes back and forth. His story turned out legitimate, so they gave the money back. I bet he sweated that one out. Turns out that the soldier in the 4th Engineers died from drowning. They went to an irrigation ditch to do laundry, and he jumped in. Tragedy. He was the first soldier we had killed. It's always tragic when it happens like that. The engineers are building an "Axis and Allies" board game from scratch. Quite comical. They have drawn the globe on one of the tables and are building all the little pieces on the computer. Hilarious. I think we will play soon.

28 May: The past two nights I have had catastrophic REM sleep disruption. The first night, we had a giant thunderstorm. The raindrops were as big as your fist. It physically hurt to get hit by them. Of course, I had no poncho hooch up, so I got dumped on. We rolled our poncho up onto the Bradley and were trying to pull it down in the middle of the storm. Brummet and I were totally confused, as it occurred at 0200. We finally got our hooch set up, and it stopped raining. Quite a spectacular storm, I must say; all my gear got soaked. It took a little while to get to sleep again ... oh well. Had the bike setup for the morning PT session. Worked pretty well. I had to ride early to avoid the crazy looks associated with riding a bike trainer in the middle of Iraq ... I guess it begs some questions. Rode for forty minutes and then woke everyone up to run. We then did our standard affair of shaving, showers, chow, etc.

After that we had school time for MOUT. I gave a class to one of the NCOs who taught all the guys the TTP [tactics, techniques, and procedures]. We did single team, single room. It went pretty well. It proved kind of nice to do something tactical again. I spent the rest of the day avoiding the sun and BSing with people. I guess it went by pretty quick. Last night Major Barnett woke me up from a dead sleep in the middle of the night. We were going to go on another goose chase off of some bad information passed up to us from one of the battalions. I was so confused by it all. Fortunately, we stood back down and went back to bed. I woke up at 0530 and just lay around until 0600. Very peaceful. We then got up for PT ... I am at twenty-two of fifty. Had a good run this morning—did 4 x 1,000 meter repeats. Felt pretty good. Now I am just hiding from the sun waiting for the 1500 respite and reading a little *Moby Dick*. It's getting harder to keep on writing, since we have the groundhog-day effect going on. It should improve once I get into command, but this month was pretty boring.

JUNE

A s June progressed, coalition forces adapted to the unwelcome prospect of continuing operations in Iraq. This involved a shuffling of forces, the development of military infrastructure, and the continuing evolution of tactics and techniques.

In the case of the 4th Infantry Division (Mechanized), units quartered among the Kurds or within pockets of northern Shia found the people generally friendly; the Sunni were far less likely to be. Captain Brown's narrative describes the migration of his brigade from its original objective areas southward into what came to be known as the Sunni Triangle. For combat troops, this was increasingly where the action was. By fits and starts, troops policing the relatively benign areas found themselves drawn into the restive ones instead.

Reinforcing and complicating this migration was the development of military infrastructure: logistical support areas (LSAs), supply routes, headquarters, maintenance facilities, airfields, and so on. Brown's comments about rear-echelon amenities and who had air conditioning and when—grousing in the finest tradition of the combat infantryman—reflected the emergence of semipermanent facilities. Over time, these would be supported by a predictably steady flow of ground convoys, but convoys and facilities alike would provide the embattled U.S. soldiers with that much more to defend.

The Army's senior leadership, aware of Iraq's logistical vulnerabilities, actively sought to generate as much support as possible from bases outside Iraq. This accorded with larger transformational initiatives to reduce logistical "footprints" within active theaters through such concepts as just-in-time logistics, split basing, and Intermediate Support Bases (ISBs). In Brown's narrative, the trend manifests itself in his surreal sojourn through Germany to obtain testimony relating to a friendly fire incident.

Brown comments that simply driving in Iraq's traffic was dangerous in its own right, borne out by the fact that a major fraction of coalition casualties would come from accidents alone. Interestingly enough, the spectacular accident Brown was involved in during this month suggested yet another hazard, organized crime. The money at the accident scene could as easily have come from robbery, smuggling, counterfeiting, or a host of other illicit activities. All that Brown and his soldiers encounter should be understood in the context of the lawlessness of much of Iraqi society. The country as a whole demonstrated a murder rate several times that of America's most dangerous urban centers, and deaths due to apolitical crimes of violence would dwarf those politically motivated throughout the 4th Infantry Division's tenure in Iraq.

In this dysfunctional country plagued by lawlessness, the collapse of the previous regime, and continuing attacks on coalition soldiers, U.S. forces groped to acquire an appropriate touch. Some argued for coming down hard in the recalcitrant areas, incarcerating thousands from the outset and relaxing gradually only as the security situation improved. Others favored a gentler, more negotiated approach. Whatever their philosophical preferences, the absolute deficiency in language skills at the unit level virtually forced the soldiers into heavy-handed solutions. It was better to be safe than sorry; the guilty and innocent could be sorted out only by those qualified to do so. Initially, too much reliance was placed on the bilingual Iraqis and informants who pursued their own agendas. Indeed, a truly reliable interpreter proved an invaluable asset.

Also, relatively large-scale operations could be forced on the scattered units with short notice. Brown describes one called PENINSULA STRIKE; another labeled DESERT SCORPION occurred in about the same timeframe. U.S. commanders quickly mustered bits and pieces from their wildly dispersed units into an operational mass while nevertheless leaving local security intact. It is a comment on professionalism and training at every level that they performed so well while doing so. It is a comment on the paucity of forces in theater that they had to.

---

2 June: Spent the past few days in the groundhog-day zone. The living conditions here at the TOC have not improved … we are idiots. I continue to get good PT daily and am currently at twenty-six of fifty-four. I finished *Moby Dick.* Made my top five list. Sheer genius. I went to Brian Faunce's and Pat Stobbe's change of command yesterday. 1-12 IN shacked up in one of Chemical Ali's old houses. Very nice, although they do not have the swimming pool filled yet. I ran into Jack Senneff and all the 1-12 IN guys. We discussed all the things going on in their sector.

The battle right now remains heavily civil-affairs oriented, but we don't want to admit this or place our efforts in that direction. We need to get the banks open, regulate the black-market gas, and get the police involved. Unfortunately, we continue to expend inordinate amounts of energy chasing phantom regime officials based on unactionable information. The blacklist, essentially a codified body count, represents our gauge for progress. The regime "ist kaput"—move on. However, the new government won't stabilize until we provide them the means to restore civil infrastructure and empower their police force … Civil Affairs. Jack and I talked about this for awhile. It's a total Catch 22. I do believe that ex-regime officials will surface the more stabilized we get the government.

After the 1-12 IN change of command, we headed down to D-Main at Tikrit. They are living at one of the bombed-out palaces. We rocked that building with a 500-pound bomb. We also dropped the bridge into the river, so they had to jerry-rig some crossing sites. D-Main had AC and a movie schedule. It's just a field version of Camp Doha. I envied them for about ten minutes. We got the plan for a new, improved giant operation with no real actionable information. We really need to work our HUMINT [human intelligence] a lot better across the board. Our ability to capture/neutralize targets is quite awesome; however, we have zero capacity to find these targets. I don't really know the answer, but do know that we do a pretty poor job of tapping into the local leaders. I think it's mostly language barrier and confusion of responsibilities. On the way back from Tikrit, we stopped at the 1-8 IN TOC. They are doing pretty good. I actually got excited to see them. The changing of the guard down there is ongoing. We have some really good guys going down there; I just need to knock out the COC inventories. All in all, it was a good, fast day. Did some PT today and have to pack up our gear. We move from "Andersonville" [named after a Civil War POW camp in Georgia] (minus the creek) tomorrow.

4 June: Packed up all my gear and launched the TAC back down to Samarra Airfield East … the full circle in forty-five days. I don't want to go south again … too hot. We used HETs since our tracks are running totally on metal [i.e., their track pads were worn out]. I stayed behind to attend Lieutenant Colonel Park's change of command tomorrow morning, and then we will launch down to link up with the TAC.

5 June: The change of command went well. I ran into all the fellas. The 1-12 IN is a great battalion, and they have done an outstanding job. I think Parks left with a real sense of accomplishment, and he caught his white whale commanding a battalion in combat. He flew out of Kirkuk right after the change of command. What a wonderful feeling that must have been. I thought *we* would leave right from the change of command, but we got caught up in all the briefings and aerial recons. I did not receive an invitation to any of those, so we watched some movies and hid from the sun at Andersonville. I almost finished reading Solzhenitsyn's *The First Circle*. I have nothing to do since I am separated from the TAC. I do good PT and hide from the sun. We have also developed the movie night routine. It helps the time go by.

6 June: Lieutenant Colonel Sassaman landed at the TOC. It was good to see him again. I guess he will shadow the colonel for this operation. We didn't leave for the TAC again today. I hate being separated from all my bags, although I did have the foresight to pack my throw bag accordingly. Now we are planning to leave on 7 June, after the 1-68 AR change of command. I broke through the halfway mark with PT yesterday. I am currently thirty-one out of fifty-nine.

7 June: The day goes pretty fast at Andersonville since so much of the time is simply spent on sustaining operations. Staff Sergeant Winters has labeled the one building on the compound the plantation house; one of the battle captains described the XO's behavior accordingly: "Never have so few taken so much from so many." I have never seen anything quite like it. I made it to the 1-68 AR change of command. Lieutenant Colonel Piscal did a great job. Talk about a guy that poured his heart and soul into an organization. Very nice event. He too flew back to the States. Both Parks and Piscal are going back to Fort Carson, and neither has a job. That must be nice. They deserve to freeload for a little while. I ran into my classmate Chad Giaccomozzi. Talk about a good deal. He will change command in July and head off to Stanford University for physics. He'll pull that gig for two years and then teach at West Point ... and I am not even in command yet. It's funny how I have fallen behind. I guess it's a function of the two years I spent stagnating on brigade staff. Oh well, that will pass here soon as well. It feels like all my classmates have these wonderful opportunities that I will miss ... two years in the brigade S–3 shop versus two years at Stanford—you choose.

8 June: After the change of command, we finally left for the TAC— seventy-two hours late. The drive took forever, and the associated comfort of the backseat of the S–3 Humvee did not shorten the experience. Everything started zinging once we showed up. Chaos and pinging ... or is it pinging to produce chaos. Whatever it is, it does not make things better or easier. I have never seen an operation as complex or with as screwed up a task organization as this one ... and I have seen a lot of confusion and messed up task organizations. We'll see how this pans out, but we have boats, helos, tracks, dismounts, MPs, CI [counter intelligence], THTs [tactical HUMINT teams], 101st ABN, 173d ABN, V Corps, etc. Craziness. Of course, we are operating 160 miles from our assigned sector in someone else's AO.

These plans take on lives of their own. I just can't believe that we committed all these assets off the intelligence tips we received. We definitely need to develop the situation more and commit the appropriate force—i.e., a company, not a brigade plus. Well, I have been pulling the morning shift since 0345 ... not fun, but it provides a chance to catch up. I heard on the radio that the HET escort detail received some RPG/small-arms fire. I can't figure out why this keeps happening in this area. Forty-five days ago we could not find anything down here. Now chaos reigns. They just don't have enough infantry guys here. We'll see how this all works out. I do know that it will prove a lot hotter down here. It's bad hot.

9 June: 127 degrees—that was how hot it got yesterday. PENINSULA STRIKE came and went pretty much according to plan. We did the combined arms rehearsal [CAR] at 0900 and then hid from the sun, conducting final precombat checks/inspections. Keven Beattie will take my place in the Bradley, and I'll stay back at the bunker with all the other assets. Major Barnett wanted me to go forward but decided to train up my replacement instead. It proved a good one to miss as the temperature hovered around 125 degrees all day and a Bradley and flak vest do not cool you down. The operation kicked off at 0100, but the initial flurry of activity began at 2300—launching birds, boats, UAV, etc. The air assault went smoothly, and the ground convoy and blocking positions all went over well.

In fact, everything went as planned until the MP battalion shot up a truck running one of their checkpoints. The truck was full of 2-503 PIR [Parachute Infantry Regiment] soldiers. No military in civilian vehicles was the rule for this operation, and they ran the checkpoint. We launched the medevac bird, and thankfully they took only superficial injuries. Everyone reported receiving small-arms fire and RPGs but no effects. I think we are still seeing the random shoot-up-the-sky-in-your-vicinity deal.

We secured all the high-value target [HVT] houses and detained 377 people in our holding facility. The THT teams are pumping them for information, but no big fish in the AO, it looks like. The informants all use us to settle personal vendettas from bygone years, and we always play along. The interpreters are working to gather all the information, but it seems all these detainees just worked for the Iraqi Intelligence Service and didn't play major roles in government decisions. The only action we did have occurred when a 1-8 IN soldier got shot with a shotgun at pointblank range. His RBA stopped the entire round, and he stood up and kept on going. I guess this body armor really works. They grabbed the guy and put him in the holding pen. The THT team leader told him that he killed the soldier and that it was his brother. The guy started crying … psyops [psychological operations]. He claims that he thought the soldier was a burglar. They are working him for information, but it sounds like he just got spooked and shot the guy coming into his house. We had to evacuate two Iraqi civilians that died of heart attacks during the mission. I guess the lead squads were moving down the street and the Iraqis came out on the porch and dropped dead. Their relatives had glycerin for them but to no avail. Obviously they had previous heart complications. It made for an interesting leadership-reaction event.

10 June: I finally went to bed about 0400, after everything calmed down. Of course, I woke up at 0730 with the sun beating down on my head and a horde of flies trying to carry me off. I spent the morning consolidating reports and gathering information. I finally broke free about noon for some personal hygiene. I was conducting a search for water when I came across the TAT [to accompany troops] box (a storage box about 3 x 2 x 2 feet) with the leftover melted ice from two days before. I couldn't resist the "canoe bath"—hilarious. I squeezed into the box full of ice water and just sat in it. It made me feel so much better. Fortunately, I had grabbed a new uniform off my Bradley prior to its departure forward … quite the moral boost. The rest of the day proved calm as everyone slept off the previous night's activity. I stayed up during the day but got to bed early. The assault CP came back; they looked awful. Everyone had sweat pouring off their uniforms and salt everywhere. They looked like Ranger School students due to all the water weight loss and bloodshot eyes from dehydration.

11 June: Woke up just before 0500. Nothing real big going on other than one of our boats got shot at on the river last night. Other than that, we are just working to sustain ourselves 160 miles from our BSA … what do they teach at SAMS [School of Advanced Military Studies]?

I did a great job avoiding the sun until about noon. The XO called and told me I was the investigation officer for the friendly fire incident two nights ago … great. I spent the remainder of the day interviewing guys from the 173d and hanging out at their TOC. Ran into Mike Fenzel and had a good long conversation with him. He hasn't changed much. It was good to see him, and he set me up for success with the interviews. They occupied the houses in the vicinity of Objective DAYTONA, so life proved pretty good for those guys—125 degrees doesn't feel too bad when you are inside. I conducted all the interviews and then drove to the scene of the incident. I consider us extremely lucky to have suffered such minor wounds on this one. The event proved far more confusing then I initially suspected it would. The confusion started with the vehicles the MPs had engaged ... a Humvee and a nontactical vehicle. The angles of fire just do not add up. I think we may have a combination of friendly fire and direct enemy action. Regardless, I have a lot of unanswered questions and a lot of work on this thing still. Unfortunately, my star witness was evacuated to Landstuhl ... makes for a tough investigation. Today is malaria pill day, and I am tired.

12 June: Well, spent all day yesterday with the MPs. We went back to the scene and re-created the checkpoint. Very interesting. I photographed the entire event, walked the scene, and took all the angles of fire. Felt very much like setting up a nonstandard live-fire range. I reached about the 60 percent solution and briefed the colonel. He wants me to go to Landstuhl to investigate further. I went through all my pictures with the MPs and then

Aerial view of typical urban terrain in Iraq

went to the scout platoon and went through the pictures with them. Each day I get more questions but understand all the dynamics better. I have to assemble each individual's actions and compile each viewpoint. Everyone has his own viewpoint, and they are all right. It's just I have to determine what happened. After interviewing all the 173d guys, I came back to the TAC and found out we had birds leaving in thirty minutes. I scrambled to type a memorandum, pack my bags, and get out to the airfield. It moved quite fast. The helo ride proved uneventful, but I did violate my no-helicopter-in-Iraq rule. Regardless of the violation, much less painful than driving. The TOC has continued to improve ... namely the plantation house. It has gotten really hot all around the country temperature-wise. Right now, I am waiting for some orders and then heading up to Kirkuk to leave for Germany. Planes, trains, and automobiles ... at least I'll be doing something. It's a crazy world. I don't know how high up this briefing will go.

21 June: Thought I would get out of Kirkuk right away. The Air Force told me they had a bird leaving at 0630, which means a 0330 manifest. I couldn't sleep, so I made some phone calls and screwed around on the Internet. Finally went to check in at 0300 and the moron told me the flight was for the next day. He asked me if I thought it was today, so I told him, "No, I normally just walk around Air Force hangars at 0300 in the morning." Yeah, the Air Force is way different. So I had to burn a day. That's easy in Iraq. Slept in until 0930 and woke up in the scorching heat. The airfield has a lot of amenities but no wind, which makes the nights quite a bit hotter than out in the desert ... and they have a lot more flies—the price of living someplace decent. I finished up my book and then went over to Finance to get some money. They had AC, so I hung out there for awhile. Ate Hot A's with the guys from 173d and then decided to go for a run ... bad idea. The food and running just didn't match up well. I then went through my e-mail and phone call routine and racked out before the flight.

Well, they did manifest and got to number 46 ... guess who had number 47? Me. It's maddening. So funny how nervous you get when they have something they can take from you; I am no longer a bottom feeder with nothing. My chance at a free trip to Germany suddenly turned me into a ravenous, caged animal attempting to escape. Luckily, they had another bird that afternoon. I remained beyond nervous and hid from everyone I knew until that bird showed up. I experienced the horrible feeling that someone would see me and say, "I didn't realize you hadn't left yet; why don't you just stay." I managed to hide out all day and convinced the air load planner to rearrange some cargo to create seats so I made it onto the plane. The cargo: 10th Special Forces Group redeploying to Fort Carson. Wow, I am jealous. Good for them. I'm jealous. Took a sleeping pill and crashed for the entire flight. Woke up, and it was cool outside. I went over to the 64th Replacement Company and got a room for the night. It was 2300 Iraq time, so I just got some food and a beer and crashed on a bed. So comfortable. Of course, the fire alarm blasted off at about 0200. I woke up, looked around, and went back to sleep. The guy I was sharing the room with wanted me to go outside, so I assured him that if I saw any fire I would jump out the window. Don't worry. Needless to say, no fire. More sleep. Woke up the next morning and had a large Army breakfast. Nothing in the world like an Army breakfast. Mess halls are the same everywhere you go, great breakfasts—pass on everything else.

After a luxurious breakfast, I walked back over to the airport to see about a rental car. It's Sunday, so everything pretty much remains shut down. I didn't have a hat to wear this entire time, but I figured it's the Air Force—what do they care. Turns out I got lucky with the rental car. I got the very last one … a silver Mercedes C180. The car just wants to drive itself. Went over to the PX [post exchange] for some civilian clothes. Of course, they have not opened yet, but they have a snotty Air Force specialist out front inquiring about my missing hat. I wasn't really in the mood to play around with him and did not want to wear my Kevlar, so I just ripped off his face instead. I guess he got the unfair brunt of two-and-a-half months in Iraq shoved down his throat at one time. Someone should have briefed him on choosing his battles wisely. I sent him on his way with his tail between his legs. It was wrong, but it felt good. He did not volunteer to escort me back to pick up my hat, and I assured him I would change into civilian clothes the second he provided me the opportunity to buy some.

I drove out the front gate on A5 heading south. Step into the AM. Total culture shock. The car hit 200 kph before I even got it into sixth gear. I slowed down substantially after that first burst. I think it had to do with Eminem blasting out "Super Mega Dance Party mit Bayern Drei." Got to Landstuhl and linked up with Specialist Johnson for some interviews. Great guy … so much different than our commo soldiers. I forgot how good I once had it. The hospital pretty much sucks, especially when they have so many war wounded. Thankfully, they can get them to this level of care so quickly. Everyone proved very cooperative and helpful, which made it easy.

I continued to run back and forth to the phone to coordinate with Jenny and Bill [his parents-in-law, then serving in Paris]. Linkup of two moving parties always proves difficult. Tried to check into guest lodging, but it was full. I had them make arrangements for me … I thought the Schloss Hotel sounded appropriate. I tried to drive over there, but they had some huge Vikingfest. After cloverleafing the objective, I finally gave up and decided to go for a run-search. The trails and trees of Germany reminded me of Fort Lewis. So awesome. The trails were so soft, and the trees so tall. The smells and woods of Germany brought back distant childhood memories. The timelessness of the German forest felt awesome. I think the fact I could do anything outside at 3:00 P.M. without bursting into flames proved a novelty in itself.

I finally checked in to the hotel. It's up on the mountain right next to the castle with 200-foot trees and paths all around. The Viking contingent sat outside drinking beers and enjoying the afternoon with trashcans on their heads and broad swords at their feet. I went to check in—my outfit: brown t-shirt and gym shorts. It's all I had. I explained to the Frau that I had civilian clothes en route. She accepted my apology and sent me up to my room. I sat out on the balcony drinking mineral wasser and enjoying the German countryside. I think Granddad's generation chose better in the countries they rebuilt, if not in the wars they had to fight. The clothes, Jenny, Bill, and Max all showed up within the hour. I had a shower with pressure, and we headed down to the front yard for beers and dinner. Sandy Ewers, Joe Ewers' wife, joined us for dinner—they are stationed in Germany. We had a great time … Jagerschnitzel and all. The meal and dessert knocked me out. I slept like a rock with the big German windows wide open and the cool air blowing in.

I woke up the next morning and ran on the trails with Bill. We went up to the Schloss overlook. I could live in Germany for a good long time. After running, we went over to the PX at Ramstein to buy random objects from my accumulated list. The flight line was packed with C–5s and C–17s. It looked quite busy. The C–5 looks like a monster. I sat outside eating Baskin Robbins ice cream and talking on the phone. I also bought a pair of shorts to hang out in. The joy of being comfortable does not go unnoticed by the deprived. After doddling around for awhile, I went back to the hospital and spoke with the doctors. Nothing real eventful, but I did refine some of my slides. I left Johnson with some phone numbers and headed back to the Schloss Hotel for Jagerschnitzel round two. The meal proved just as good as the night before.

I finally bid adieu and headed back to Rhein-Main to await transportation to Kirkuk … sad face. Needless to say, I did not peg my anxiety over getting a flight out. I checked into guest housing at Rhein-Main; unfortunately, the only room they had available was for colonels and above … so I encouraged them to pretend I was a captain in the Navy. They saw my orders and took pity. The next morning I did laundry, Internet, PX, and the gas coupon extravaganza. I followed the signs to the Esso station and ran into the beach for Ironman Europe in two weeks. I had to stop and take some pictures. Of course the beach was packed, and I joined in the melee. Swam for thirty minutes along the Ironman route and then just sat on a park bench enjoying the lake. Typical German beach with the Speedo brigade and scantily clad, saggy women named Helga. I have very distinct memories of countless summer days at the German Schwimmbad with all the associated pommes-frites, bratwursts, and soda without ice.

I stayed there until my desire for food outweighed my level of comfort and my clothes had completely dried. I then walked around downtown looking for a restaurant. Found a Greek restaurant … bingo. I had a huge plate of gyro meat and lamb chops. I forgot how much I love German-Greek food. I stuffed my face, and then went to gelativille for some ice cream. I then headed back to turn in the rental car. Of course their computer broke down, so I kept the car for another night. I checked on flights out and then headed back to the O–6 billeting. I couldn't go to sleep just yet, so I went down to the Amigo and drank some Jack and cokes while eating chips and salsa. There was a bunch of National Guard finance guys talking about the toughness of their summer assignment to Germany and how they weren't authorized rental cars. Pretty funny the disparity of wants, needs, and desires. I talked to them for awhile and then went to rack out.

Got an e-mail saying to try to come back through Baghdad if I couldn't get Kirkuk in the next twenty-four hours. Baghdad would prove a nightmare. Thankfully, a Kirkuk-bound C–17 had diverted into Rhein-Main for computer problems. I managed to get manifested on that one … as the only passenger. I then turned in the Mercedes with a tear in my eye, ate some Brotchen, drank a cappuccino, and bid civilization farewell. Kirkuk Airfield proved depressing. I couldn't sleep due to all the flies and mosquitoes that somehow figured out my mosquito net. I got up the next morning early and went for a run. After cleaning up, I went over to the ALOC and waited for transportation to the TOC. Mission complete, morale crushed.

Leaving is always the double-edged sword ... so hard to come back. It feels like Christmas break at Ranger School, or Plebe Christmas at West Point. It's so hard to return to the gloom period. Instead of returning to the gloom period, I returned to the summer solstice. Redeployment to America seems so far away. Found out upon return that we were moving south in the next couple of days. Not good. We need to go north. Fortunately, I received numerous packages. I am thinking of selling baby wipes to the Iraqis now. If we could teach them about personal hygiene, we could make a killing. The TAC had not changed at all; they were all filthy and sleeping right next to the wall urinal because it had the most shade. Wow. I am back to the world of thinking for 35-year-old men. I made the NCOs move them away from the latrine. I don't know if I really care whether or not they get dysentery, I just don't want them giving it to me—Realpolitik on the microscopic level. You just get beat down by stupidity here, and these guys know better. I guess stupid hurts ... really bad. I finished the briefing and am waiting to get on the division commander's calendar. Once complete, I'll start COC inventories. The one thing that I learned from my travels: we are living worse than anyone else ... and it is our own fault. Oh well, we are moving. The plantation house screamed in agony. Ha, small victories.

22 June: Spent the day working on some slides and hiding from the sun in the Plans van. The HETs were supposed to show up to take us south; but they proved late, of course. It got too late to ride around on HETs, so we spent the night and the TAC left in the morning. The CG is supposedly coming today, so I can brief this investigation and move on. It's my last official act as a brigade staffer ... unless Keven goes on emergency leave and then I have to stay in the TAC. I just can't break free. I was doing a great job of being expendable but not quite worthless up here at brigade ... sage advice for aspiring company commanders. This investigation wouldn't seem so bad if it wasn't backing me up against a change of command.

23 June: The CG came for the briefing, and it went smoothly. He wants me to brief all the brigade commanders now. I guess the final stretch to command is going to prove a long one. I hit up the brigade commander about my status, and he said not until the completion of this operation. I guess no one feels the ticking of the clock except for me. On a good note, Hancher got the new "NOFX" CD. It's really funny. The weather proved a little bit cooler today. I guess we passed the summer solstice, but it will continue to get hotter. Speaking of the solstice, I have developed a new primitive holiday centering on 21 June. When I returned from Germany, I had a bunch of boxes and mail.

I decided to open one each night as the sun went down. It's my version of an Iraqi Hanukkah. I tried to explain it to Abbas, our interpreter, but he didn't seem to get it. He couldn't get me a menorah either. What kind of Islamic fundamentalist nation is this?

26 June: The most dangerous thing we do here in Iraq is drive. We had a very cogent reminder of this coming down the Jabal Hamrin Ridge with the command group (two BRT gun jeeps, the CSM, colonel, and S–3). Four Arabs in a car came screaming past our little convoy. About three minutes later they slammed into an Arab truck coming up the ridge ... total chaos. As we pulled up, we established security and assessed the situation. The driver of the truck crawled out the windshield uninjured, but his load of fruit scattered to the four winds. The entire engine compartment of the car collapsed into the front seat. Not good. The trunk blew open, and millions of Iraqi dollars went everywhere. A guy in the chase car was wailing, but somehow through his sorrow he managed to collect up all the money. I don't know what these guys were up to. Oh well.

I moved with Staff Sergeant Harrison to the car with our CLS bags. We put on some gloves as the other Arabs started dragging a guy out of the back left seat—completely disregarding the idea of neck and spine stability, but we really couldn't communicate that fast enough. As they got him out I moved to assess the other guys. The driver had a broken neck and no face—real dead. The guy riding shotgun had a smashed face and spinal fluid leaking everywhere. The guy sitting in the back right had no pulse. Three guys real dead on impact. About the same time, the Arabs had sprung the back right guy free. He was a really big dude. We went to work on him in the messy scene of gas, oil, and blood. I had the Humvee drivers and other BRT establish security and stop traffic around us as we worked. The guy had a pulse of 60 and was snoring—totally unconscious. Told the colonel to start working an aerial medevac if we wanted this guy to live. Sergeant First Class Barreto took the 9 Line and started trying to get FM while Schwartz worked the TACSAT. This all happened incredibly fast. Everyone seemed to know what they needed to do—made it very nice.

Harrison kept the guy on his side while I cleared his airway with an MRE spoon—I don't know why, but that morning I stuck my brand new MRE spoon in my pocket. We thought his teeth were all busted, but I think he just had bad teeth. His face was pretty messy—broken nose and shattered jaw. Blood drained all out his mouth. About this time, a senior medic showed up with more gear. I told her I would work the airway and cardio while she continued with the secondary survey and started the IV. Harrison and I rolled the guy onto his back and I measured him for a J tube. Harrison got the J tube and started jamming it down his throat. I quickly reminded him of the roof of the mouth flip technique. The tube then went right in, but totally filled with blood. Sh—. We rolled him back on his side and drained him again. Of course, we ripped the IV out when we did this—oh well, we're the JV team. Once we drained him and got the IV back in, I went to check on the medevac status … nothing on either radio or iridium cell phone—we were in a commo black hole.

I made the decision to move east and continue calling the medevac bird. At this point, one of the Arabs started yelling at me—"Alive! Alive! Breath!" I went over to the passenger side of the car and straightened out the guy's really crooked head where the Iraqi pointed. As I got his airway straight, he started agonal respirations as his lungs collapsed. Totally freaked me out. Nasty. I now had his blood, sweat, and brains all over my hands and a demonstration of agonal breathing reminiscent of a scene from a horror movie that I won't soon forget. I told the Iraqi that he was dead and went back to the only guy we could really help.

We still didn't have communication with anyone outside our convoy, so I had the medics clear out the back of their 5-ton and get a sheet of plywood out—our new stretcher. We loaded the guy onto the board. I took his pulse—80 and he still had good respirations when we loaded him. I taped the IV bag to the top of the 5-ton and then helped the medics in. I told them they were in charge of the patient now as we got everyone turned around and headed toward Tikrit. I gave their captain instructions to drive east until he could get a hold of the medevac bird on 3355 plain text and then talk the pilot in. I then got in with the rest of the convoy after policing the scene and collapsing our perimeter. We got through to the TAC and had them relay the information up to the main in order to get police out to the gruesome scene. I wonder why they had all that money? Major Barnett thought they were up to no good … makes you wonder.

We finally made it to LSA ANACONDA and linked up with the TAC—not a bad location—they have a chow hall here. This place reminds you of the "haves and have-nots" of war. It's run by III COSCOM [Corps Support Command]. They have lots of AC, hot chow, and luxuries; they have a soldiers' club here with weekly dances. Crazy. I call it Cam Ranh Bay, Iraq. We are now allowed to run in shorts along the airfield. They say this is our final set. No one is falling for that one again.

I linked up with 1-8 IN. They are in the process of doing a 180 with regard to the leadership and capabilities of that battalion. They just sound confident now. I am in the midst of right-seat rides for this mission, after which I start COC inventories. Lieutenant Colonel Sassaman set the date for 10 July—actually works out nice. Sassaman has that battalion chasing bad guys. He's very aggressive, which is what this AO needs. It's the worst section of Iraq right now, and they had zero infantry here. Well now, these jackasses are getting knees in their backs and the screws turned tight on them instead of having free rein to lob RPGs at medevac vehicles. Big-stick diplomacy after nightfall. Hopefully, the area clears up with all these dismounted patrols. The 3-7 CAV just doesn't have the MTOE [modified table of organization and equipment, alluding to their lack of manpower, supplies, and equipment] to get this region under control. I guess that is why we had to move so far south. Tactically, we are just hunting bad guys. Our DIVARTY lost two soldiers the other day … kidnapped from a checkpoint they set up for demolitions. TF 20 sounds like they got a tip and are launching this morning. We'll see how it goes.

30 June: It's been a crazy few days. I managed to escape the clutches of brigade. The TAC jumped from 1-8 IN's location, and I just stayed … fait accompli is the only way to get things done here. Had a good conversation with Sassaman … three-hour counseling session with an A CO PL [Company A platoon leader] and myself. He takes so much time to get guys on the team. He has really established the command climate for this battalion.

After that, I finished my book *Appointment in Samarra* [by John O'Hara] and racked out for a couple hours before commencing Operation SIDEWINDER. We went with the engineer company on Objective OHIO. Good learning experience … we are winning the "hearts and minds" over here. We rolled up a farmhouse full of women and children. They had three guys of age but nothing else significant. We had 100 guys roll into the objective area at 0100 in the morning with helicopters and APCs [armored personnel carriers] all over the place. We found a scythe. Can you say "busted raid?" We flex-cuffed all the men and placed them outside on the front lawn with sandbags over their heads. The women freaked out. I grabbed the translator and had him go talk to them. The THT teams are very unaggressive. You have to jumpstart them on every single question. I am just going to give them a list and yell out numbers for them to ask on the objective ... too easy, and how long have we been doing this?

We got back real late, and I just crashed in the hangar. Slept in until 1000, but it got crazy hot. Went to shave and clean up and got a call saying I needed to report to the brigade TOC. Great. Turns out I had to brief all the brigade commanders on my investigation. We flew up to Tikrit. Division is fighting a different war—living in the palace complex with central AC, satellite TV, etc.

The briefing went well. Kinda funny—battalion commanders were standing along the back wall and the CG and I did all the talking. [Maj. Gen. Raymond T.] Odierno is a phenomenal commander, and the briefing went well. All the advantages I gained from the AC at D-Main got quickly erased as I entered the sauna box of the Black Hawk. They fly doors closed here because of the dust, so you just suffer from the heat in the back. Got back to the airfield and talked to the medevac guys. Turns out the Iraqi we treated the other night is still alive. I don't think he is doing so well, but he lives. Minor victories. Of course, they will probably blame the Americans for the whole incident, even though all we did was help. Not much else to report. We are jumping over to 1-8 IN TOC today. Hopefully, living conditions improve. I know that they are at brigade. I can honestly say you never really worried about the living conditions at brigade because you had so many other folks more worried than you. Battalion is a different story. These guys don't even have cots. Going on three months now and they are living like total animals ... the disparity of this war.

JULY

J uly deepened the recognition that the battle for Iraq was going to go on for awhile. On 4 July an audio recording of Saddam Hussein urging insurgents to resist coalition efforts made its way onto Arabic airwaves. A mosque in Fallujah suffered a devastating internal explosion that clearly indicated bomb making had spread to religious buildings. Attacks on U.S. troops continued, driving the overall total of combat dead past 147, the benchmark established by Operation DESERT STORM in 1991. On 22 July 101st Airborne Division soldiers surrounded and killed Hussein's sons Uday and Qusay in a spectacular shootout in Mosul. By 29 July Hussein was back on the airwaves, praising his sons as martyrs for Iraq and urging others to emulate them. Perhaps even more ominous, about 10,000 disaffected young men joined the militia of Muqtada al-Sadr, the emerging voice of Shia opposition, in the holy city of Najaf. The extension of armed hostilities from the Sunni minority to the Shia majority would be troubling indeed. Angst over all this was incompletely offset when Ambassador L. Paul Bremer, the presidential envoy to Iraq, introduced a broadly representative 25-member Iraqi Governing Council (IGC) to guide the nation toward free elections and a constitutional government.

Continuing unrest was accompanied by a shift in tactics. In June the insurgents had attempted a few direct-fire ambushes on combat troops. These went badly for them. Even an isolated Bradley platoon packed far more firepower and lethality than the insurgents could hope to muster. By July they were placing increasing reliance on improvised explosive devices (IEDs), RPG potshots at soft targets (unprotected or unarmored targets), and mortar rounds lobbed in from hasty positions that were as hastily abandoned. Logistical support areas and the routes into and out of them became favored targets. Although the odds of inflicting significant damage were low, the odds of disruption and publicity were high and the possibility of evasion without contact was high as well. Captain Brown's first missions as a company commander were cat-and-mouse exercises to snuff out fleeting mortarmen before they could fire again.

Tactics, techniques, and procedures continued to evolve, with both sides warily pacing themselves against each other. The durable M1A1 tanks and M2/M3 Bradleys were everywhere: guarding fixed points, escorting convoys, overwatching patrols, and taking the fight to the identified enemy. This in turn ramped up enormous demand for spare parts and maintenance, which the theater, still bruised from the maintenance shortcomings from the march on Baghdad, was unprepared to handle. This situation would affect Brown, and it would become worse. Commanders worked with what they had.

Tactics, techniques, and procedures also involved making an appraisal of and gaining the confidence of the local Iraqis. This would have been a complex undertaking even had the Americans spoken the language. Balad, the town most prominent in Captain Brown's narrative this month, had a Shia core surrounded by a Sunni hinterland. The disparate reception of the Americans was not as simple as Shia versus Sunni, however. The web of relationships, loyalties, and jealousies had to be picked through tribe by tribe, clan by clan, and family by family. The situation was complicated by the fact that all knew the Americans would balk at wanton bloodshed and murder whereas the insurgents would not. Fear for the safety of their families governed the behavior of many, if not most Iraqis. Despite these risks, by the end of July we did see Iraqi police in new uniforms out on the streets of Balad—and the overworked U.S. infantrymen grateful for their presence.

The American attitude toward Iraqi opponents was hardening and hesitation to open fire receding. On at least two occasions Brown intervened personally to keep his soldiers within the boundaries of the laws of war. Heat, fatigue, surreptitious attacks, combat stress, and Iraqis caught in calumny or untruths fired a spirit of resentment in the men routinely in pursuit of the enemy. Ironically, the Iraqis were not alone in perceiving the truth as they would prefer it. Brown observed with bemusement as a messy series of events—where his company took out three mortars, captured a dozen suspects, returned fire in a built-up area, paralyzed the battalion command net for an hour, killed an innocent mother, and weathered a major row with the locals—morphed into a single report emphasizing the triumphs and ignoring the tragedies. All that was said was true, but not all that was true was said.

---

1 July: We got to the new 1-8 IN TOC location. Huge improvement. Probably the nicest location I have spent any amount of time at yet. They actually have AC operational … some of the time. We have a decent building with a porch for chow time. Lots of rooms and it remains relatively clean. We take one step at a time. Not a bad place to hang my hat for a few days. I went through all my gear; I have a ton of stuff. I don't know where it all comes from. It's such a pain jumping vehicles since you just accumulate stuff as you go. We ate dinner at 1500—way too hot for T-rat lasagna. Well, I won't have this computer for too much longer. Brigade is screaming for it.

I guess two computers per TOC captain ain't quite enough. It's funny how fast those guys can frustrate you.

Today proved one of those crazy days. It started out easy enough ... waking up on the roof of the battalion TOC outside Balad, Iraq. Lieutenant Colonel Sassaman wanted me to ride with him today ... very interesting. We walked over to the police station and harassed them for not painting over the anti-Saddam graffiti. The MPs continue their leader-teaching program with those guys—just not all that aggressively. We messed around there for awhile without an interpreter; I don't know how effective our conversation proved. We then rode out to Charlie Company to get the scoop on the bad guys they caught last night. One of the kids was the nephew of the Balad mayor. That should prove interesting since we have a meeting with the mayor at noon. They had six detainees for the S–2 to run up to Samarra Airfield East. What a painful process they make us go through with these guys. We left there and went back to the police station to link up with the 3-7 CAV commander for a joint meeting in Balad. The people in Balad itself love Americans; it's the punks in the urban sprawl that hate us—Ba'ath Party suburbanite flunkies.

We had to walk along the street to get to the meeting. I was walking out front while Sassaman and the 3-7 CAV commander walked behind me. After about 100 meters I looked back and saw that I was alone. Not good. I went back to the only building they really could have gone into and walked around the outside. I started getting a little nervous seeing how those two guys who were kidnapped ended up dead. I didn't want to walk into the building since I could get surrounded with nowhere to run, so I walked all around the building looking in each of the windows. Crazy feeling being the only visible American. Eventually, I heard Sassaman laughing and figured out what room they were in. I gladly rejoined the two battalion commanders.

The meeting proved pretty productive; it always does when you bring the press and $10,000 in cash that you just hand over. It wasn't our operation ... not very well run in my opinion. They gave us a bunch of information, but the Civil Affairs guys seemed uninterested in it. It's funny—they are trying to win the hearts and minds passively while we continue to win them over with our "bullish" tactics. Well, they get ambushed every night and never catch any bad guys, whereas we bring in ten a night. Drinking tea and eating random meat only gets you so far—you have to continue the raids. The meeting broke up, and we went to eat some more random meat. I think I am starting to regret that decision now; however, I was starving. We did the project list and went through the TTP. Basically, Lieutenant Colonel Sassaman took everything over even though it isn't his AO yet. No one has done anything in this area for three weeks; we will make it all happen in two.

We left lunch and had to deal with the freak show associated with the arrest of the nephew. Sassaman got the mission of personally escorting the kid back to the mayor. Not good. We brought him back and explained all the dangers associated with celebratory fire. The scouts almost smoked those guys with .50-cal. We left the mayor's house and headed back to the TOC. As we passed an alley, I spotted two guys with AK–47s. I yelled for the Humvee to stop, and we all piled out for the chase. These guys freaked out; the unit assigned here never chases guys. They ran down to a corner; Sassaman, the master gunner, and I started maneuvering on them. I had a fleeting shot but didn't take it due to the abundance of little kids on the street. We started running the alleyways using the gun jeeps in support. I took cover behind a corner and pulled security on an internally opening gate. Well, it opened, I switched my rifle to semi, and drew a bead … on a four-year-old little girl. Fortunately, I didn't fire, and she ran back in after my hand signal. We rummaged through the AO for awhile but realized we didn't have the combat power to seal off the area.

I don't think I will forget that whole scene. I brought the command Humvees up, and we drove the area; but the locals informed us the AK bandits had escaped on motorcycles. It's funny how much goes through your mind in those situations. You have all the adrenaline, the breathing, and the heart rate for the chase. I couldn't take that shot because of the kids even though the ROE clearly authorized me to shoot. I am a little pissed at myself for not taking the shot, but it was a bad shot. The good guys know: AK–47 = you get shot. In our little AAR [after action review] (we AAR every contact), I stated the only thing I would have done differently is to fire warning shots. I always forget how hard it is to "break the seal" on live fire, especially two-way.

Well, this week has proven adventurous. I guess it's a new month and all. I reported up to battalion on our little contact, and then we went to link up with Major Gwinner (new XO, real strong). We went on some recons of potential future TOC locations since Colonel Rudesheim dictated to Sassaman that we had to move out of the nice house … aren't we the conquerors here? Those two are always fighting. Sassaman was none too happy about it all.

We did find a good TOC location. It's a school. They are out for the year and desperately want us to move in and fix it up. I told them we would leave by 20 September when classes resume. Everyone wins.

We finally got an interpreter—Ed from Chicago. He's quite funny and really good. We finally returned to the old TOC location. Battalion life proves fast and furious. We had a little welcome ceremony for Ed. Sassaman is so good with building the team. We had an update in which the battalion staff openly mocked the company I am taking over for half an hour. It's good to know all the problems … bad to have your unit dragged across the coals.

I should have fired warning shots. Still frustrated with not getting those guys. The next time I am just going to run as fast as I can—no soft-clearing anything. I am just going to chase them down and scalp them. I get so pissed at these guys taking potshots at our supply convoys, and then when I see them I don't shoot since they were in a crowd. Now they will probably shoot at someone else tonight. It's so frustrating when our contact remains so fleeting. I guess it's best not to endanger the civilians, but they have to flush these guys out. I watched another beautiful Iraqi sunset and then we had story time about our day's activities. Hilarious. Sassaman just had his 9-mil, so I had to bust him out about being a Keystone Cops look alike. All in all, it was a good day … but I didn't kill the guy with the AK.

2 July: Today was not quite as interesting as yesterday. I had the chance to clean a uniform this morning, and then we rolled up to LSA ANACONDA. I saw how the better half lives. I got to pick up my deployable hand receipt from the property book officer and had a good discussion with those guys. Looks like I have fourteen pages of inventoriable items for the company COC inventory. This could prove painful. Oh well, I have until 10 July.

After that, we linked up with Bravo Company for a trip up to "Military City." Basically, it's the housing area for all the Balad Air Force pilots. They really don't have a vested interest in screwing with us. They merely want to maintain their current standard of living while preventing "Ali Babba" from getting all their goods. They all work on the airfield for us. I went over to talk to five of their guys while Lieutenant Colonel Sassaman spoke with brigade on the radio. While I was perfecting my Arabic dialect, I heard a blast of machine-gun fire less than fifty meters from my location. I ran back behind the Bradley for cover and to assess the situation … one of the Bravo Company squad automatic weapon [SAW] gunners had an accidental discharge. Turns out he was using a piece of shrubbery to hold the trigger mechanism in place. Are you kidding me? The branch broke, and bullets flew. Great first impression, guys. That got the blood boiling for the rest of the day. We had a long discussion with the town leadership following our self-imposed "contact." It proved smoking hot, and I got hungry. We headed back to the CP to link up with the colonel. They went out to release some detainees back into the community; I just chilled out at the TOC and printed counseling and command philosophy stuff.

3 July: I went to bed about 2230. I was totally racked out when *Boom!* Our entire building shook. I had earplugs in and was totally confused. I then heard a bunch of small-arms fire. I rolled off my cot and started putting on all my gear ... okay, so it was all Tim Knoth's gear. I ran out front and tried to gain situational awareness. Best we could tell, someone launched an RPG or threw a hand grenade at us. The guards and scouts started chasing some guys down. We remained busy on the net for a little while and then things died down. I went back to sleep with all my gear on. About 0330 Major Gwinner woke me up and told me we had some intelligence on bad guys in the village. We started putting together some teams to clear the joint at first light. We had the mortar platoon come over to help out the TOC guys. We took the informant and drove around throwing chem lights in the bad guys' front yards. After that we came back, divided the town into sectors, and then started our Keystone Cops raids. I had a bunch of twenty-year-old aggressive, inexperienced kids on my team ... good, I'll follow *them.* It's funny, the more experience you have, the less desire you have to kick the door and go in first.

Our little team cleared three buildings. Total squalor. Not much in our buildings except for some old timers and the one-per-house AK–47. Half these guys work for the police force. We detained all the males for questioning. We then sent the meat wagon around to pick all these guys up. Major Wright, Lieutenant Colonel Sassaman, the S–2, and I sat at a picnic table with the masked-up informant for some questioning as the sun came up. I saw pretty early on that we had a busted raid, so I left to go get some sleep. This country is so poor ... and hot. Of course I couldn't sleep past 0800, so I got up for my morning monkey bath. After that we went over to the police station to link up with 3-7 CAV for our mayor meeting in Balad. We rolled into downtown Balad and had our little chat with the mayor and the imam [prayer leader]. I guess we picked up someone last night who was causing some intertribal conflict. This caused a long-drawn-out debate. Turns out we picked up this guy because they were beating him up because of his regime association. He's in the hospital, so there really isn't much we can do for Sheik Haji-Turkeman. What a name.

After our meeting we went out to lunch ... way out in the country. We ate on the floor of some chicken farm—no shoes, no chairs, no plates. We had some giant fish and rice. Very tasty. You just eat it with pieces of bread and hope you don't get some horrible dysentery or kidnapped for that matter since you are way out in the boondocks. Crazy country. We basically ate a giant fish on the floor of a barn with the ranking officials of a 200,000-person city. What a country. Pictures and words cannot describe the things we do here. After our dinner we went over to Matt Cunningham's company. They are doing really well; they are attached to 3-7 CAV. We journeyed back to the TOC for naptime. Very nice but so hot. When you sleep during the day, you just sweat bad. The ideal thing to do would be to set up with air conditioning in a super-dark hangar, operate solely at night, and just rack out during the day. Hopefully, I'll reach that state quickly with Bravo Company. We continue to plan our Fourth of July party. It should be fun. I think I will launch a bunch of rounds into the air. Time is going faster now.

4 July: Last night proved pretty uneventful. We walked a little foot patrol around the perimeter and then just racked out. Not too much going on. I just hung around this morning and straightened out my gear. I start COC inventories tomorrow. We are supposed to barbeque sometime today. It's a pretty lazy day thus far. I did eat some crackers and Italian tomato-paste dip while drinking Perrier. That sounds pretty weird coming from the squalor of Iraq.

6 July: I lost the computer. I guess the brigade arcade was not complete without it. I am back to the pad and paper. We had a good Fourth of July dinner. They brought steaks and hamburgers up from Kuwait. Lieutenant Colonel Sassaman went around to all the companies and gave awards and inspiring speeches. T.K. and I feel like he is the "Gladiator." We played a little music and threw horseshoes until the mosque started blaring its call to prayer. Tim McGraw versus Mosque music. The dichotomy of this place never ceases to amaze. I spent one more night in the lap of luxury prior to heading down to the company with Sassaman. We hung out for awhile, and I inventoried some stuff. We then did some PT. I think we scared some people by running in the heat.

Eagle Six (Sassaman's Bradley) at the Balad Mosque

LSA ANACONDA took more mortars last night. You can see them from our bunker complex. It's reminiscent of the scene in *Band of Brothers* where they are in the back of the truck watching the artillery in the distance. ANACONDA remains a very easy target … 18,000 people who don't patrol. I guess we had eighteen casualties there the other night—that is unacceptable. We spent the rest of the night looking for the mortar crew. We took down a few houses—some were the same houses from the week before—and confiscated more weapons, but mortars are tough to find if you don't get a Q36 radar hit and you have to action on crater analysis. It's maddening. You can lob a few mortars and be gone before we get helicopters and the QRF [Quick Reaction Force] notified, let alone get to that grid. You have to be there waiting for them … that's what I will do once in command. The area they fire from is in my AO … guess where B 1-8 IN will be the evening of 10 July. The company is struggling with maintenance right now, particularly generators for the Brads. We need to figure out some systems to keep things going. Ted Bryant (the old CO) might get evacuated because of some sort of *Jurassic Park*–looking foot infection. That would make things very interesting, to say the least. Well, I need to get going on those inventories.

9 July: It's been a crazy few days. The COC inventories just eat at your time. I haven't done anything tactical with the company—it's just been way too crazy. The TOC and UMCP get mortared every other night and I have to go up there to inventory my equipment ... I go during daylight. There is a Mad Mortarman north of LSA ANACONDA that someone needs to get serious about catching before he hits something big. I ran into Hancher today; he had a similar hide-under-the-cot experience that I did with the RPG drive-by ... too funny. I went up to Tikrit with Lieutenant Colonel Sassaman yesterday looking for a Bradley to no avail. I did get to really see how the other half lives—unreal. They live better there than at Fort Hood. Central AC in a palace with all the associated MWR [morale, welfare, and recreation] stuff makes it easy. Saddam lived large and so do these guys. I would rather be stationed in Tikrit, Iraq, than I would Fort Hood, Texas. Of course I didn't find the Bradley, so back to square one. It's attached to the division assault CP down in Baqubah. Oh well, the COC will happen; they'll have to sign my giant missing-items memo. I spent all day getting that typed and then swung by the brigade TOC to find out what's going on. Everyone is moping a bit since the latest redeployment date is 1 April. Great! Well, chow is here; it comes at 1400 scorching hot.... Never worry about getting a cold plate. I heard an initial report that a guy in A/1-12 IN (Jack's company) got shot with an RPG and lost his leg. That sucks! Makes you feel a lot less sorry for these Iraqis and their cowardly ambushes. What happened to the Arab pride stand-up-and-fight ideal we read about?

11 July: It's been a crazy couple of days, that's for sure. I took command at 1000, 10 July 2003. It was a nice ceremony. I used the Normandy flag speech. The guys just need something to be proud of. Major Barnett was very sad/excited with the whole ordeal. He was like a proud father, and the colonel actually gave me a coin. Immediately following the COC, the BC [battalion commander] and brigade commander gave me an expanded AO

Bravo Company, 1-8 Infantry, at LION FOB

and the license to hunt the Mad Mortarman of Balad. I gave a quick Frago and met with the platoon sergeants to go over my command philosophy. This company is so ready to take off. They just need a modicum of guidance.

We built a mini-range on the perimeter, and we will shoot there daily. They love it. We also started working some quality of life issues. We have a great battalion staff who's willing to work it for us … if we ask. It's amazing how that works. Had my guys go in early to do the Vietnam patrols and set in counterambushes while I went to the 1800 battalion Frago for the mission on the twelfth. Everyone then rolled out to my sector. I had a squad in contact when I showed up and had to deal with a bunch of communications issues in my Humvee. I got on my Brad, and things started to click for me. I got the AH–64s down on my net and started working the sector. We were working the AHs with our lasers, and they were giving us good spot reports with theirs. It worked really well, and Lieutenant Colonel Sassaman got on the net and told everyone to take notes because school's in session. We always talk so much trash on the net. It felt good to be back making things happen. All in all, it was a good long day—0230.

I got up this morning and worked the Op Order piece. I had the platoon leaders in here working it with me—a little parallel planning. I think this will work out quite nicely since there is no time. I had all the officers working except for one who I thought was at the UMCP. It turns out he was 200 meters away in his bunker pulling "weapons guard" while his platoon was up at the UMCP for their maintenance day. I spoke with him, but I don't know if the lights are on for this guy. We have aerial QRF tonight, so it should be a good mission, but we still need time to prepare for the next. I have zero time now as a commander; but everyone works very hard for us, so it's great. I guess a soldier in 64th (one of Dena's) was killed yesterday. It's under investigation but not due to enemy contact.

12 July: We have a company operation going on tonight, and the guys are pumped. Right now they are out confirming zeroes and test-firing weapons … that haven't been fired since Kuwait … BS. I went out on the mission last night. We had an inordinate amount of lessons learned. We got two UH–60s for the operation. I had the platoon do the whole thing … with a little prompting. I thought we were a total soup sandwich, but then the higher-ups all started singing their praises for the platoon and the indirect mission we fired. I guess we worked it out enough on the company net to make it sound smooth on battalion. I had them clear a cemetery area where Q36 picked up radar hits and then exfiltrate back on the birds. I think I overwhelmed them with tactics, techniques, and procedures with the helicopters. The irony was that all the mech guys were doing an air assault raid while I, Roy [Maj. Darron Wright] from 82d Airborne Division, and Sassaman watched from our Bradleys. Yeah, they got lots of advice and lessons learned. I was a little pissed until I linked back up with them and saw how excited they all were … it was the first helicopter ride for some of them. That made me smile. Guys were coming up thanking me for getting the birds. What a different perspective.

It's a crazy feeling riding the roads of Iraq at night. We rolled up to the battalion CAR this morning at 1000. Right when I showed up Sassaman grabbed me and dragged me into the FAS [Forward Aid Station]—he was pissed. Charlie Company took two casualties from ten grenades thrown over the wall of one of their platoon compounds at 0600 that morning. They had zero security. He made me examine every single wound like I was a surgeon. Thankfully, no one was killed. We got lucky. I briefed all my guys on these dangers. You just can't live next to Route 1 like they are doing up there. I prefer the wide-open space inside our armor battalion's perimeter. We had a good rock drill with the company and fired our weapons—they are going to be great.

14 July: Large chunks of time just fly by when you're in command. The mission went pretty well. We went into Tu-Pac Shakur (our jihad town) with a north hook and south upper cut. The city lies on a "C" with MSR [Main Supply Route] LINDA. It's a crazy Mogadishu-type city … except we have Bradleys. We did a simultaneous takedown of five houses. One house was separated and I sent the XO, Jimmy Bevens, and Red Platoon to that one. I went to the block of houses that we had labeled X2–X5. I had White Platoon establish outer security and Blue do the search. We dismounted 800 meters from the objective, and the infantry moved forward to establish the infantry cordon. Once that was emplaced, we breached the doors and established the Bradley outer cordon. I had two Apaches working the area for me, providing external security on my company net. It worked out nice. I had some initial troubles getting the infantry moving; but, once launched, it went down well. Blue went over the wall for initial entry. It was pretty funny watching them climb over with all their gear on.

We flex-cuffed everyone. A couple of the men wanted to fight back … yeah, that didn't work out well for them. After some initial scuffling, they started cooperating. Once we had them tagged, gagged, and bagged, the first sergeant rolled through with the paddy wagon to both objective areas. We uploaded them and moved them to the S–2/THT team at L7. We had twenty-two total. We then did a detailed search of the houses. We found all kinds of IED materials—blasting caps, RPG sights, plastic explosives, etc. These guys were bad dudes. We dropped them at the interrogation point with the battalion S–3 (Roy), and they proceeded to question them … two of them are going much higher and the others sang like canaries. All in all it was a really productive raid—some real bad dudes taken off the street. They had twenty-five IEDs … this town is bad.

I got back to the CP at 0430 and got about an hour's worth of rack before the Apaches came up and sent us on a morning of wild goose chases. What a party. We went to Military City and checked out a truck with aluminum in it. Then we went to scour some haystacks before finally going down to the Tigris River for some Vietnam patrols. Smoking hot down there—no fun. I had a guy fall out for heat, and we took him to the BSA. I came back to MACHINE CP for a nap and then headed out for the night mortar hunt. We hung out there for awhile and then did a gun run through Tu-Pac Shakur to keep the Abu Hishma tribe under wraps. They so don't follow the curfew. I got good sleep last night and am now getting ready for the night's order. It's Bastille Day.

16 July: I got a run in last night. We also worked on improving our positions. Of course, 1-68 AR tankers want us to move so they can have more room … I will resist. Wars change people. I used to feel compassion for the people. Now I am only willing to work with women and children. This generation of Iraqi men is lost. I think this was inspired by my up-close experiences of the past few nights. I thought we would conduct our standard mortar search last night. I got off my track to do some coordination with the platoon leader. They were maneuvering real well with a purpose. They had guys covering one another's movement, doing bounding overwatch, as they left the track. We had a discussion about that the other day. I was thinking, "Wow, they look motivated." As I was walking over there, I found out why. *Crack! Crack!* goes the AK–47 into the field to my front … game on. I hopped back in the Bradley as my Blue Platoon laid waste to the house the fire came from. I maneuvered the other platoons around to block off the area and then I shot up into the center of the city to block it off. We then proceeded to clear the block of houses. We detained all the males in the courtyard out to our front and called for THT support.

"Eagle Ed," our interpreter, came and spoke with the guys from the shooting house. They, of course, said they weren't firing at us ... there was a wedding and some of their friends were firing. Pathological liars, all of them! We asked him to take us to the house where the wedding and shooting occurred, knowing he was lying since it came from his house. We had him stand up in front of the family and tell them what he told us. The other family was pissed—you could tell by the fusillade of Arabic and gnashing of teeth. This tribe declared jihad on the coalition, and now they have to pay the price for their boasting. We questioned them for awhile with the interpreter but decided they had zero intel, so we moved on, keeping our lying friend. We told him he would spend the rest of his life in Guantanamo Bay, Cuba, if he didn't tell us the truth. He was terrified but continued to lie. He has a full beard and tells us this story about taking tests the next morning for school. We ask him what grade is he in ... ninth? Does he think we are that stupid?

We moved back to the EPW area and released the guys not of value and then did another gun run through the perimeter before returning to the CP. Funny, we no longer get scared when shot at ... just really pissed off. Of course they decided to launch a mortar early the next morning, so no sleep and off to work in the midday 125-degree heat. The Q36 radar kept on pointing to a cemetery area. The irony of the day proved that my plans to attend my first Catholic priest-led mass were replaced with driving through a Muslim cemetery with one of my Bradley platoons. We minimized the damage, but those bastards asked for it by using the place. I found a bunch of 60-mm. fuses and some other demolitions. They are definitely using this area as a cover for bad guy operations—smoker of a day.

We ate dinner at LSA ANACONDA (the most dangerous place in Iraq for any number of reasons, most notably 18,000 guys with their weapons wrapped in trash bags in a small area) and then headed right back out to enforce the new 2100 curfew and hunt for the mortars. I guess word spread through the town about the "Machine," because they all went inside. They either smile and give us the thumbs up, or they run. I can't change my bullish tactics because they only understand force. We are at heightened security from 14–17 July ... that means I run more missions. I am still trying to finish initial counseling and roll out for the witching hour, all at the same time. It's game on after they launched an RPG at Roy, the battalion S–3. Yeah, he caught them. I am pretty confident they regretted shooting at him. When they caught the guy with the smoking RPG launcher, he tried to deny that he had fired it. Well, got to go hunt the white whale … hopefully without the white elephant.

18 July: Victory! We got the white whale, and it felt awesome … then things went downhill quickly. I was doing some initial counseling when a mortar went off right outside the front gate of the LSA—right where the XO was waiting for me to link up. The Q36 gave us about six grids to search. On the way to look, the scouts and Roy saw three dudes run into a hut. They went to the hut and found two mortar rounds. They grabbed those guys and started searching the field and found 82-mm. mortar no. 1. About the same time, my 1st Platoon stumbled on some scorch marks in the earth. The XO noticed some upturned dirt. They started digging … 82-mm. mortar no. 2, just fired, complete with base plate. I got my 2d Platoon into an adjacent field, and they started chasing a guy who had a bag filled with AK rounds. He got away, but they found mortar no. 3. We got lucky! As anyone who has ever been to JRTC [Joint Readiness Training Center, Fort Polk, Louisiana] knows, it's like looking for a needle in a stack of needles.

After we collected up all the mortars, we began to clear all the houses touching the orchard. They of course knew nothing; they are far more scared of the guys launching the mortars than they are of us. Too bad, because if they would lift one finger to help us I would turn on the Civil Affairs projects. Until then, we can continue with our jihad versus crusade in Abu Hishma land. We had the interpreters work that place for awhile and then went back to house X4 to see who was there. No one in the house, but five guys hiding in the chicken coop. Bad choice, guys—they get a ride to Samarra East in the paddy wagon. It was the house with all the IEDs in it, so they were definitely up to no good.

We continued clearing in and around the orchard for bad guys until about 0200. We then had the interpreters question the detainees for awhile. I had one platoon pull security while the others went up to Cemetery Hill to form a company patrol base so we could scour the area at first light. After we finished with the detainees, I started to move back to the base in my Humvee and my Brad ran over a huge role of concertina wire. We spent the next five hours of the night cutting it out of the tracks—painful! The guys we searched the night before started coming out of their houses for morning prayers, and guess who was still there? When we went to take the side skirts off the track, the pressure from the wire jammed the final nut in place—no way to get it off. Finally, Sergeant First Class Berg came down with all his tools and went to work on it. He made it happen, but it took forever.

We went mortar hunting once the sun came up and then rolled back through the LSA at 0900 for breakfast after zero sleep but with three mortars ... LSA heroes. Came back to MACHINE CP and the AC was fixed so I racked hard from 1000–1600 and then got up for the night mission. It felt weird missing an entire day. One of the sheiks informed us of more mortarmen in one of the towns, so we did the chem-light clearing technique. I put the company in a line, drove through the town with the informant, and threw chem lights at bad guy houses. The trail element then moved on the houses and detained all males. We had a monumental amount of confusion since the streets were so small. One of my platoons rolled and detained the informant by accident as he stood pointing at a house. Lieutenant Colonel Sassaman and I could not stop laughing about that one. Now we just have to find out if the sheik was lying. It is incredibly difficult for anyone in this country to tell the truth ... and it just makes us a goon squad for whatever informant wants to deceive us.

We collected thirteen EPWs and moved them along the dike. The families saw them and started wailing, crying, and screaming as only these women can. The women would grab dirt and throw it into their own faces. Two months ago I would have felt awful, but now I saw their distress as an opportune time to do some questioning. Of course they knew nothing about a "howen" [Arabic for mortar] even though we've heard it fire from the very fields they work in. We told them their husbands were going to Cuba (our new favorite psychological tactic) to rot with the other al Qaeda terrorists, and the only way to get them back was to turn over the howen. We probably already have it, but we think there might be another one. Once we saw that they didn't have any information, we told them the truth about their relatives. We've become so callous. They had this man who looked about 150 years old— no teeth, all stooped over, and boils on his face. We told them we thought he was firing the mortar. They looked at us incredulously, and then we all started laughing. They wanted us to take him off their hands. They actually do have a sense of humor here. Then they asked us to tea. After we broke in their door and carted off all their men, they asked us to tea! Unbelievable! Maybe the reason they have so much trouble with the truth stems from their unwillingness to remember what happened ten minutes prior.

We had no more mortar attacks. I am keeping my fingers crossed—so painful hunting these guys. I heard the LSA commander is giving money to the sheiks to not fire on us. If true, he must be a real moron. My policy is to take it to them. Mortar fire comes from your village, we come to your house.

Never change from bullish tactics over here. So instead of sitting at the gate pulling heightened security like some units did, we went on the offensive all over from 14–17 July. Happy Ba'ath Party Birthday and overthrow of King Faisal II, Iraq. Never give up the offense.

19 July: This country is so assbackwards. Everyone sleeps on their front lawn. I guess I have seen that done in America before, but it usually involved a pretty crazy party with a plethora of alcohol. Here, it's the norm. I felt pretty good about the progress we were making the last time I wrote—both as a company and within the region. Now I'm not so sure about either. I guess every dog has its day. It started out easy enough. I gave a little focus session on patrolling to the platoon leaders and sent them on their way. I wanted to get a haircut (I looked really bad) and shower before linking up with them for the witching hour (2000–2100). I got my haircut and went for a twenty-minute run around the perimeter.

I got my shower stuff and was getting ready to shower and get all the haircut hair off my body when we got the call that Famasili was shot and White Platoon had contact. They had found some mortar scorch marks in the field behind a house. They went to investigate the house and came upon a cache of weapons. One of the men from the house bolted on them and they opened up, hitting him and an Iraqi woman in the crossfire ... these streets are so narrow and packed with people. Of course their power amps were down, so they couldn't talk to us. Instead of moving to where they could talk, they got on the battalion command net (which is retransed throughout the area). Jimmy Bevens was two miles away and attempted to get the situation under control, but it quickly devolved into a commander's worst nightmare ... a platoon RTO [radio telephone operator] broadcasting on the battalion command net all sorts of crazy reports. As I hop in my Bradley, the situation I understand is one friendly slightly wounded in the arm, one Iraqi man shot but stable, and a civilian woman with a grazing wound to the neck, with all casualties sent back to 21st CASH.

We cordoned off the area and began systematically clearing the houses. I could tell battalion was pissed about the whole reporting thing; I reminded them that's the type of information I had to deal with daily but that I would fix it. We searched the area for awhile and found nothing. The interpreters got on scene, and they found out that the woman shot had not been taken to the CASH but picked up by her family and taken to their front yard. That made sense since she was reported as slightly wounded. I am still about to crush the platoon leader at this time for the total amount of confusion his reporting has wreaked on the situation.

We asked to go see the lady and take her to the hospital. They tell us that she is dead. Lieutenant Colonel Sassaman instructs me to go take her pulse while he talks to these guys. We get to the house area, and I go in with a team. All the women are lying around screaming and crying—totally freaky. I go into the center of it all and they have a sheet covering the woman. I ask to look. She has an American GI bandage on her neck. I pull it off and find the entrance wound … not grazing. The exit wound blew out the back of her neck. I do the polite thing and check the pulse and breathing, but rigor mortis has already set in. She's way dead. I call the platoon leader over: "So this is a grazing wound to the neck! Yeah, I'd call it right *through* the neck." About this time, they bring over a little baby to Sassaman and me—two months old, and it's hers. Winning the hearts and minds one day at a time.

By this time we are all pretty upset about the whole thing. We try to explain to the family how we came under contact when we discovered a large cache of weapons (numerous AK–47s, RPGs, IEDs, a mortar site, and various machine guns with ammo) and that their relative was caught in the crossfire. They didn't want to hear it. We explained to them that we had an American soldier shot as well. They denied this, saying he was injured while wrestling. What? They are such pathological liars and can no longer distinguish what truth is. How do you get a bullet hole in your arm wrestling? I don't think they have even a concept of truth.

The Iraqi "police" show up, and one of the guys says we took money from him when we confiscated his uniform. We gave him his uniform back, but he insists he had 200,000 dinar in it. Okay, yeah, right! That's a rice bag full of money and well over ten years' salary for these guys, and he expects me to believe that it was in his left coat pocket. He informs us that he'll settle for $200 American. Yeah, go home, Bud.

About this time, the Iraqi male that caused the entire incident arrives at the CASH … dead on arrival. Hey, are there any other brilliant reports to send up? Meanwhile, I'm getting pummeled by battalion on these grazed, slightly wounded, stable personnel dying. I have my other platoon down here for security, and I start talking to Andy Sinden, their platoon leader, about the whole thing. The confusing nature of the whole event was that Andy was reporting it and Andy's guys treated the male casualty. I couldn't figure it all out. Turns out that my other platoon decided to let the guy bleed out in the field, and then Staff Sergeant Reagan and Blue Platoon found him and treated him. Now I've got the ass. I just ask them to show a minutia of understanding of the big picture and to demonstrate a few of the Judeo-Christian values our culture espouses. If nothing else, it is outstanding medical training. This war hasn't been that bad to make you that callous.

We wrap things up on the objective area and head back to see Famasili—he's the only one they diagnosed correctly. He was really funny when I came in. Big Samoan kid strung out on morphine. He stands up and salutes inside the hospital. I get the lowdown on the dead insurgent and then move out. Next morning I collect up statements from the guys on the night's activities and move out to the TOC. It's like we take one step forward and two steps back here in Company B and in Iraq. We are doing a big award ceremony for all the good things we have done. The previous administration gave out the following awards: none. I have already signed twenty-seven AAMs [Army Achievement Medals] and five ARCOMs [Army Commendation Medals], and I am on Day 10 of command. Yossarian in *Catch 22* developed two ways to deal with big screw-ups … fire the guy or make him a hero. The final report that went up to division: 1 insurgent killed, 1 civilian killed, 1 friendly casualty returned to duty, large cache confiscated. I guess when you combine it all together into one paragraph it makes sense and sounds good.

The platoon from last night spent the night up at ANACONDA on QRF. I swung by to talk to them about the whole deal. I informed them that they were not under investigation, but that while they were in my company they would do combat lifesaving on the injured in the following order: friendly, civilian, enemy. If they had a problem with that, I would move them to a company where they do not have to treat civilian wounded. If they totally lack any sort of value set, they can look on it as nothing else but live medical training. It's so frustrating, but I guess that is why we have leaders on the ground to make the calls and enforce their standards. I had a good talk with Sassaman about the night's activities. He told me not to worry about the reporting thing—and that we all get haircuts now and again. He also told me that he and Roy were playing soccer with the locals in Balad proper (a much more permissive environment). It made me feel a little better. You can't be everywhere at once, but I must always be everywhere with some people. I ran into some of the guys that work at the brigade TOC. They were all excited because the reports they received were that we came under fire and attacked and seized three mortars while killing the enemy. Yeah, and that's probably how it went up to division. Combine all the days' activities into one story and we sound heroic.

Sassaman came by our AO and told me that he went to sign the death certificates at the hospital and they brought the baby to him ... dead. They let it dry up in the hot sun. This town is just a bunch of f—ing savages. Back to square one. Tomorrow has got to be better.

21 July: Well, we have had two relatively calm nights in a row. We fire illumination rounds at 2100 and 2300 to signify the two curfews and then we perform our curfew run. The only excitement occurred when the insurgents' mortars fell short of their target and hit up the street from us. I was sleeping in the bunker and never heard it. Apparently, it was quite loud since the tankers went to investigate. Either the Abu Hishma tribe will start cooperating now or it will devolve into a bad anarchy scene. I told Sassaman that we would pour on the Civil Affairs if we have another five days of cooperation. I hope we do, but it's so hard to run operations and work Civil Affairs at the same time. Very confusing for all parties involved. I got a digital camera; now I have to figure out how it works. That will be my activity for the day ... to beat the heat.

The Armor guys want to start increasing all our security, especially between 0430–0530 ... a time when no attack has ever occurred in Iraq. Our fixation with the French and Indian War is comical. We normally don't get back in until 0330—total reverse cycle for us. My solution to the problem is we shoot our ranges during that time. Their TOC proved a bit incredulous when I told them my security plan ... man our bunkers and shoot at the range. It is better than doing the Ranger School sit out on the perimeter thing ... we are shooting guns. I don't think anyone would probe a mechanized company doing live-fire training. I sold them on my idea of security.

22 July: Another uneventful night last night with the Abu Hishma tribe. That's good for the battalion as Charlie and Alpha Companies more than made up for our quiet night. I guess we had an informant tell us Saddam Hussein was in this house, and they ended up just blasting it. Recon-by-fire-type attack. They had 25-mm. and Apaches pouring 30-mm. gun runs on this housing complex. When they went into the house they found four terrified civilians. Of course they proceeded to trash the house but didn't really look for anything as the battalion commander walks in and finds multiple untouched safes. He was pissed. They found only money but totaled the house. I guess their actions got us out of the doghouse. We have a big meeting at 1400. I think it's designed to rein everyone in.

Alpha Company killed a guy last night because he ran away from them after curfew. They also shot up a motorcycle that turned around and ended up hitting a bunch of kids in the process. It's covered in the ROE, since we continue to operate off wartime ROE. That's fine, but you just have to overlay a semblance of Christian values. Everyone has become so frustrated. The longer we stay here the more harm we do. No one really gives a rip if we kill Iraqis, we just have to come up with a smidgen of evidence that they were bad. I won't allow that attitude to prevail; we will be surgical and precise in our application of force. We still have to rebuild this country. I think that I've deliberately tried to avoid contact in my city the past few days so that I can justify sending the Civil Affairs guys in. Once we get a couple of projects going, they will talk and we can become the local sheik's goon squad. Still no mortars fired from my AO. Two more days and we can start winning the hearts and minds financially. Apparently, all the sheiks save one want to start toeing the line. We will pay a visit to the instigator in the next few days. I am sure we can convince him to play ball.

Glad I wasn't part of the Elvis sighting [Saddam hunt]. Last night sounded painful. I guess they have to go back to the house and do all the claims. We also heard pretty definitively that we would be here a year. That is going to break guys—especially the ones that still don't have cots. One year is a long time to sleep in the Iraqi dirt. Apparently, the higher-ups are pissed off at 3d ID's attitude. Yeah, they have really jerked their chain, and I don't fault their attitude. If you want to piss guys off, tell them they are going home each month and then don't send them home. They are breaking the morale of the Army with their carrot-and-stick leadership tactics. Lieutenant Colonel Sassaman asked about mid-tour leave, and no one really wanted to let guys go. I guess they are scared that they won't come back. Oh well, we all think the care for soldiers in Vietnam was better, but WWII was far worse.

24 July: Well, it has proven a couple of pretty calm nights for the Abu Hishma tribe. We have a standard rollout time of 1700. We fire some illumination rounds at 2100 and 2300 and do curfew patrol. Yesterday we had a marksmanship OPD and standardized all our equipment on our dismounted weapons systems. I think everyone got a lot out of the discussion. I want them to use science in order to employ force surgically. I think they all bought into it. It's a combination of maturity, leadership, and training to mitigate the blasting of hundreds of rounds to shoot one guy and then injuring a bunch of civilians in the process. Our efficiency rate will go up. Guys are coming back from the range and asking me all kinds of questions, which means they are experimenting and learning. It takes some time, but they have the concept. This company is so ready to go to the next level.

We had another mortar "informant" yesterday. We went on the goose chase. It's funny because we have gone on thousands of these things and dealt with thousands of informants. This one came through the brigade—hilarious how they deal with these guys versus how we do. They try all these tactics and use methods to develop the informant when all the guy wants is to get his neighbor in trouble and get money for doing it. I told him to take me to the mortar … dry hole, of course. Then we go to the target house … right across the street from his house. I am certain it's some sort of feud, but we will keep eyes on it. It's like the "Jerry Springer Show." I told brigade I didn't want to action on the single-source intelligence anymore unless they showed me weapons. We have played the random goon squad way too much in this area … and the mortars haven't fired since we got those three last week and policed up the bad guys. Brigade concurred. I think the folks on the LSA just don't want our actions to interfere with Salsa Night at the club. We fight two very different wars.

I got a run in this morning before it got too smoking hot. We have more nighttime now, so we have more survivable temperatures. I honestly think I can feel it cooling down. Yesterday the high was only 120 degrees. It didn't feel bad at all. The low temperature gets down to about 78 degrees, which feels quite cold. I figured out the digital camera yesterday, so I should get some good pictures. I have used it to develop plans for potential raid targets. Works pretty nice, since we don't get any external intelligence support. Intelligence and targeting is all bottom-up driven, and companies and battalions do it all. I have found that I can make my sector as calm or hot as I choose, based on what I go looking for. Lately everyone wants this sector to remain calm, so I just gather intelligence on the bad guys and wait for the word to bring them in. They are terrified of my company but not of the truck drivers from the LSA. They don't stay in uniform or keep their weapons at the ready, and the locals know the difference.

I talked with some shepherds yesterday about the howen. They knew nothing, so I reverted to psychological operations with them. I told them the mortar had killed a shepherd and a bunch of his sheep. He then started telling me everything he knew ... all the town gossip. I think I am learning how to deal with my village—apply force and straight-up lie. The interpreter and one of my platoon leaders were impressed with my ability to get them to talk. I told them I learned it from being a little brother. I also exploit the deaths of Uday and Qusay to my advantage.

We put the informant in the back with one of the soldiers. As I closed the hatch, he rotated the handle around, smashing my thumb in it. It hurt so bad I wanted to cry ... but Sergeant First Class Berg, one of the platoon sergeants (total funny guy) was there, so I played it off like it didn't happen. I quickly walked over behind my track and almost threw up. By this time it started throbbing, so I got us moving really quickly and held my thumb high up in the air. Now I mark my time in Iraq by the advancement of the dead portion of my thumbnail ... it would have been nicer to use a calendar.

I also got eleven packages yesterday. Wow. I ration them now. It's very nice receiving mail. Amy's [Captain Brown's sister, a securities lawyer in Denver] law firm sent me fourteen bottles of shampoo and conditioner. I don't think they have seen my haircut. We have our gravity showers set up, so I now supply the company with shampoo ... it doesn't take much. I have got to go work on our big awards ceremony for the twenty-sixth. It will be the first time these guys have gotten awards in a very long time—the previous administration proved a bit stingy with the ribbons. My guidance to the platoon leaders was that everyone leaves here with an ARCOM and an AAM—or an Article 15 [nonjudicial punishment]. I went to a platoon "party" for two of the guys that are on end term of service. It was a good thing for the platoon to do. We had a very nice little farewell picnic. I didn't even know these guys yet. Gustafason and Frayne—I told them to capitalize on the GI Bill. One is going back to college; the other is going to become a rancher in North Dakota. They told me that they would have stayed in the Army if they knew they were going to get to do all this training. The platoon is very excited. They are so pumped with all the new shooting and training that we continue to dream up. I am convinced the Army can be fun if we allow it. Too many people get caught up in the bureaucracy. Fortunately, wartime company commanders can totally ignore it.

25 July: Last night was quite the party. We threw track out in this orchard area. That really made for a long, sweaty night. All the kids from the town came running over to us.... "Mister! Mister!" They have about the same vocabulary as I do. I took some pictures of them, and they loved it. They think my digital camera is magic. Of course they want to touch all your stuff until you yell, "Ali Babba." Then they all jump back and say "No Ali Babba." Hilarious! They wanted water, and I asked them if they need a doctor. They say no and point at their stomachs for food, so I ask them if they are pregnant. My phrase book is very limited. They all laugh and fight for attention and the honor of asking the next question. Of course, they want you to go home with them and drink tea. We were shooting illumination that night, so I acted like I called in the fire missions from my camera and then pointed at the sky. Our technology blows their minds away. I enjoy the kids. We chased them all home for curfew yelling "Ali Babba" and shining our flashlights on them. They enjoyed it thoroughly.

In the beginning these kids had thrown rocks at us as we drove by. I was terrified we were going to run over one of them as they darted all around us.

As we interacted more and more, they began to see it as a fun parade. Many helped us search for mortars and weapons caches out in the farm fields.

The teenage crowd. They really wanted to trade things, ask about Hollywood actors, and look through my sunglasses.

We finally got the track fixed and moved back to the CP. I put my name on the list for the cell phone and actually got to call Kris. It was great to hear her voice, but it was tough to wake up at 0330 when my name came up. I felt guilty since we still had guys waiting to use the phone, but they get to use it when they pull maintenance at the UMCP. I, on the other hand, haven't used it in a month. I woke up this morning and went to shoot a Bradley zero range up at Samarra Airfield East. It's quite a drive in a Bradley when it's smoking hot. One of my mirrors is out, so I had to figure out the "Kentucky windage" (adjusting fire based off where your first round hits) until the mechanics/ missile techs can look at it. We got back to the CP in time for chow and our first live-fire OPD. I had all the leaders out there and ran through our CQM [close-quarters marksmanship] table one. I think they really are catching on, and everyone seems to want to move in the direction I want them to. I spent forever trying to zero my M68. I had a great shot group but couldn't get it to move where I wanted it. I was getting really frustrated, so I took it to the armorer. Yeah, my barrel is loose. We have to turn it in. That made me feel a lot better about my marksmanship. It's so frustrating when your rounds are so tight, but every time you get up to check your target the barrel changes position. We'll get it fixed. Tomorrow we have company PT and the awards ceremony. It should be a good day. I am inundated with boxes.

26 July: We had a great day today. Started out with a company run around the inner perimeter followed by racing the same route. It turned out quite a smoker. At the end I passed out all the little pocket flags that Amy's law firm sent us. We then showered and had an awards ceremony. They told me that there hadn't been that many awards given out in Bravo Company in the past two years. I will never figure out why we don't give awards. Lieutenant

Colonel Sassaman had a really good time with the guys yesterday. It's always good to bring your boss down to see things going well ... makes it much easier on the company. He gave out coins to the victors of the race, minus me. They told him the "terminator" doesn't count. We passed out twenty-seven AAMs and three ARCOMs. Then we went and got some outstanding company pictures with the digital camera.

Of course the good fun had to end, and we had to go out looking for another mortarman ... wild goose chase, and it's so smoking hot out in those fields. I guess someone got pissed because we were ordered to fire HE [high explosive]. The FSO [fire support officer] and I went up to this giant 300-foot-high water tower and watched the sun go down and dropped rounds along the banks of the Tigris River. It proved a total smoker climbing the tower in all our gear, but the view was awesome. The first two rounds proved duds due to the soft soil, so they fired variable time. I had no clue what we hit, or really where we hit since it was so dark. I just knew the azimuth and distance it should hit. I worked it off flash to bang ... and some pretty rudimentary math. Sound travels at 330 miles/second. It took ten seconds for the sound to reach me; therefore, we must be on target since my azimuth lined up ... fire for effect. We shot a battery two [i.e., a battery of guns firing two rounds each]. Glad I didn't sign my name on that one. We probably blasted some farmer's storage shack. Each day we alienate the population more and more in the Abu Hishma tribe. It's one of the towns that would best serve Iraq with a MOAB (mother of all bombs) placed in its epicenter. Well, I guess I have to go meet the CJCS [Chairman of the Joint Chiefs of Staff], General [Richard B. Myers, U.S. Air Force], today. He is coming to the battalion TOC. The meeting should prove interesting.

27 July: Well, the CJCS came and went. He did a great job talking to soldiers but proved incredulous when we told him how we were hunting down and killing the bad guys. I don't think they understand back in Washington that we continue in this ongoing war ... and wars involve shooting and killing. Fortunately, we have had very few American casualties; but that doesn't mean there are very few Iraqi casualties. Their weapons suck, but they continue to use them ... and die trying.

I think that is the farthest forward I have seen anyone from America come ... to a battalion TOC. This war doesn't seem half bad if you visit corps support commands. All the decision makers need the opportunity to search for mortar caches in an Iraqi orchard at high noon and roll through RPG alley at midnight … with an infantry platoon. Then they would truly understand that this place blows. Until then, don't tell me that a year is not a long time in the big scheme of things.

The thing that kills guys about staying here a year is the total lack of a meritocracy. The Army does its rotation policy like its promotions … just wait it out. If they told us you could leave when your region has an active police force pulling 24-hour operations; a hospital/evacuation system capable of level-two care; a viable school/youth activities system; a democratically elected, American-approved governing body; and a balanced, sustainable agrarian/industrial economic system, we would work so much harder. Instead, they tell you plan on leaving 1 April. Okay, now I really want to go bust my hump setting all this stuff up during the day while hunting bad guys at night. We'll just sit inside our wire, play volleyball, take weekends off, and wait for 1 April like the rest of the "lob-cockers" on the LSA. Hell, they don't shoot at me. I guess the only thing that keeps us going out there night after night is pride and the desire to do a good job.

One of the JAG lawyers told Lieutenant Colonel Sassaman that we were alienating the Iraqis each time we conducted a raid. He lost it. He basically is going to force her to leave LSA ANACONDA, for the first time, and come out on patrol to show us how to win the hearts and minds of the people shooting at us. Bottom line: if you haven't left the wire, don't talk to me about strategy … you have no idea. I begged to get them on one of my patrols, but I think they might be overloaded with a plethora of work that just won't allow them to leave the front gate. Two very different wars, two very different worlds. Enough ranting.

29 July: The mortars have started again … so much for a sense of normalcy. The Easter egg hunt started up once again. This time we got the engineers' metal detectors. We found a cache of rounds: forty-three 120-mm., ten 82-mm., and cases of antiaircraft rounds. Of course we didn't have enough demolitions to blow it all, so we had to guard it through the night and wait for the engineers to come down in the morning. We set up a patrol base and instituted a rest plan—or lack thereof. Trying to sleep in body armor with your helmet on just isn't that restful. We went to scour the area at first light to no avail. It's so hard finding these guys. I chased some apple pickers through the orchard. Then I had my infamous conversation with the tomato picker, informing him that we would blow the cache and he needed to go home. He, of course, didn't want to cooperate. They just don't want our help. The engineers brought us the demo, and we blew the cache ... huge explosion. Luckily, we had the Iraqi police force go around and tell everyone to go home. It proved fortunate because rounds went everywhere. The police now have uniforms, and they are proud of themselves and their new car. I finally got out of there after the cache blew ... we were so tired. We headed back to the CP and racked out from 1100–1500 ... until the mortars started again. We had an 1800 command and staff meeting. It lasted three hours and then I headed out into the town. Pretty boring night.

30 July: Shot a bunch of ammunition last night since I got my barrel back. We had another boring day up in Abu Hishma land. It made for an early evening, and I got to get some PT in. Things are slowing down throughout the region, it seems. We are kind of getting into a routine around here, but it always has its hiccups. I am attempting to run and shoot six days a week. Of course, it never quite works out for me. We found a .50-cal. machine gun last night down in the Military City. They obey all the rules but provide you with the "Mister, Mister, Mister" ambush. I made the mistake of taking the kids' pictures. Then they just demanded that I take more pictures of them. It turned into "Mister picture, Mister picture" barrage. They would bring out rocks and sticks for me to photograph. The first time it's pretty funny, but after the fifteenth stick they bring me to photograph it gets kind of old. We ran into the Iraqi police on curfew patrol for our town ... very nice. They are making it happen with their new car and shiny uniforms. Of course they use the siren every time they drive. Hilarious scene. It makes our life much easier. I really don't know what we are going to do if we stay here a year; it is starting to get boring.

AUGUST

In August world news concerning Iraq was dominated by car bombs. The most spectacular of these targeted civilians. On 7 August a car bomb killed eleven people outside the Jordanian embassy in Baghdad. Jordan numbered among the Arab nations attempting to be significantly helpful in the reconstruction. On 19 August suicide bombers destroyed the United Nations Headquarters in Baghdad, killing UN envoy Sergio Viera de Mellis and twenty-four others while injuring over a hundred. On 24 August a car bomb killed three security guards at Ayatollah Mohammed Baqir al-Hakim's office, and on 29 August another killed al-Hakim himself and eighty others outside a mosque in the holy city of Najaf. The insurgents seemed to be turning their attention from U.S. soldiers, who were proving difficult and dangerous to kill, to the process of reconstruction and reconciliation itself. The choice of technique suggested foreign assistance and involvement, and from this point a Jordanian al Qaeda affiliate named Abu Musab al-Zarqawi would increasingly gain infamy as a terrorist leader.

Analysts surmised that the car-bomb attacks were intended to derail the reconstruction, push the Iraqis into despair, and exacerbate tensions among the ethnicities and allies in Iraq. In this they had at least partial success initially. Believing that the security situation was beyond control, the United Nations and humanitarian agencies began evacuating Baghdad. The mass mourning of al-Hakim transformed into a Shia anti-occupation protest as well.

---

1 August: "Cunningham, we're taking off once I finish with this FM [radio] update," I said.

"All right Sir," Cunningham drawls back.

"Remember to use common sense, take care of soldiers, and always do the right thing—this is fighting. Eagle Six out," Sassaman concludes as he does every night. I grab an ice-cold water from the cooler and head out to the track. I sit on the semi-padded bench seats in the cramped, dusty dwelling in the back of the Bradley mixing my pink lemonade. My efforts to capture all the sugar granules in the bottle prove fruitless as my makeshift funnel falls apart. Add lemonade mix to the plethora of moon dust in the cavern. I crawl through the turret hole and pop out up top. The pink lemonade slides into the antennae housing group off to my right side—a perfect fit. I grab my CVC and plug in the spaghetti cord. It's the communications umbilical cord that connects me to the rest of the company and battalion. The helmet is worn out. The padding lumps up in spots that I smooth out to no avail. These lumps will smash on my head for the next six hours. It's an ever-losing battle. I key the mike, and we start rolling out the front gate of our compound. Once on the highway we race toward the logistical support area. We pass through it onto the north side of our sector. We roll down the south edge of the airfield; the guard towers snap pictures of our little parade as it passes. I wonder what they think of us. "You're going outside the wire?" Yeah, we live outside the wire. Two very different wars.

As we drive in the relative security of LSA ANACONDA, I pull out my Garmin global positioning system and plug in the grids for tonight's patrolling. We're heading back into the orchards and farm fields along the Tigris River.

"Red One, Machine Six," the radio squawks.

"This is Red One," he replies.

"Roger, the Assault CP is going to do some dismounted patrolling vicinity MC 39226234 [reference map coordinates]," I inform him.

"Roger," Red One replies.

"Yeah, so don't shoot at us," I say jokingly.

"Wilco," he laughs back.

The Bradley finally comes to rest next to the ever-present tomato field. My body continues to rattle even after getting off the track. Our suspension systems and track in general is shot. Of course, we won't see any more parts until September, according to the ADC-S [assistant division commander for support] visit today. Yeah, so my question is, if our mission is so important that we stay here a year, then why don't they fix our broken equipment? Or do you just need to say: "We currently have 150,000 troops in Iraq … 500 of them are actually outside their bases doing something." I think this negativity stems from the soreness in my lower back. Man, this body armor kills my back … between all the protective plates and gear strapped to the front, I feel like a pregnant woman at the end of a long day—everything pulling forward on my lower back.

We get everyone together and give a little on-site brief as to where we are going and then head off into the undulating, overgrown orchard. The Iraqis have dug up this entire area with irrigation canals to water their various trees. Unfortunately, the grass covers most of these canals, so you constantly fall down, especially at night. The first step into the orchard area is actually a leap from one bank to the other. Then you place your weapon at port arms in front of you to break through the initial external barrier of the orchard. Once inside the orchard, you can hobbit-crawl along the various orchard lines—picking the poison of the muddy ditch or the overgrown high-grass thicket. We alternate back and forth, depending on our desired direction. After about 200 meters of breaking through some *Jurassic Park*–type brush, we can see a main trail. To get to the trail requires a very delicate maneuver called the turn and bounce. You back-ass through the really thick briar brush until you are just free of the brambles—you are going down into an irrigation ditch, so this maneuver requires delicate timing. Once you reach the delicate juncture of breaking free from the brambles and falling into the ditch, you turn and bounce with all your gear across the ditch. Many a man has back-assed straight into the ditch or jumped too early, thereby landing in the ditch. The maneuver requires a degree of skill and precision learned through countless nights of orchard navigation. I flawlessly execute the turn and bounce. I am safe on the farmer's trail.

Once out on the trail, we spread out and look for telltale signs of the mortarmen. We come upon one of the thousand pump houses in the region. It's always interesting how these things work. The water table in the region lies four feet below the surface, so they pump the water from the ground to feed their crops. The pump ends in a tube approximately 120 millimeters in diameter that sticks up at a 45-degree angle, the exact specifications of the Iraqi mortar we seek. I have chased after more than my fair share of these pump tubes. The pump houses normally straddle the irrigation ditches, so we experience minor victories when we find one. We no longer have to perform the turn and bounce maneuver—we can walk across the pump. We cross the pump and hop onto the east-west farmer's trail. We walk about 100 meters down the trail when it comes to a "T." I stop the patrol, and we all take a knee. Just then, an Iraqi comes running up to the pump house. I level my weapon and take aim. As he gets closer, I whistle to him … facial expressions prove priceless. He nearly jumped out of his skin. I signal him to come over. He's unarmed … Charlie Company probably would have shot him at this point.

"Ayna Howen?" I demand.

"No Howen," he retorts … I've had this conversation before. I signal that we have heard it back here. He points over in the general area where we found the huge cache three nights ago.

"Ayna Sila/RPG?" I demand again.

"No Sila/RPG," he replies.

I know he speaks the truth because he's terrified. He still has his hands raised in the air. I've had this conversation with a million Iraqis now. Everyone is just a farmer who has seen nothing. Our buddy starts jabbering about fixing the water pump and points at his wrist. The FSO asks me what he is saying … like I know. I tell them that he said in fifteen minutes he would take us to every mortar in the Balad area—he has their locations memorized with a ten-digit pluggered grid [encrypted military GPS]. Everyone laughs. The farmer remains perplexed with hands raised high. I let him go, and we continue with our search. We head north to the river as the sun sets. I decide to start heading back since the orchard can prove murderous at night. We get back on the trail and head west. The canal continues to prove uncooperative. We can't find a place to cross, and it continues to lead us into the hinterlands. Finally, we find a suitable area to execute the turn and bounce. Unfortunately, we now have more distance to cover, and it's dark … zero percent illumination. It's a new moon and all. Our circuitous route leads us back through some new crops. I think it's actually cotton. We break through to a clearing; a MIG–23 lies trashed off to the side. I'll never understand the haphazard placement of military equipment in this country. From the MIG, we head south across some freshly plowed ground. The darkness causes multiple spills, but we persevere. We reach the final ditch between us and our Bradley. We have the last opportunity to excel with the turn and bounce. As I approach the site, I slip and fall flat on my behind. Fortune smiled upon me tonight, and I didn't slide into the water. I just sat there and looked up at the sky.

"Hey sir, are you all right?" someone asked.

"Yeah, I'm just enjoying another beautiful night in the central Tigris River Valley ... one of many left to come," I reply. They laugh and we all chill out for a minute. The most beautiful aspect of this country is the view, the view of objects far, far away. I guess that's irony. This country's beauty lies in the sunsets and the night sky, things far away that remind us of home. I finish up my internal pontifications, jump the canal, and get back on the Bradley. I'm covered in sweat. I can't think of anything quite like a nasty, sweaty Kevlar head band to wear for four months straight ... awesome. I check in with battalion and then drop down to the fires net. We are firing some intimidation illumination rounds over the city again tonight. I don't think it remains all that intimidating after three weeks of doing the same thing. I have actually grown bored of it. We start up the track and start heading back to the CP.

"Hey, Cunningham."

"Yeah, sir."

"Congratulations."

"On what?"

"It's 1 August, another tax-free month in this Middle Eastern paradise."

"Sh—."

"Cunningham, you're living the dream ... people would pay to switch places with you for a day."

"Yeah sir, but only for that day."

"True dat, True dat."

2 August: Headed up on patrol last night and decided to stop by the brigade HQ to get all the Q36 radar hits. Of course, the only person in was John Hancher. We talked for awhile. The primary focus for them right now remains gravel ... six inches to keep the dust down. So glad I am not spending my tenure over here tracking gravel drops. Hung out there for a little while and then headed north out the gate.

"White One, Machine Six."

"White One."

"Yeah, did you find the weapons?" I joked as my open liner to every situation report.

"Yes," he replied, not joking.

"Really," I inquired, feeling the practical joke setup.

"Yeah, we uncovered a cache with 10 AK–47s, 2 shotguns, 1,000 rounds, 20 RPG rockets, and 27 electrically primed explosive devices," he said proudly.

"Sweet. That's the play of the day so far. I'll come down and check it out."

We rumbled through Tu-Pac Shakur annex, through a field, to a dead end. Great, turning the Bradleys around always proves high adventure. I got back out on the canal road and headed to a linkup point. I performed the hobbit crawl into the orchard and checked out the cache. Some pristine-looking weapons, if I do say so. They look better than ours—all freshly lubed and wrapped in plastic. I start heading back through the orchard to call battalion and instruct the platoon to clear the house next to the orchard.

"Yeah, go in soft. I'll be there in a minute," I tell the platoon leader.

I get on the radio and tell my Red Platoon to set up a flash checkpoint at L6 [Checkpoint 6 on Route LINDA]. We then start moving the weapons into my Humvee and getting an accurate count. The house turns out to have four AKs … well outside the Iraqi weapons policy, so we detain all the males and I call for an interpreter. Of course, none are available.

"Okay, send me the interpreter or I am just going to let these guys go," I tell battalion.

"Brigade has none," they reply.

"Brigade has none, or they are all out contracting for gravel?" I ask.

"Yeah, gravel and stuff," battalion replies.

"Okay, well, these guys aren't shooting at the infantry, so I really have no reason to keep them. Their call if they want them. I don't have the transportation assets."

Someone hands me another microphone and tells me Red has contact. Great. An Iraqi ran their checkpoint, and they opened up on him with small arms. "Any of our guys hurt?" I ask.

"Negative," he replies.

"Did any of our weapons malfunction?"

"Negative."

"Did we shoot the Bradleys?"

"Negative."

"Any collateral damage?"

"Negative."

That conversation represents the prioritization of my thoughts on the subject. I go search the house that we just secured, ask a few questions, and then head back to my vehicle to go see the checkpoint.

"Machine Six, what do you want us to do with the guys in the car?"

"Oh yeah, what's their status?" I absentmindedly reply.

"Two slightly wounded in the arms and one shot twice in the chest and once in the cheek."

"You guys are doing CLS, right?"

"Yes sir."

"Are they cooperating?"

"Very much so."

"Okay, I'll support a ground evacuation to the 21st CASH then."

"Roger."

"Hey, make sure someone pulls security on them in the back of the Bradley."

"Wilco."

I head out onto the road in time to see the section speeding off toward the CASH. We do the mandatory Texas lazy-hand wave and head up to the checkpoint. I get on the ground and walk through the whole scene with the platoon leader and all the shooters. We AAR every contact. Turns out the Iraqis had no brakes and nearly smashed into two soldiers. Luckily, the squad leader fired a shot and knocked out the front tire, causing the vehicle to exit stage right. They fired fewer than forty rounds, with twelve of them hitting the car. It had two flats, and the window was shot out; our marksmanship is definitely improving by leaps and bounds. A month ago we would have fired 7,000 rounds and missed the car. Precise, surgical, scientific application of force … they are probably sick of hearing me on that but they are shooting better. I talk to them a bit about the CLS skills utilized tonight and our marksmanship program. It was an overt checkpoint with lights flashing … Iraqis' fault, investigation complete. I relay everything to battalion and instruct the platoon leader to get a status on our daily Darwin award [semi-fictitious award given over the Internet for stupidity] winners. We then head back to the CP. Every night is an adventure. Fortunately, all the Iraqis will live and will be a little smarter next time. I wonder how they planned to stop if 1st Platoon hadn't been there to shoot out their tires? An object in motion will remain in motion unless acted upon by an opposing force … it's all physics.

3 August: We had a pretty lazy day yesterday. No hot chow, no LOGPAC [logistical package], no mission—just had to perform a payday brief. It proved pretty harmless, and Lieutenant Colonel Sassaman really just wanted to come down here and hang out, do PT, shoot, and be away from the insanity. Today I'll work on our room-clearing SOP [standard operating procedure] and give an OPD. We try not to patrol on Sundays … it's our focus day for training and self-sustainment. I still have not seen a priest since I deployed. I guess they really are short on Army priests.

6 August: We've had a couple of fairly boring days. Found a weapons cache last night and searched a few houses. The people got confused about the mud hut we found the cache in, and they brought us the key ... no clue that we had found the cache already. We took them down there, and the key to the broken door worked ... we flex-cuffed those guys. Of course, they wouldn't send us an interpreter, so I just let them go. I guess they are all tied up with gravel contracts ... I am pretty bitter about the gravel.

I had a good run this morning and then got the morning crisis call: "Stop the war! The CENTCOM [Central Command] commander is coming to the LSA." Of course, that is not how it got reported to us. The TOC told me I had to have eight Bradleys up at the LSA for the COSCOM change of command. I told them to pound sand, I'll send four. We went round and round with that one until they finally provided a little better task and purpose. Every day you have to fight stupidity. However, this time I got left holding the bag since they all acted like I was denying the CENTCOM commander, when in reality I was denying their stupidity. It all worked out, and, of course, it's not happening until tomorrow. They expect everything to turn on a dime around here. It's good to make the battalion staff do a little homework before they start randomly tasking my whole company out. I don't know if I have ever seen eight Bradleys in one spot yet. It's good that they act like we have nothing better to do than jump through hoops. Should be a party ... it's 125 degrees.

We held this car for a few days, until we could determine the rightful owner.

7 August: Time just rips by for me here in Iraq. I spent all day in the sun preparing to execute the two minutes of security operations inside a perimeter of 18,000 soldiers. They wanted to start rehearsing at 0700. I watched a lieutenant colonel from COSCOM sit in his AC office all day and then make hourly checks of my guys to make sure they were still in full battle rattle. Of course, he was just wearing a soft cap: no Kevlar, no vest, no weapon, no standards, no spine, and no brain. At about 1000 I basically told them to pound sand, we would be back one hour before show time.

I went over to brigade. Very nice living conditions over there. I actually like their building here more than I do the one at Carson. However, morale is absolutely rock bottom there. My guys live in a dirt field and eat MREs and still have twice the morale of the soldiers at brigade. There is just more for us to do. The NCOs are screaming to get out of brigade, and the officers are all dropping their paperwork to quit. Well, my guys proved pretty excited about the whole day, seeing as how the MWR tent AC broke down and the thermostat broke 130. They were all just trying to hide from the sun. We looked like a bunch of refugees compared to the rest of the LSA.

The visit went well. The general rolled in, waved to us, and went inside. We then waited until the end for them to walk back out. We did get to eat some of the leftover hors d'oeuvres. I linked up with Pat Connely from division staff, and we sat around drinking sodas. I told him my town was probably getting ready for a full-scale invasion of the LSA since I hadn't patrolled there in two nights due to all the preparations for the hand wave. He's a really good guy and super talented. He was the first captain [at the U.S. Military Academy] when General [John P.] Abizaid was the commandant, and I think that was why he attended. The ultimatum to the sheiks to fix the Sunni Triangle came and went, but they made us stay up there until the general landed in Baghdad. I left a platoon at the airfield, and everyone else went over to the MWR tent. It was R&B night there. It's a very, very strange subculture. They had the soul train going and were all getting freaky in their PT uniforms. It was like a really bad dance club in America, except you had all these E–6/E–7s getting freaky with these private first class/specialist females. I could take it only for about twenty minutes. Fascinating study in human dynamics and it really is a different kind of war. We rolled back to the CP and racked out ... and then the trial began.

9 August: "Hey sir, brigade says they have a mission for us at 1200," the RTO announces to me, as I sleep in.

"Yeah, that's a great time to execute it! I hope someone from ANACONDA is going to leave their AC and come on this mission with us."

I get up and go try to collect the details. They give us a six-digit grid, an Iraqi name, and a description of the house—it has grass in the front lawn. Okay, someone needs to leave the wire and go look at this town because you just described 200 houses within that six-digit grid. Of course, battalion is jumping through hoops to get us information that no one can provide. Dave Gray, our S–2, tells me he will put together a target folder for me to pick up at 1100. Sassaman tells brigade he ain't doing the raid unless brigade's informant comes with us. They tell him the informant is too fat to go on the raid without being conspicuous. We tell him he can go in the back of the Bradley; he still doesn't want to play. Thanks for protecting the informant.

I roll over to the TOC and go over the hit with the S–2. Guess what, the house is the same one I went into two nights ago when we dug up the orchard and confiscated four weapons. Wow, our bottom-up intelligence is great. Brigade is saying this guy has multiple weapons in his house and some buried in his orchard. I tell them everything is past tense … they had a bunch of guns, now I have a bunch of guns. Okay, now they want to detain the guy that drives a sky-blue Mercedes—Yassin Taha Attalla. Where were you guys the other night when I demanded an interpreter but he was busy on the gravel contract? Turns out, this guy might be the head of the Wahabi group—some real bad fundamentalist guys coordinating the vast majority of the attacks in the Sunni Triangle. They want us to do a simultaneous takedown of his office in Baghdad and his house in Tu-Pac. Guess what, guys. We might have tipped our hand when I had them all out in the front yard and rifled through their house prior to letting them go since I couldn't get any interrogators pushed down to me to question them about the family's European vacation, rifles, and money. Now I have to go find Yassin and his nice Mercedes. I explain to them that the house they were after is still under construction and has nothing in it. They just want the guy. I decided to do a drive-by of the place en route back to the CP and see if the Mercedes was there. I had big doubts about that, though.

I rolled into the town and drove up to the house, and we had a black Mercedes across the street. I called it up. It's not sky blue, so they are skeptical.

"Listen, this town has one Mercedes in the whole thing … and it's very nice. You want me to just let it go?" I asked.

"Well, they said it was sky blue."

"It's the only nice Mercedes I've seen lately. Why don't you send the interpreter."

"Okay, we'll work it."

I walk into the building under construction and start talking to the head engineer. He knows a little English, so I start working him.

"How much can I buy this house for?" I act very interested.

"We don't want to sell it," he replies a bit incredulously.

"Is it your house?" I take the angle.

"No, it belongs to a man named Yassin Taha Attalla." He sells out.

"Great! Where is Yassin? I have much money for this house," I lie.

"He is over at the mosque praying."

"Okay, we'll wait until he comes back in one hour."

I go down and instruct my guys to shoot out the tire of the Mercedes if it even attempts to move. I get on the radio and call battalion, telling them about my conversation and then call forward a platoon to help me out. The platoon shows up and surrounds the mosque, and we wait. At 1300 they come out of the mosque and we have them all sit out front in the scalding Iraqi sun. We then start looking for Yassin, who is of course in Baghdad. Pathological liars. I then tell them we need the keys to the Mercedes to check out some of the paperwork, or we will have to break the window. They tip their hand, and ten minutes later we have his two brothers ... and we are going to lunch at their house. We apologize to the mosque crowd, and I make them all come by and shake my hand to ensure they are not wealthy guys leaving. It was like a receiving line.

We walk down to the house across the street and go in. It's the house we raided the other night. Fortunately, we did not trash it. We went soft. I talk to all the guys that we had detained out on the front lawn because of the weapons cache. They have us in, and Sassaman shows up for our conversation with the interpreter. Turns out that Yassin really is in Baghdad, but he will come to lunch with us on Sunday at 1300. Wow, I've done all kinds of takedowns and building entries ... ballistic, demolitions, mechanical, and now the walk-up-and-invite-yourself-to-lunch. Hilarious. We eat a big meal and have a good conversation. They want their shotgun back, and I tell them I'll give it only to Yassin. They say on Sunday ... and, Roger, I'll bring it. We have some outstanding Iraqi tea and then head back to chill out. Of course, right after dinner we get the call that a mortar fired in another company's area. Guess who has to go look for it? We roll out to the grid and then get told not to go look for it. We were going to clear some houses, but I guess they thought we were too tired and let someone else in on the action. So, we head back again.

Wham! Sparks fly everywhere. I lose sight of the Bradley in front of me. We slam on the brakes and get out. We start pulling security and bring up the other Bradleys. The lead Brad is off the side of the road tilting at a slight angle ... facing the complete opposite direction. The entire right side track is lying in the road in front of me. I run up to the Bradley and ascertain that everyone is all right. They are terrified and a little banged up but all right. I go back and look at the track ... catastrophic failure of the shoe, bushings and all. We all take pictures of it because no one has seen it fail like this before. We call for some recovery assets, set up security, and wait. We pull the track back on the road and attempt to self-recover. We work on it for awhile until a bus shows up. It's 0200 and the curfew is 1100, so we clear the bus. It's packed full of people returning from Najaf ... way to the south. Once we get all the people off the bus, we clear the bus. They did not stop for anything. They just crapped and pissed right inside the bus for well over fifteen hours. It smelled horrific. I could not believe what I saw. I witnessed the nastiest bus in the world. What is wrong with these people? After some more questioning and checking for fedayeen tattoos, we let them go and I headed back to my Humvee.

"All stations this net, be advised that the Ace of Spades, Saddam Hussein, is traveling north through our sector on a bus with approximately fifty people," the TOC radios.

"Stop the bus, stop the bus," I yell as I run toward it.

It has taken off down the road. We all climb into the Humvee and race after the bus. We are in a high-speed pursuit of a bus full of crap. We race around to the front of it and slam on the brakes. We put a machine gun right in the front window and block off the road with a Bradley section. I run up to the door and have everyone get off the bus and look at their faces. We then thoroughly clear the bus and pull their luggage from underneath ... nasty. I call back to the TOC and inform them we don't have Ace of Spades on our bus. They tell me that it was actually a bogus tip. Still, it provided us a great Keystone Cops chase, and the track should almost be recovered by now. They are almost complete and heading back up to the UMCP, so I head back to the base and try to get some sleep. We got super lucky tonight with not flipping that track and killing someone. It went up on its side. Everyone did the rollover drill properly ... way too scary, and the condition of our tracks and operational tempo is no longer funny or something to scoff about.

I finally lie down and go into instant REM sleep. Fifteen minutes later the RTO wakes me up ... four mortars and fifteen rounds just hit the LSA. They must have my sleep schedule down. Nothing for two weeks and then wham, we have a coordinated attack. We get the attack helicopters on our net and start working the area. I go to the site down by the Tigris River ... wow, it's smoking hot. Two-and-a-half hours later we have an 82-mm. mortar. Battalion is stoked. We also uncover a weapons cache of AKs and ammunition. As the temperature breaks 120, we break contact and head back for some sleep and cool down time. I get about three hours and then head back out to the bush. I swing by the brigade TOC and pick up the Q36 printout as the platoons move into sector. They work the area for a little while, and then we link up.

"Hey, I want to stand on the grid from this printout," I say.

"Okay sir, we'll go around from the north side."

We drive up into the town and park in one of the fields ... incidentally, it's next to a house that we have watched for awhile. We get back there and beat the bush out toward the grid. It's getting dark, so I bust out my giant mag light.

"Okay, I'm five feet from the mortar ... 4, 3, 2, 1 ... there's a mortar at my feet," I say jokingly in the thick bush. The squad laughs at my sarcasm. Ten minutes later the mine detector picks something up; we dig and find a full-up 82-mm. mortar. Sweet! Everyone is stoked, and they don't know if I was joking or not.

We pull the mortar from the field and head to the house. We detain all the males and wait for Sassaman and the interpreter to show up. They had a couple of weapons but nothing of note. As we wait, the mayor and sheik of the town show up. I've never met them since I pretty much work the night operations and allow others to run the city council.

"Ismee Sadiki Bob." I tell them my name is Sadiki Bob.

We exchange amenities, and they ask me what's my rank.

"Captain."

"You Captain Brown?" they ask.

"Yeah, that's me."

"We love Mister Captain Brown."

"What?"

"Yes, you and your soldiers very good, very good."

"What do you mean?"

"Yes, you are very firm, but you help us and don't break our stuff."

"Yes, my men are very disciplined," I say, feeling pretty good about things but knowing they were just trying to butter me up.

We talk about the mortar and the mortarmen for awhile, and then they go home. Of course, they invite us to dinner at their house, and we will set up a date later ... because I still have to eat dinner with Yassin. Oh yes, they are coming to dinner with us. Maybe Yassin will show after all. All the higher-ups are very interested in hunting him down and snatching him ... and I have a lunch date with him tomorrow at 1300 ... my birthday.

10 August: I finally got to sleep in a little bit, seeing as how it was my birthday and all. We rolled up to the house at 1300. It proved another brutally hot day. We got to the house and put in the security force in some shaded areas. Roy and Sassaman showed up a little later. Yassin came out and shook my hand. I in turn gave him a shotgun and some candy for the children. We definitely need to use this form of takedown at NTC/JRTC. It works very nicely as a TTP. Eat lunch, distribute weapons, and exchange gifts. We go inside and proceed to violate the no-soda-during-combat-patrols-between-1100-and-1600-due-to-the-heat rule. The meal is awesome. They bring out a huge spread of kebabs, lamb, rice, garden products, and fruit. Sassaman has everyone sing me happy birthday in Arabic and English, and then I blow over a kebab stuck in the rice. Strangest birthday party I've had. We chow down and talk over matters with Yassin. Higher will not give us the informant, so battalion will not give them the HVT. No informant, no detainee. That is our rule since we have so many blood feuds going on in this country and a ton of Jerry Springer raids. We have a great meal, and then they bust out the tea. It's awesome tea. I present Yassin with a bottle of sparkling grape juice that Aunt Margy sent me. They are thrilled by the gesture. I told them in America it is a tradition to bring the host a bottle of wine, but since we were in a Muslim country I brought them a nonalcoholic bottle of sparkling grape juice.

They then ask me to give a little speech. I tell them we are growing in our friendship each day. The first time I visited them in the middle of the night; we rummaged through their entire house and took weapons from them. The next time we just talked in the street. Then we came to their house for a little meal, and now we are partaking in a large feast. I told them it was very symbolic of the growing relationship between Iraq and America. They ate that up and all came forward hugging and shaking hands. It's a very affectionate country. They all want me to come to dinner at their houses now. So funny. I tell them I can't relax until I find all the mortars and caches to make Iraq safe for Iraqis and Americans. They agree to help. They love a little diplomacy. Of course, right in the middle of our fruit desert the Q36 radar picks up on a mortar fired ... but no impact. Launch the QRF to the area ... it's 7,000 degrees and we are probably dealing with a false radar read.

Sassaman tells me that the brigade commander wants to meet all the guys that found the mortars at 1700, so we converge on the brigade headquarters. All the guys are amazed at the building ... better than at Fort Carson. I let them go into the ice-cold AC and tell them to pretend it's a library ... very quiet. "Hey sir, what's a library?" one of the smart alecks asks. The CG lands and hands out coins to the guys. He comes up a little short, so Chuck Armstrong, the aide, gets all in a huff. He owes me six coins now. The brigade commander hands out coins and gets pretty excited, yelling "Hooah" real loud. Sergeant First Class Berg looks over at me and says, "Sir, you told me to pretend it was a library." We all started laughing. We headed over to the nice mess hall after the little awards presentation prior to the night's patrol.

11 August: The night proved moderately eventful. We found a small cache of demolitions- and IED-making materials. We found the guys who owned the field and detained them. Someone went over to Military City and got an interpreter ... one of the ex-pilots. We talked to them for awhile and then let them go. I told them about the weapons-buying program, and they very much wanted to cooperate with us. I told them I would cut them free if they followed my instructions. They agreed ... I sent them home to tell everyone they knew about my weapons buyback policy that I just made up. They proved very grateful. I sat out there and talked to the pilot for awhile, and then we headed home after we figured out how to carry the demolitions outside the Bradley. What a smoker of a couple of days.

12 August: I continue to chase phantom mortars around the countryside with no relief in sight. The LSA is such an easy target; they have these huge lights on at night, and all you have to do is haphazardly aim and shoot. Then just bury the mortar or run with it to the local tomato patch and throw it away. The people remain terrified of anticoalition forces, so they don't talk about anything. "No howen, mister," has become a cult classic with this town. Every policeman I see, I give him the case of finding the howen. I always promise them a promotion. They, of course, reiterate all their accomplishments and the success they have had digging up weapons ... most likely their own. I did have a little birthday party last night, courtesy of my mother's ingenuity ... the XO assembled the whole company for a surprise: chocolate cake.

Birthday cake and party courtesy of my mother

14 August: It's been a decent couple of days. The howen has fired only once. Of course, it went off at 1130 and it was an hour drive to get to the location. Striker 5 [the brigade XO] was on the scene offering his expertise after returning from a shopping trip. Thanks, is this your first time out of the wire? Of course, it was 1,000 degrees, so he took off pretty quick. The area he told me he cleared … yeah, right. We didn't get back in there until later since it was already cleared … and guess who finds twenty-seven recoilless rifle (RPG-size) rounds and sixteen 82-mm. mortar rounds? Thanks for clearing that for me, sir. Of course, he disparaged our reaction time, but I don't choose where I live or where the mortars shoot. Oh well, it gave Sassaman good, humorous information for the brigade update.

We came upon a kid out in the field. I started talking to him, and he gave us some information … amazing. He told me the mortar was mounted on a gray truck. It makes it a little easier to search for. Of course, the kid proved terrified of the whole ordeal and made me walk him home … holding hands. Hilarious. Everyone was laughing because the kid wanted to hold my hand and no one else's. I told one of the guys he acted the same way the kid did the first time we went on patrol together. We all got a good laugh out of that. The kid couldn't see at night very well, and he kept falling down whenever we turned off our flashlights. He dragged me to the ground one time. What a war. We dropped off the rounds with LION TOC after our drive back.

The next day we had a meeting with [Lt. Gen. Ricardo] Sanchez [Coalition Ground Forces commander]. Kind of a downer. No coins for the guys, and he guaranteed that we would be here a year if not longer … sad face. He did say they were working on mid-tour leaves but not everyone would get to participate. The 1-8 IN would get to send five guys on leave … sweet. We'll see how well that works out. We came back to the CP and hung out for awhile before heading up to drive through the town. It proved pretty unadventurous, although I did work on my Arabic. I am inspired to learn since we will probably be here a very long time. The people love our efforts to learn the language, and before long they swarmed us with all kinds of random questions. I had them show me their houses, families, and cattle since that was the direction my daily lesson took me. They found it very entertaining, and they had some chant going when we left. Hopefully, it was a good chant … it was a very loud chant, whatever it was.

15 August: Sometimes I feel like Iraq is not all that bad; the mission is good, and it is worth all the time, money, and energy that we daily invest.

Sometimes we shake hands with the locals and play with the kids. However, sometimes you shoot the locals and become mentally mired down in all our efforts. I was leafing through the *Army Times* dated 11 August. I skimmed over the semi-morbid, semi-heroic picture article, "Human Toll."

Down in the right-hand corner stood a picture. It seemed out of place ... it was an officer and I knew him ... well. Josh Byers was killed in action 23 July outside Iraq. He was the deputy honor captain at West Point for our class. He roomed with Joel Newsom across the hall from me. We shared the same giant latrine. He was an armor officer who volunteered and went to Ranger School. He was in my squad. We had three officers in the squad: me, Mike Moon, and Josh Byers—all West Pointers. We all graduated together, quite a rarity. I ran into Josh later out at Fort Carson. He was the general's aide and waiting to get into command in 3d ACR. Whenever I had to deal with guys at 7th ID, I would always swing by to see him.

He tells a hilarious story about this girl Melanie whom he wrote his entire plebe year. Turns out, he thought he was writing to Melanie when in actuality he wrote to a different girl, Melany. They had met at some leadership camp before he shipped off to West Point, and those letters carried him through the thick and the thin of plebe year. Turns out, Melany proved a lot thicker than thin Melanie whom he thought he wrote. His account of their long-planned five-star rendezvous and preparation/anticipation leading up to said event had us all rolling with laughter in the north Georgia rain. I've heard the story at least four times, and each time I crack up laughing.

The last time I talked to Josh, he was planning on getting out of the Army. The aide job had burned out him and his wife. We talked about exercise equipment for the basement and other mundane subjects. That was last December. I saw him out running a few more times for PT prior to coming to Iraq. I still don't believe it happened. I don't even know what happened ... just that he is dead. I think he is my first classmate killed in action, and it just doesn't feel real yet. The tragedy doesn't strike home because currently I was not interacting with him everyday. I hope someone writes to his relatives. He was a great guy. I think that news made Iraq time stand still for me. It begs the questions that all the papers are starting to ask: how much longer, how many more deaths, and for what end state? I feel terrible for the guys in Vietnam because they probably asked those questions every hour. I just can't believe he is dead. I never gave him his boots back from Ranger School—they are sitting in my garage.

17 August: I had a couple of good, decent days. We had an OPD and were chilling out at Alpha Company's CP after playing a soccer game on a grass field. After their awards ceremony for their first sergeant, we went over to talk about officer moves. It proved pretty boring. I was going to roll back with Kevin Ryan, but he took off while I was talking to Tim Knoth about Josh Byers. I gave him a call.

"Hammer Six, Machine Six."

"Did you already leave?"

"Roger."

"Okay, I'll see you later then."

We got everyone in the Humvee and got the Bradley ready to roll. I started joking around with the driver.

"Hey, which way do you want to go home—Route LINDA or Highway 1?"

"Which way is faster?"

"I don't know, but LINDA is safer."

"Okay, we'll go LINDA."

We rolled out the TOC and started heading west. The S–3, scouts, and HHC [Headquarters and Headquarters Company] commander (Kevin Ryan) were about five minutes down the road. We were listening to them talk back and forth on the net as we rolled down the very familiar road.

"IED! IED!" Kevin Ryan yelled on the net.

Boom! The IED exploded, hitting one of the scout Humvees. The chaotic chatter of the net heats up as everyone attempts to gain situational awareness. Roy, the S–3, starts directing traffic, and they start firing H&I [harassing and interdicting] fires in the direction of the wires heading south. No real targets but the bad guys are over there, and they won't fight if we are shooting.

"Eagle 3, I'm two minutes away with a Bradley—friendlies on the road," I report.

"Roger. We are shooting coax [the vehicle's coaxially mounted machine gun] to the south," he excitedly reports.

"Anyone injured?"

"Scouts have two down, two down," he rapidly reports.

We get on the scene and establish security. They are calling for a medic; they'll just have to settle for my rudimentary EMT skills for now. The S–3 calls in the medevac bird. I get the CLS bag and start directing the buddy aide. The gunner on the scout Humvee has a dime-size hole deep into his lower back below the vest. I roll him onto his stomach and start treating him. His pants are blood soaked, but he is conscious. I put on surgical gloves, bandage him, and get someone over to keep talking to him, monitor his breathing, and check for bleeding. The guy is pissed, so I know that's good. He tells me that he can't feel his right leg. I grab it hard, and he curses.

"Yeah, you're gonna be okay," I reassure him.

"But I can't move my leg."

"Don't try to move them—so long as you can feel them, you're good. You're gonna be lying down for awhile anyways. Where are you from?"

"Tacoma."

"No kidding. Well, drink a beer at Jillian's (a popular Ranger hangout) for me when you get there," I say.

He laughs ... he just turned twenty-one. I move over to the other casualty. He is sitting in the Humvee. Conscious, but his face is full of glass and covered in blood and his eye is swollen shut.

"Give me a thumbs up," I say. He does, good. He can talk but it hurts him bad. I bandaged his face—just threw the bandage on there and then started secondary survey. He has small shrapnel wounds in both his legs. I bandage those and head back to the other patient and conduct a secondary survey on him. He has some other small shrapnel wounds that we start to bandage while they put the IV in. I yell to increase security and then go find the S–3 to argue to conduct ground evacuation. The helicopter is already in the air, so we go by air … that's the rule. This is the part that sucks … waiting for the helicopter to get there. There is really nothing more we can do besides treat for shock and manage the fluids, bleeding, and IV.

Our battalion physician's assistant arrives shortly on the scene. He was an SF [Special Forces] medic in Vietnam … he's seen this before. He comes up to me and asks me my assessment. I give him the report of the injuries and what I did to treat them, and he just looks at me and says, "Good job." Nothing more we can do out in the dark. We pass the flashlight around and he looks at the wound and dressings. About that time, I hear the helicopter coming. I get over on the radio and have someone key the mike for me so I can talk without getting blood all over the hand mike. Pretty comical scenario. I directed the bird in, but, of course, they brown out [lose visibility because of dust listed by the rotor blades] … twice.

Finally, they land 100 meters up the road from us. I launched one of the engineer tracks forward to help us with security. We have only one stretcher (all vehicles now carry stretchers), so we have to buddy-carry the guy with the face wound. I run down the road and talk to the medevac medics as they bring the guys forward. Total chaos loading the face guy onto the bird with the helicopter blades spinning and dust everywhere. Everyone was yelling too. The bird took off, and we recovered the Humvee to the engineer TOC. I put the Bradley up front and told him to run over anything in the road … just flatten it with the track. You have to go Bradley up front these days. The ride back proved uneventful, but our paranoia and frustration proved high. I was pissed. Why don't these guys fight us straight up? I, of course, know the answer to that, but it still doesn't stop me from wanting to just tear this country apart some days. My mood toward these people is so sinusoidal. They are almost as Dr. Jekyll and Mr. Hyde as me.

Fortunately, I think those guys are going to be all right. Life expectancy was never an issue, but damage management will be. Funny, but I would have been in that convoy if I hadn't stayed to tell a story about Josh Byers—and yesterday was my first day with my new religious medallions. "Hey Holcomb, you screwed me … we should have gone Highway 1."

18 August: Time is flying by. I thought I would have a couple easy days following the IED. It turns out the facial injury was way more serious than I thought. He nearly died due to brain swelling. But he is doing well now and no real brain damage. I screwed that diagnosis up. I got into a decent routine with PT and all, and no one was lobbing rounds at ANACONDA.

The only excitement we had was an ambush on the TAC along Route 1. They hit Roy's Bradley with an RPG; it must have been an improved one because it penetrated to the turret. Fortunately, the halon [fire extinguisher] bottles blew and contained the whole thing. The Brad drove away from the attack—with a hole in the side and some lucky guys on board. The insurgents opened up with AK–47s and injured two scouts in their Humvees (flesh wounds to the neck and through the leg). Yeah, I don't roll in the Humvee anymore. They got the attack helicopters up and blasted some insurgents. Unfortunately, you just don't know if you got them all. The S–3's Bradley lost internal commo, so the driver just floored it out of the kill zone. Unfortunately, if he had stayed they could have totally annihilated those jackasses. Better to err on the side of caution and luckily no one got killed … Americans, that is. We just keep HE punched up nowadays, and we shoot at known and suspected enemy locations with 25-mm. It's easy to shoot once you've broken the seal. Recon by fire authorized and encouraged. If nothing else, they are in violation of the curfew. Fortunately, my sector already understands the heavy-handed tactics, and the sheik cooperates with old Sadiki Bob.

20 August: We got another Q36 hit—at 1130. Great, it's quite temperate at that time. We rolled up to check it out. Had to drive back down some Mogadishu-like streets, and we got stuck pulling an Austin Powers–type turnaround maneuver. The Bradley went into this small ditch, and the driver revved it to get out. Yeah, we smacked a tractor … hard. The neighborhood erupted with screaming women and men. You would have thought we ran one of them over. I got down and implemented my mob-mitigation techniques. I gave them a claims ticket and told them to go to the base. That won't work, but it bought me some time to get some money from the commander's discretionary fund. I worked that issue with battalion as we continued to search at a dry hole for the mortar—so frustrating. I seem to communicate much better after my eleven-day Arabic crash course. They at least enjoy my efforts. Unfortunately, the only person that spoke English in the crowd was a Kurdish woman who did not speak Arabic. She looked like something straight out of *Arabian Nights*. Of course, we found no howen there. We rolled on back after near heat casualty status and returned at night to look some more. The Tigris terrain and heat proves absolutely brutal.

The next day we kind of chilled out and waited to go meet General [Peter J.] Schoomaker, the Army chief of staff. We are getting inundated with the big whigs as of late. I guess they like all our stories and ever-growing arsenal. The visit proved uneventful, and we did get steaks for dinner. Put on the show. No peas and carrots with potatoes au gratin like we had for the past ten days. So I did get a steak and a fully functioning MP3 player out of the deal. We patrolled the area with the IED en route back. They don't screw with a platoon of Bradleys … especially since we are just waiting for an excuse to lob rounds down range. The engineers were patrolling that AO too (it belongs to them), but we always like working with them. "The Giant" (Eric Paliwoda) and I get along real well. We got back to the CP about 0100—no issues.

21 August: "What time is it?" I ask.

"0500, sir."

"They really don't want me to sleep, do they?"

"No sir, I guess not—here go the grids."

Sergeant Smith hands me a piece of paper with five Q36 hits fired simultaneously on ANACONDA. We roll out the gate fifteen minutes later. It's a 45-minute drive to the north side, so we give the grids and Frago over the radio. Fortunately, the BRT and engineers are working the AO as well; they are located much closer. We get down to the river, and I walk to the ten-digit grid. About five minutes later, the platoon I am with finds a mortar bipod. We go down by the river and see some broken reeds along the bank. Crazy Harrell tells me he thinks he sees the tube in the water.

"Well Harrell, you know either you or I have to swim for it."

"Yeah sir, that water is looking pretty nasty."

"Yeah Harrell, that's why I'm thinking it's gonna be you swimming for it."

Harrell laughs, and we move on looking for a stick or something to fish out the plastic—not believing that there is a tube in there. I come back a minute later and Harrell is soaking wet and covered in nasty mud, grinning ear to ear with an 82-mm. mortar tube. Sweet! The XO and I carry it out. That's the deal. If they find the tube, we have to carry the whole thing out. Fortunately, it isn't far. We load up triumphantly and head out to the other grid assigned to us. Red Platoon is working the area. We make a couple wisecracks about them taking too long to find the mortar. We get on the ground and head toward the search grid. It's starting to get hot, so we move fast. We are on the scene about ten minutes when Red Platoon strikes gold. We get the ever-elusive 120-mm. mortar, an 82-mm. mortar, and a cache of rounds—with the leftover casings from the fired rounds. Victory!

"Hey sir, you and the XO are still gonna carry all this stuff, right?" one of the privates asks.

The XO looks at me incredulously, and I shake my head. There is a reason they affectionately call that mortar the "big bitch." It's not really portable by man, especially in this terrain. We drag it out to a trail, but there is no way a Bradley could fit down that trail. I called for a security element, and we walked into the town.

"Ayna Abu?" I ask the kid for his dad.

"Abu fil Beit." He points to his house.

"Ed her lee Abu." I tell the kid to take me there.

The father and I go back and forth on the usage of his truck in Arabic, but finally he is convinced to let me borrow it to move the mortars—I had to threaten his chickens, though (limited conversational skills and all). The XO rides up front with the dad, and we ride in the bed with Abu driving. Of course, the thing has no brakes and the kids are all running behind us. Hilarious scene. We load the howens and move them out to Sadiki Bob's debaba (tank). We then move to the engineer CP and await the formation of the sheik council to talk about the mortar problem with the brigade commander. We found all of the mortars this morning—six in total. This is huge!

22 August: I have to go to all the sheik council meetings now … colossal waste of time. The sheiks love teaching me Arabic and showering man-kisses upon us … that's easier for them than rebuilding their country, I guess. The meeting ends with everyone in agreement to meet again and fully cooperate with coalition forces. We have a never-ending circle of cooperation that leads nowhere. I finally arrived at the TOC for the Annual Training Guidance and drink about twelve Fantas to stay awake. We are going to start doing platoon live-fires in October, so battalion laid out the glide path to get us there. Unfortunately, mission requirements will dictate the schedule. This war interferes with everything.

The meeting broke up, and we headed back to the CP. I had to drop off $100 in Tu-Pac for the smashed tractor. That represents about two years' worth of their gross national product. We speak for awhile with the locals and finally have them sign for the money. Of course, now they want $500 and are pissed off about the busted tractor that probably never worked to begin with. We argue for awhile and then he asks me to dinner and tea … crazy. I decline, and we head out. I look back and they are stoked about all that money. Figures. They are such a society of bargainers. All the men in the town were scowling at us, so I used my new tactic of throwing candy to the kids. They go bonkers and love Americans. It causes the men to get pissed at the kids and smack them around; but candy outweighs the beatings, and the kids love us, which drives the Arab male ego wild. Pound sand. I finally get back to the CP and get to listen to my new MP3 player … what a day. Now the battalion TOC is getting mortared—their first time. Can't believe those a—holes will shoot into their own city with such an indiscriminate weapons system. Hopefully, I'll get to stay in my bunker tonight.

25 August: Well, just when you thought you've seen it all … someone does something even more incredibly stupid. Two nights ago the RTO woke me up and told me Datray and Cobb were safe (two of our chapter cases—soldiers kicked out of the Army for discipline problems). That's great; were they in danger? I don't know. Yeah, they are at ANIMAL CP (A/1-68 AR). They were supposed to be on the CSM detail at the TOC for extra duty. How the hell did they get down to A/1-68 AR? Turns out, after they finished their detail, they walked out of the battalion TOC's wire, hijacked an Iraqi car at gunpoint, bought some whiskey, and started driving south. Driving through the Sunni Triangle with a tank of gas, one M16, a Caprice Classic (no brakes), and three bottles of whiskey is definitely worthy of the Darwin award.

Apparently, these geniuses decided to head south and catch the next plane to America. I guess the hamster upstairs stopped turning for a little while, and they thought they could just go AWOL … something they had done before. No one informed them about the war going on in their vicinity or the difficulty of getting a plane ticket! They also forgot to get a map prior to heading out on their excursion. The battalion TOC had no idea they were gone until 1-68 AR called up. They fired warning shots at a car that tried to run their checkpoint ... since it didn't have fully functioning brakes. Luckily, they identified the DCUs as they came by. We got them back the next morning and detained them in our little jail cell. They spent a bad afternoon with us prior to shipping them up to brigade. I got to deal with the Iraqi whose car they had stolen the day before. Of course, he proved a pathological liar, and it made for a very interesting sworn statement. It should be a fascinating court-martial.

SEPTEMBER

On 7 September President George W. Bush requested $87 billion from Congress to cover military and reconstruction costs in Iraq. The following day the British announced that they would send a thousand additional troops to reinforce their embattled forces in Basra. Recorded messages from Saddam Hussein went onto the airwaves to spur on the resistance, and attacks against coalition forces continued. Meanwhile, the original logic for the war seemed shaken when UN arms inspector Hans Blix announced that he believed Iraq had destroyed its weapons of mass destruction ten years before.

Pundits threw around such terms as quagmire and exit strategy. All realized that the only viable exit strategy involved developing Iraqi forces to assume the load and continuing to develop the Iraqi capacity to self-govern. Attacks on Iraqis cooperating with the Americans continued. Most notably Aqila al-Hashimi, the most prominent female member of the Iraqi Governing Council appointed by Ambassador Bremer, died of wounds several days after an assassination attempt. The fledgling Iraqi police force increasingly was the target of anticoalition forces. What was worse, the coordination between Iraqi police and coalition soldiers was uneven at best. On 12 September U.S. soldiers outside Fallujah killed eight Iraqi policemen pursuing bandits in a terrible case of mistaken identity.

Stretched to the limit as they had become, U.S. commanders could not afford to leave units as capable as Brown's nurturing their relationships with and refining their grasp of such relatively benign sectors as Balad had become. Twice during September Brown's company hastily deployed to undertake demanding combat operations in tougher neighborhoods. On each occasion, local familiarity and interpersonal relationships could not transfer as readily as troops could be moved. Insurgents were sufficiently mobile to relocate to areas where the coalition had relaxed its grip. A certain "whack the mole" aspect began to characterize operations, as U.S. forces concentrated on one area of unrest and then another. Witness, for example, how often Balad had to be reworked—albeit on each occasion from a higher plane—or how often Samarra would be resubdued in the coming months. The long-term solution would have to be loyal, capable, locally familiar forces—an Iraqi constabulary—that could maintain control and surveillance indefinitely after the mole had been whacked.

---

5 September: Computer … yeah, broken again; now I am stuck having to transport all this data. It's been a crazy few days with the omnipresent highs and lows of morale and rebuilding. We did a big operations order and were basically told to patrol the same area, but we might have another mission. We continued with our daily routine for a few days with the only real excitement being in Charlie Company's AO. An Iraqi launched an RPG at one of their checkpoints … they quickly turned him into an experiment of man versus 25-mm. HE. The Iraqi lost that one pretty badly.

The next morning I found out that my company would conduct an air-assault raid on a village area used by Saddam Hussein and [Izzat Ibrahim] Al-Douri [former vice president of Iraq] for sanctuary. Its location proved just west of the Jabal Hamrin ridgeline where Blacklist #1's mother's tribe was from. My company would go in on two Chinooks and one Black Hawk, landing right on the bridge to isolate the objective (my idea). The mission was right up my alley … albeit out of the comfort zone of most people here. Felt like a total Ranger battalion refresher course—except it's for real, and there is not too much experience in the company for this. We went in totally like light fighters. I had this huge rush of good ideas coming back to me from back in Ranger days—everything from air-assault operations to skedko resupply [supplies delivered on a sled-like litter]. We take so much for granted with the Bradleys. The whole mission got juiced up a little bit at each level, so by the time I briefed it we were expecting to IMT [individual movement techniques] off the Chinook like the 1st Ranger Battalion did in Afghanistan. It's funny, but I didn't even have a dismounted radio assigned to me prior to this mission. We just assembled an assault force out of scratch. Fortunately, we had a little time to deal with it since recon would prove heavy; Americans had never been to this region before.

Everything for the mission went really well. Dan Rather showed up to static load training. I was pretty much running the show on that, so they all came over to my bird—hilarious how many reporters showed up for this one. Fortunately, an equal amount of brass showed up to give them all sorts of made-up sh— to gain airtime and "Pentagon points." Funny, but they eventually just wanted to talk to the guys getting on the bird. A few of them came over to me and were asking a bunch of questions. Of course, by this time I was in my chill-out mode, hanging in my bare feet since we were going to sleep on the tarmac. They started badgering me about getting on the helicopters for the mission—I told them they could if they got all the way in the back. They loved it and kept telling me all their qualifications to do all this stuff. I just told them this was my first time in a helicopter, that I couldn't hit the broad side of a barn with my rifle, and that I hadn't been in charge of this many people since the high school band. They didn't know what to think, but they kept writing stuff down. They'll probably put my picture in the paper with the caption "Band leader enjoys first helicopter ride."

Dan Rather and other members of the press covered our static load training.

We did the Eagle Prayer, our 4th ID rock ceremony [a good luck ritual wherein each soldier touches a rock from UTAH Beach, where the 4th Infantry Division came ashore on D-Day, 6 June 1944] and our ready break. Adrenaline was pumping—unfortunately we had to deal with the infamous sand fleas of Samarra Airfield East. That place absolutely sucks. We boarded the aircraft at 0420 in order to hit right before daylight. We would do the first hour in the dark under NODs. I packed everyone on the bird, and we did a final offload rehearsal and reloaded. I took the door and told everyone to follow my lead. We had five guys in the company who had been on a Chinook before—hell of a time to start experimenting with things. I just did everything I thought Sergeant First Class Pippen would do, albeit in a more urbane manner—the press was watching and all—what a feeding frenzy. I am sure someone would have taken over my role, but no one really knew what I was talking about. I feel so much more comfortable doing this stuff than I do in the Brads—but the Brads do instill a huge degree of confidence with all their firepower. I had forgotten what it was like to talk about hand grenades, AT–4s, and M240s as primary weapon systems instead of 25-mm. chain guns and TOW missiles.

The birds came in hard and a little east of their briefed landing zones. We moved to our blocking positions, but the satellite imagery proved very deceiving. Our canal was a muddy trail, and our bridge was merely a pipe running under the road. I found a bridge along the river and isolated the objective from that area. A good call—the only trafficable crossing point of the Al Uzaym River for 100 kilometers. I stumbled onto the linchpin for the isolation of the objective in the pitch black and called battalion to request setting up there. Of course, I couldn't talk to my other platoon, so I got a squad and moved to their objective. Turns out they had landed pretty much on their objective, checked the plugger, and moved out because the plugger showed them one kilometer off. The plugger was busted ... please fight the enemy ... objectives never look like you expect. We got it unscrewed and waited for the cavalry to arrive so we could move into the village area.

A routine operation, not much going on

We passed off the battle positions and then started moving to clear buildings. Everyone was moving so slowly, so I went to see what the holdup was—they were doing interviews on the uncleared objective. I chewed a little ass on the radio. Everyone was "celebrating" the air assault, so I had to reestablish the tempo. I kinda expected that to happen, though. The briefed building layouts, our numbering system, and the plan for clearance did not coincide with reality. I guess I was struggling to get my point across, so I told them the HQ element would start clearing houses and they could join the mission when they were ready. I rolled into the first housing complex and started clearing with the HQ (we are actually a pretty damn good squad). Since the locals all sleep outside, I use my new clearing plan—walk up to the toughest looking dude in the group, holding my rifle in my left hand, and start parleying. I assign locals the role of entering the building first and have them lead through the house and all danger areas. It works pretty well.

The locals think I am crazy because I introduce myself as "Sadiki Bob, the Hungry Lebanese" ... and they always offer me food for my hunger. They are dumbfounded by our size, blond hair, blue eyes, and "Lebanese" accents. I did the first house, and then everyone started moving. The reporters all converged on me, so I remained on my best behavior. About halfway through my southern objective, I got a real interpreter pushed out to me, so our intelligence and conversations improved drastically—from talking about the family, donkeys, and chickens to local politics and tribal affiliations. They kept on saying "Laji," which means refugee. It turns out they were Arabs who moved into Kurdish territory during the Arabization program of the late eighties to early nineties. Well, the Kurds returned the favor of moving them out and one-upped them by saying Saddam lived there and they were concealing WMDs in caves to the east. It took me about fifteen minutes of talking to these dudes to realize that neither was true. Evil dictators would much rather rot in prison than live in the abject squalor of "Albu Talhah"; but once you are there, you are going to clear everything. Just keep looking until you have twenty-plus heat casualties. I ate a powerbar with one of the reporters, told him not to bonk [when an athlete "hits the wall" and has to drop out of a race due to dehydration], and then told the locals about my magic blue water (Gatorade).

This town was straight out of the book of Leviticus. They were going to slaughter and eat a full-grown flawless ram to cleanse the village's impurities. Yeah, but will it make the temperature cool down? We finally got to the last street (footpath) via climbing over a wall. I kept a security element with me and moved the rest of the company back to the blocking positions. We got to the nicest house in our sector (the one with the roof) and started gathering intelligence on the area. I do the old Jedi mind trick and ask for the prominent, powerful people in the river valley so I can pay my respects as the new military commander in the region. We all sit down to chai and a discussion of the tribal layout for the region and any caves in the area. They sing like canaries in the mental mind trap, and we now have our next five follow-on missions. Of course, our initial read of the AO is very far off. Yeah, our number 3 guy on the list is Sheik Mobarek, who was great friends with Saddam but has been dead for eight years. I thought for sure someone was going to make us dig up the grave and determine the cause of death. Actionable intelligence is tough in this country.

We finish up with the tea—of course, one of the cameramen got right next to me as I drank it down. I haven't talked to them at all, and they've been following me for three hours now. They can be a pain in the ass. However, I looked at the camera and broke my stoicism. I started laughing and said it's one hell of a war and jokingly asked them if they were going to make me famous. "Hell yeah, we are," the guy from "60 Minutes" said. I just started laughing. I called higher HQ to pass on my assessment, but they are paralyzed by the media. They are staging some BS scene between the brigade and battalion commanders. Sassaman is not cooperating, so they keep reshooting the scene to get the right mood. Are you kidding me? Very funny—when is the movie coming out?

We just wait. We screw around with the locals—have them put on our flak vests and watch them crumble under the weight. We get the follow-on mission of clearing villages to the south—same squalor, different town. We did shoot a dog that one of the guys thought was going to bite him. Yeah, now go bury it, moron—standard funeral scene. It sucks digging a grave at 1300 in the Iraqi sun; but, if I have to suffer through the family chant and request for money for a wild dog that just happened to be next to their house, then the dude that shot it gets to partake in the festivities. Party for all.

Well, we clear until the eleven guys from the Black Hawk start puking their brains out and pass out from the heat—combination of bad food, no sleep, and clearing buildings in 120 degrees with flak vests for eight hours. Of course, someone calls up from the air-conditioned TOC asking why these guys passed out. I dream of answering questions like that. Are you outside? Are you wearing any gear? Have you slept in thirty-six hours? Did you clear any buildings today? What did you eat for dinner last night? Have you been in direct contact with the sun for more than two minutes at a time in the past three months? Are you outside the wire? Okay, you just cannot understand what I am telling you. We spent about an hour getting those guys fixed up. Bottom line, once you start puking water in this country, you've got about an hour before your body crashes on you. It's that delicate a balance with the heat. You miss an hour of taking in fluids, and you will be heading to the hospital. I don't care how tough you are. We got those guys passed off to the forward aid station and then continued to clear, haphazardly waiting to be told to stop. Of course, we have to sleep out here again with none of our stuff and then go clear the other side of the river. No one sleeps—bugs, heat, and dehydration headaches ensure that, along with Op Orders and security requirements.

We roll out to the river at 0400 and head to the most desolate village I have yet seen. This place was totally cut off from everyone. We rolled up on these guys sleeping at this well. They woke up to two Bradleys staring at them (I got a platoon of Bradleys after clearing the village). Facial expressions are awesome—sun coming up, Bradley chain gun aimed at you ... first call. I snapped the picture, and we left them alone. Total squalor town—no farming and lots of World Food Organization bags of flour. They did have a donkey tied up. I tried to ask them why "el hamar" was all tied up, but they don't speak Arabic. Time warp. Apparently, they knew how to tattoo because the women's faces were totally covered in tattoos. Step into the AM. We screwed around on the east side of the river denying the enemy sanctuary prior to flying back to the CP. Tactically, it was a great mission and phenomenal training. Not really lucrative if we are trying to keep the budget in check ... 1 AK–47, 1 RPG, 1 Saddam Fedayeen, and a dead evil dog. We did manage to clear 900 mud huts.

"Hey sir, what a busted raid," Holcomb said.

"No Holcomb, it was a success. Just think, when you're at Virginia Tech drinking an adult beverage next month, you can tell those college girls that you used to be a soldier and that you were part of the air-assault raid into the Al Uzaym River valley denying high value targets sanctuary in the towns and cave complexes of the Jabal Hamrin Ridge. Although we did not find Saddam, we confiscated numerous weapon systems, captured Saddam Fedayeen paramilitary members, and pacified an untouched portion of Iraq through the integration of close air support, attack helicopters, lift helicopters, Bradleys, and good-looking infantrymen. All that coordinated through the box you carried on your back," I replied.

"I guess it's all in how you brief it. Could you give that one to me on a card?" Holcomb retorted.

"No, you're going to be dangerous enough in college."

We popped the "purple magic cloud" [smoke grenade], the giant grasshopper landed, and the camo tribe climbed into the belly as it leaped away. It's all about perspective. I wonder what they'll put on "60 Minutes."

Someone snapped this photo of me running off the helicopter in the 123-degree heat.

8 September: I thought I would get to come back here and take it easy for awhile after our big mission, but the jackass mortarmen laid siege to the LSA … starting at 1300 the day of our return. No sleep and lots of heat. We did eventually find the 82-mm. mortar. We were having the battalion AAR at the battalion TOC, and I thought we would get a hero's welcome for getting the buried cache—wrong. The brigade commander was pissed because we didn't get the guys firing it. You never will, back in those orchards. Hence, the term guerrilla warfare and the invention of the mortar. They don't shoot when you are there. On the way back, they fired again, and we got the base plate and another cache. We are shutting them down, but there is just so much crap buried out there for them to fire at us.

The higher-ups won't fire counterfire despite what everyone says … fire it. Apparently, the LSA commander got called down on the carpet at Baghdad for all the attacks … fire counterfire. We are such pansies about shooting our artillery. Every time they get a ten-digit Q36 we should fire it up with white phosphorus. That is the only way you will get them … unless it's in the town, but it hasn't been. I don't know. I guess we are concerned about the crops or something. The only way insurgents learn is through violence. The guy Charlie Company blew away was on their new police force … not so great, but we haven't had any RPG attacks on Route 1 since. Word gets around.

I put my entire company out in the region where the mortars were firing from … and they fired from a different area while we were sitting out there. We didn't hear or see anything back in the orchards. We just got the radar grid and called for counterfire … denied. Will someone please take off the skirt? It's all right because my CP is well outside the mortars' range. Your attitude changes drastically when someone gets hurt in your unit and you get American blood on your hands. Fortunately, Lieutenant Colonel Sassaman and I are in line with one another on that one. Since they wouldn't fire counterfire, we did. We went to the grid and stood on line with all the M203 gunners and lobbed rounds into the orchard. Sassaman wanted to shoot his mortars into the AO, but they still had to finish registering. We detained a few Iraqis near the site for questioning, and they thoroughly enjoyed us shooting up their orchard. Really weird. We went into the field to look for the mortar, but by then it was pitch black … this sh— just won't end. I did have some fun with the sheik and the farmer whose orchard we blasted. He had us in for tea afterward. Everything is so messed up. We got our turn with the iridium phone for morale calls yesterday—it's the double-edged sword. Families are crumbling back home, and there is nothing we can do with our ten-minute phone calls every ten days to stop it.

9 September: My AO has gotten a lot of attention lately. We are in the midst of Operation Tu-Pac Siege. We rolled into the town with psyops blasting the curfew message, then we played a little Metallica, Blink 182, etc. It's taken the place of H&I fires inside the cities. We worked the town over for a little while, checking all the graffiti and advertisements and crushing Saddam supporters. We take the curfew violators (who always claim they had no idea about the curfew) and place them right next to the loudspeaker and play the message. Pretty effective method for reinforcing the curfew times.

Sassaman, Roy, and I drank tea at one of the houses that we pulled a cache out of a month ago. One of the brothers is still in jail, but they were happy to see us. Every time I go anywhere with Roy, the locals have a hilarious story about him. I guess he knocked some dude off his bike—unfortunately, it was one of the higher local police so we had to assuage him and tell him we didn't realize he was a cop since he didn't have on a uniform. I see that guy all the time now, and he is always wearing his uniform.

After teatime we set up a checkpoint in the middle of town and hung out there. A pregnant woman came through, and I thought for sure I would get to deliver the baby; but she was en route to the hospital, and they had time.

About ten minutes later ... *Boom!* We all ducked and then we see four flares in the sky. That doesn't make sense. I'm thinking 3-29 IN fired, but I can't figure out the flares and why it sounded so close. The FSO is saying that he thinks an A–10 was dropping flares and we were arguing over that one until ... *crack, crack, crack* goes the snap of the rounds zinging by. I jump into the Bradley ... wrong one, so I hop off and get into mine. We roll out toward the fighting and the battalion TAC with the S–3 and commander.

An IED detonated in front of Sassaman's track, so we started in on the firefight. I got down and linked up with the guys at the end of the IED wire (they initiate these things with 100-meter-long strands of stereo wire). I confirmed the TAC's frontline trace and then took over the fight. We started bounding forward on line emptying a magazine every fifty meters and lobbing 203 rounds to keep them close. We finally hit a canal that the wire was running across; Sergeant Hays and I tried to get across, but the mud, water, and reeds were way too thick and our gear was way too heavy ... so I just ended up covered in murky, nasty water. The Brads meanwhile were moving around the flank of the firing position, and they reported a bridge. I had the M203s blasting the far side, keeping the bad guys hemmed in. We got around the far side but couldn't find the body—just all his gear and some blood.

After searching the area for awhile in the dark, we pulled back and fired 155-mm. HE. It was one hell of a company live-fire right on the outskirts of the town. They must have freaked out when we opened up with the 25-mm. HE. It had to be an outsider because that town knows we shoot back ... a lot. I am sure they got the message yet again. It was an awesome unrehearsed display of firepower; we sustained no friendly injuries, but we did blast a mechanized company basic load at three dudes using every weapon system except missiles. We continued the psyops campaign on the town with rock music. They proved very cooperative after that.

10 September: The TOC got mortared today; one of the logistics guys, Specialist Gray, got hit bad in the leg. He is in critical condition because they can't stop the bleeding in his leg. Fortunately, HHC organized a blood drive; their determination caused the doctors to go the extra mile, and they ended up stabilizing him two days later. He was much closer to dying than we all thought. Guess what, we didn't counterfire again. Lieutenant Colonel Sassaman has taken over the clearance of fires in our AO. I think shooting back is the right move ... very ballsy of him to unilaterally take it over, but if you ain't out here at night you really can't understand the fight. We continue to fire H&I fires into the IED field. It serves as a curfew reminder and offers us a fantastic opportunity to test-fire all of our weapons in addition to eliminating that canal as a threat. In typical Iraqi fashion, the mayor of Tu-Pac invited us to his house for dinner … great fish, no leads. Unprecedented irony.

19 September: I had some great training days. We are flying aerial QRF for the brigade; one platoon is up at Samarra and the other in services. So I get to shoot a lot now and catch up on things. We have been rolling the mounted section up for QRF; but when your sector is 200 square kilometers, there really isn't a good place to position yourself to rapidly respond to every threat. I was actually starting to have a little fun shooting and working out. My guys were guarding the front gate of 1-68 AR FOB [Forward Operating Base] when two guys dressed like Iraqis rolled up. They had beards, long hair, and rags on their head … but they spoke perfect English and absolutely no Arabic. My guys were freaking out about the whole deal.

"Yo man, is Todd there?" one of them asked.

"Who?" the guard asked, thinking something is really weird.

"You know, Captain Brown—isn't he your CO?"

"Yeah, are you guys Iraqis?"

"No man, we're 'friends' of his."

"Are you in the Army?"

"Yeah, dude."

"Okay, let me check on this."

They called me up. It was hilarious. Some guys from Bragg wanting to shoot at our range. I told them I would trade weapons for secrets. They said they wanted *my* secrets. Great dudes and we knew a lot of guys in common. I got all the squad leaders out on the range, and we shot with them for awhile. It was great. Just confirmed a lot of the things we already were working on and teaching. Sometimes it just takes seeing a guy with really long hair do it to give you some legitimacy. The company was so stoked after they came down, but I think they spoiled us seeing all their new gear. Standard Ranger setup, though. They gave me a huge credibility boost just by showing up.

We were flying high, and the range is awesome. Shooting walls and a very liberal range fan. Great close-quarters battle training. Those guys took off, and it was back to the grind … a little better trained. We did the aerial QRF deal that night. I had to go out to the TOC in the morning to talk with the 1st ID guys doing their six-month-out recon to replace us … six months more??? Lieutenant Colonel Sassaman told me about Kevin Norman, one of my classmates from West Point, dying in a plane crash. Total tragedy. I got back that night, and we did the aerial QRF again. I stayed home and worked on the new computer.

The next morning I found out that Private First Class Pease, one of my guys, had taken shrapnel in an IED attack en route from Samarra—he is attached to the other armor battalion. We drove up to the CASH and talked to him. He was fine and in good spirits. He was a little drugged up and couldn't feel his lips so we gave him an MRE and watched him eat. We all got a good laugh out of that one. Fortunately, his injuries were all superficial. Route 1 sucks … we need more up-armored Humvees—or just go with Bradleys on it—our company rule. I am trying to get them to contract out clearing operations to the Iraqi Civil Defense Corps [ICDC] and let those guys walk up and down the median looking for the bombs. They are begging for employment opportunities. If we pay them for finding them, they will do it forever … regardless of the consequences. There is money to be made. After Private Pease went back to his room, I went over to see Kevin Ryan about calling the rear detachment commander. No one below the rank of lieutenant colonel has any phone service in the entire Sunni Triangle right now … it's ridiculous. They said the CASH could take care of it. He asked me if I had heard about Brian Faunce, a former fellow brigade assistant S–3 and now the B/1-12 IN commander.

"No, what's up?"

"He's dead."

"Are you kidding me?" total shock and silence. I was sick to my stomach.

"What happened?"

"Electrocuted by a live wire that he was throwing off his track with both hands."

"No way. How many times have you thrown wires off your track?"

"Everyday. They just hang so low in the cities," Kevin said.

"Yeah, I know … I always bat them with a pole," I replied.

I can't believe it. I ran PT by his Bradley this morning … clueless that he was dead. He was in my small group at the advanced course, and I used to always kid around with him because he was so type A. I can go on and on about all the funny things we did. A year on brigade staff together is a long time … MOUNTAIN STRIKE, NTC, WARFIGHTER, this command. He and Cheryl had just bought a house down the street from us. We were planning barbeques and good times. I can't believe he's gone. I just ate dinner with him five days ago and was busting him out for skipping the 1-68 AR command and staff brief. I remember his cubicle, the coffee cup, his lawn mower boots, his sewn-up cooked-white BDUs, and his Volkswagen Jetta that we used to drive down to the chow hall when it was cold. It's so maddening and so random. I don't even know what to say because you go through the whole range of emotions … denial, anger, vulnerability, and just plain sorrow. Indescribable.

I went through the whole day in shock and then mounted camo poles on the Bradleys to pass the wires over the top. Then I went to the range and shot … extremely well. Too many tragedies this past twenty-four hours. I think they might move my company up to Samarra … just when things were getting comfortable and we were getting settled in. I really don't want to get attached to an armor battalion. Oh well, if they let you pick your assignments, we'd all be back in the States right now … like they originally briefed so long ago. I can't believe this sh—.

24 September: It's been a good couple of days. We turned our sector over to a National Guard company that they attached to the battalion so we could head up to Samarra. I have got mixed emotions about going up there. It's a town that we have neglected with infantry for a long time, so we will have to lay down the law. Unfortunately, they don't have a place for us to live up there. We are back to the start of this campaign … out in the field with the bugs. The brigade commander told me it would last only a week, but it's tough to leave the comfort we have grown accustomed to down here. I went up to Samarra with Sassaman, Roy, and Jimmy for a little recon. Not much has changed up there since April. They just don't have enough boots on the ground in that city. The recon went well but confirmed that which we already knew ... they aren't ready to receive us. Out in the open field again. We have had some phenomenal training time down here, and the guys have really built up their bunkers for comfort. I don't think I have shot this much ever. You forget how much you have shot until you shoot with the new guys. I got two new lieutenants this past week and took them through a good first day ... CLS, zero weapons, run six miles, CQM table one, enter a building, and clear a room. I keep myself extremely busy despite the down time we have had prior to the Samarra move and its delayed timeline. I think I don't want to think about Brian, Josh, and Kevin so I just continually do stuff.

I had to go to the Article 32 hearing for my two car-jacking deserters. I don't think things bode well for their near-term future, especially since I am a witness for the defense. I guess no one briefed them that I want to send these guys to jail. The Mad Mortarman has laid siege to ANACONDA once again, and I don't have to go investigate. It's really quite Pavlovian: when I hear the mortars fire, I think I have to go beat through the bush in some forsaken orchard. However, now old Gator Company from the National Guard gets to play that game. Poor guys. I think they already miss us, and we haven't left yet. We have had a couple of good days with regards to eliminating the bad guys. Some of our Brads saw some bad guys sneaking around with RPGs and leveled them with 25-mm. The AC–130 Spectre Gunship also saw guys setting up a mortar and wailed at them from the sky. That must have totally confused the bad guys. I don't know what they must have been thinking when 40-mm. just rained down from the sky ... "in shaa' Allaah." That's what they always say when you find mortars, RPGs, and AKs in their backyard: "God willed it."

27 September: Our appointment in Samarra is quite scary, to say the least. We did the whole wait-on-the-HETS-and-ride-up-here ordeal. Route 1 still remains a tough road. The ride proved uneventful enough, and we rolled on down to their battalion TOC for the latest. I received multiple briefings on winning the hearts and minds, dignity and respect, etc. We ate dinner and got settled in. We still had to send out the observation post for 2d Platoon since they had been attached up here for awhile. I tried to get out of it because it has proven quite worthless having guys sit out there for twelve hours at night.

My intuition proved right. As they were driving down to the site with the armor guys, an insurgent leveled an RPG at the platoon leader's track and he went to acquire the target. Well, the RPG missed, but the platoon leader did not: 25-mm. HE versus bad guy. Split him in half. They immediately started moving with their seven guys to apprehend everyone. Battalion sent the QRF of two tanks; I sent five Bradleys loaded with infantry. Apparently, the locals are not used to the hunt because they hung out in the area. We got the infantry clearing everything in the vicinity, and we detained seven guys, all wounded, who were serving as spotters for the RPG firer. We just swarmed the place and started policing up bad guys. It only takes a couple of actions like this to get the word out to all. The body was still holding the RPG launcher, and when they went to pick it up the arm fell off. Pretty gruesome, but hey, don't shoot at us. Battalion made us police up the body. I say leave it there with the RPG launcher, but I guess that is a little overboard. We did make all the bad guys walk by it for deterrence purposes. The brigade commander came up the next day and handed out some coins. One of the TOC rats was giving the patrol leader the third degree.

"Hey, why did you open up with 25-mm. HE?"

"I don't know."

I was standing right there and knew he was really talking to me indirectly ... so I answered: "That's what he had punched up." End of conversation on that one. You don't get much better action than RPG in hand, target destroyed. They have had so many incidents of getting fired at but not killing the insurgents in return. We finally get some results and it's like we did something wrong. Oh well, that's why this town is so awful—lack of response to shooting. We had the brief that 95 percent of the people love us and it's the 5 percent in the city still fighting against us ... my read is 95 percent of the people are not actively fighting against us and 5 percent are actively fighting us.

OCTOBER

October witnessed important shifts in the Bush administration's footing with respect to Iraq. On 2 October David Kay, leader of the U.S. search for weapons of mass destruction in Iraq, reported that no weapons had been found after a three-month, $300 million search. This, combined with the continuing lack of a demonstrable connection between Saddam Hussein and al Qaeda, undercut much of the original logic for the invasion of Iraq. Arguments supporting the war increasingly turned to the bloodthirsty tyranny of Saddam Hussein as being a disaster to his own people and ultimately, if not immediately, a danger to the rest of the world. The replacement of his pariah regime with a functioning democracy in strategically located, oil-rich Iraq would have a salutary effect throughout the troubled Middle East.

This grander vision for Iraq required more in the way of effective reconstruction and international support if it was to succeed. On 5 October National Security Adviser Condoleezza Rice assumed control of the reconstruction of Iraq. This migration of responsibility into the White House underscored a renewed emphasis on building Iraq into a viable state. Diplomatic efforts on the part of the United States and the United Kingdom secured a unanimously approved United Nations Security Council resolution supporting an international force, led by the United States as executive agent, for Iraqi stabilization and reconstruction. The practical effects of such an endorsement were not immediately apparent to the troops on the ground.

Meanwhile, death and destruction continued. Indeed, 27 October was the bloodiest day since the fall of Saddam Hussein, with thirty-five people killed and twenty-two injured in suicide attacks on the Red Crescent headquarters and three police stations in Baghdad. Ba'athist diehards were still a threat, as were foreign terrorists determined to derail the coalition vision for Iraq and a not-particularly-Ba'athist native resistance to troops too often perceived and portrayed as infidels and occupiers. Cooperation among these several sources of resistance was difficult to ascertain. It was probably messy, as was the relationship of all three groups to common crime and criminals. Iraqis surveyed during this period believed themselves more vulnerable to crime than to political violence.

Foreign terrorists were not geographically constrained and could strike virtually anywhere, though they were more efficient if they had safe havens from which to *base themselves. Ba'athist hardliners were diminishing in number but tended to locate in the pockets of native resistance. This resistance did have a geographical aspect to it. Television viewers were becoming familiar with the so-called Sunni Triangle and such hotbeds of resistance as Fallujah, Ramadi, and Samarra. Insurgents within these sizable towns actively contested the presence of coalition troops. Over time they wittingly or unwittingly provided havens for foreign terrorists, Ba'athists, and criminals as well.*

Captain Brown's foray into Samarra should be viewed in the context of attempting to pacify a geographical center of resistance. By and large the fighting, though chaotic, went his way. As we shall see, during his second fortnight in Samarra his command was attacked only once; whereas during its first week it was attacked several times a day. Achieving this relative security necessarily involved heavy-handed treatment that incarcerated hundreds, cowed thousands, and tenuously persuaded the remaining population that cooperating with the coalition was the better option. There were, however, no reliable Iraqi military forces or political infrastructure to turn the city over to after it had been subdued. There also seemed to be no practical limits to insurgents' capabilities to replace appalling casualties.

---

2 October: We did the Op Order for Operation INDUSTRY CLEAN UP in the morning and then rolled down there for a daylight leaders' recon. What a huge chop shop! It's about 500-plus buildings of car shops and machine shops. Our hit time is 0700, and we are the main effort. Funny, I've been here twelve hours and we are the battalion main effort already. They are really pouring on the support for us, so that's a good deal. The neighborhood is rough. We rolled out with the tanks in lead; they isolated the area and used the ICDC to keep people back. They actually are a good asset when told exactly what to do and fixed in place. We were supposed to do a walkthrough and investigate suspicious-looking areas ... okay, that's all of Iraq for you. We roll in and go through a couple of shops. Within five minutes we got seven RPGs, fifteen AKs, and a bunch of demolitions for IEDs. Okay, this place gets rolled. Every lock comes off every door, and every room gets searched. We go into a frenzy. Guys are bashing locks with sledgehammers and crowbars. We start pulling stuff out of the woodwork. Multiple IED labs complete with initiating systems. Weapons market–type activity ... fifty RPGs in a shed, blasting caps hidden in air filters ... game on.

We detain some guys out in the street, and they get cuffed and bagged. I get them with the psyops campaign. I start teaching them some Spanish words so they can get by when they spend the rest of their life in Guantanamo Bay. They freak out. One of the four-foot-tall, 250-pound mothers comes out and starts pleading for us not to take her son to Cuba. I tell her the only way he can stay in Iraq is to tell us the owner. They, of course, sell someone out … probably not the owner, but he will be of equal intelligence value. The lady starts kissing me all over. The guys are laughing and snapping pictures. She holds her face up to mine, cheek to cheek—hilarious. I tell her we won't send her son to Cuba, but the rest of the guys are going. They start crying and selling out everyone. The MPs start moving the 5-tons forward and policing up the material … they have to get a flat rack and do multiple turns for all the crap we are finding.

They push a psyops team to us. They have this huge speaker system and start blasting the command message. I police those guys up and give them a new mission: rock and roll music. We get "Welcome to the Jungle," Metallica, and all kinds of other stuff. It's hilarious. The locals are terrified of us. We are all in BDUs and camo'ed up. Even our interpreter is frightened of us. He keeps asking me what kind of special unit we are. The scene is classic. Guns and Roses blasting down the street and 100 infantrymen smashing locks and pulling out mortars, blasting caps, recoilless rifles, AKs, machine guns, ammunition, RPGs, Russian Mark–19s, sniper rifles, and weapons we had never seen before. It was the largest collection of weapons the brigade had found since April, when the stuff was still in bunkers. It was the largest cache outside of bunkers that I have ever heard about. It was pretty funny because Lieutenant Colonel Sassaman said I'm giving you forty-eight hours to clean up Samarra and then I'm coming up there to check on your progress. Morale was sky high, although we were smoked. It was pretty cool doing a mission this size and being the ranking guy on the objective … talk about free rein.

We finally finish up the objective, and I get the word we still have to run the worthless all-night OPs. My guys are smoked. I can't believe it. We leave the objective and head back to get the guys chow. I plan on inserting the OP … with the entire company and section of tanks. The tankers love us now. They are struggling with the whole self-imposed restrictive ROE. I can't believe no one came down here and searched this place. Oh well, you lose your rights when you harbor weapons for terrorists. I sent up the report that we broke a couple of locks and knocked down some of the doors of the more suspicious areas … I didn't say it was 500 locks and suspicious doors and multiple cars (they had a report of a vehicle-borne improvised explosive device). The higher-ups are absolutely thrilled. That always helps. The BUB went well, and the battalion commander told all the guys that went on the battalion mission that they did a good job.

3 October: Apparently, ANACONDA is under mortar siege again, so our absence was noted. Competency is a curse. We came back to our dirt field and got the guys ready to insert the OP. I missed breakfast, lunch, and dinner. I did have a powerbar, though, vanilla. We rolled out to test-fire our weapons—a novelty around here.

As we were getting ready to shoot, a call comes across the net that they got a man down and need an aerial medevac out on Route 1. I got the company ready to roll. The TOC kept on denying these guys assets. They want a better grid, description of injury, condition of vehicle, what happened, who the unit is, the helicopter can't land out there (what, in a desert?), etc. I am getting furious. The guy is pleading on the net, and we are talking about recovering the truck he got hit in. I am furious. I keep on trying to get a grid, but no dice. I can't get through. We rolled the whole company south hoping to get something. The attack aviation guys finally just took charge of the situation and worked it from their angle. You can just hear the guy bleeding on the net, and I felt so absolutely helpless. I sat on the Bradley and cried with frustration. By the time they relayed the grid to us, attack aviation had the medevac bird inbound. I was so pissed. They were calling up about applying a tourniquet, he's going into shock, amount of blood lost, tourniquet ineffective, lips blue, starting CPR, continuing CPR. Yeah, thanks for the bird—you're about thirty minutes too late. Our policy is any wounded American in sector means it's a race for all combat vehicles to get there. Here, it felt almost like what is the minimum I need to do to get through this. I and the XO were both incredibly frustrated. I don't know if they could have saved him, but we sure could have done a helluva lot better on that one.

We drove down and set in the OP and then ran the gauntlet back. Very scary place. After that incident, I just had everyone punch up HE. "I'm trying to level this town without my boss finding out." (I adapted this from the British: "I'm trying to burn this country to the ground without my boss knowing about it … the problem is he can see what I am doing from the base camp.") It is peaks and valleys here. You destroy a weapons market and an American soldier dies (first reports are he was the Air Defense Artillery Battalion CSM). Tragedy. I think the politicians would have a completely different perspective on this country if they spent twenty minutes dealing with the a—holes I have to deal with out here. I don't know if I should feel good about finding all those weapons or just scared at how much stuff is out there. Oh yeah, they are supposed to launch surface-to-surface missiles at the battalion TOC tomorrow. Hopefully, we found most of those missiles today.

4 October: We had a couple of boring periods of time. We rolled the whole company out after someone told us they were going to attack; but they wouldn't let us go into the city, just around the base. I figured we would go test-fire some weapons at the range for a deterrent. Of course, someone at battalion no-goed that idea because we couldn't see far enough to clear the test-fire range ... it's a berm. People just don't all think the same. I was standing outside by the track when *Whoom! Whoom!* Incoming mortar rounds ... great. I jumped into the XO's track, and we closed the ramp. We had guys just standing around outside watching the explosions. I started yelling for them to get inside the buildings. Once they realized what was going on, everyone ran for cover. I guess we just got used to loud explosions all the time. They fired six rounds, and then we rolled out looking for them. We set up a traffic control point and worked on really inconveniencing the people of Samarra. They really do piss you off.

Our daytime patrols have not been very eventful. We just question the guys that are rude to us and go search their houses. This one kid was acting like a punk toward me, so we searched his house. I told the dad the only reason I entered it was because of his kid acting like a punk. All the women just started wailing at the guy. Good action. We did the nightly OP insertion. So nerve-racking driving down these alleyways with zero standoff. They have every advantage in the world ... zero standoff, surprise, and very easy escape if they act swiftly. We dropped the OP and rolled back. As we were driving along, we smacked a wall that we couldn't see due to the washout from all the light on our NODs. Pretty funny. It was in the industrial area that we pulled all the RPGs out of the other day, so no heartburn about running into stuff down there.

We came back up Route RATTLER when all of a sudden my vehicle lost internal commo. My driver stopped according to standard operating procedure, and the convoy kept rolling. We had a break in contact of about 800 meters by the time I got down and told the XO what was happening. Fortunately, my radios still worked, and we just had the XO pull forward so that we could follow him. This sucks. *Donk!* RPG zinging left to right across the field by the lead formation. You got to be kidding me. This is like one of those Ranger School missions where they throw all these variables and mishaps at you. I can't talk. They are shooting RPGs at my brand-new platoon leader; he reports being attacked by bottle rockets, and we have a break in contact. The dismounts get out and start shooting at something, so I think we are taking small-arms fire ... total chaos. We pull up to the dismount point, and I hop down to try to figure it all out. We start talking to the locals and find out the getaway vehicle was a white Opel. They must have thought his Bradley was the trail vehicle. It took forever to gain situational awareness, and you just don't have that kind of time. We have to action left immediately and start suppressing suspected enemy vehicles and locations. We cleared some houses and then came back home without incident and without commo. Contacts like that are so frustrating.

6 October: Well, we are still sleeping out in the moon dust and it's day seven ... great. I am sure we won't leave by day ten. We did our daylight patrol down by the Golden Mosque. They had all kinds of shops and cool crazy stuff going on. We saw an Arnold Schwarzenegger gym with a bunch of dudes working out in it ... probably coordinating their next attack. The Golden Mosque has the tenth and eleventh caliphs buried underneath it, so it's quite a historical site. There were thousands of people out there giving us a mixed reception. We practiced all our urban movement techniques, and the guys looked really good doing it. They have definitely come a long way with MOUT. We rolled back for the BUB and dinner prior to making the nightly gun run.

I guess the battalion had a rough night last night. An RPG hit one of the tanks and took off a guy's arm and took out another guy's eye. They were sitting at a site pulling fixed security on a dam. The same place every night for the same amount of time. Ridiculous. Violates every rule in the book, and I just can't get them to listen to me about that kind of stuff. Well, that sucks. We went out on the gun run. The dropoff was good, and we moved back with the infantry walking by the burnt-out hotel. It took us a little while to get moving, but it looked pretty good. *Donk!* Here comes the Roman candle ... It's so surreal. You just sit there mesmerized watching the RPGs fly by your face. So pretty.... Oh, sh—!

"Contact front," I yell. "Start firing coax forward now," I yell. My turret is facing left, and my gunner opens up on the empty shop stand.

"No not you, turn it to the right." The XO's track keys off our blasting at the shop, and he opens up on it. What is in that shop? Right now we are engaging two areas: my "evil" shop and the target area. The infantry lays down a base of fire on the two targets. We start the infantry moving after the initial fusillade. Rounds you fire make a certain sound. Rounds fired in front of you make another sound. Rounds fired from behind you forward make a third sound, and rounds fired at you a fourth. All four combined with an RPG floating by makes for quite the experience. Looked crazy. Rounds just zinging down the street … fortunately, after two seconds they are all ours. "Cease fire. Is anyone hurt?" We start taking the Green 2 [standard status] report and trying to get situational awareness. It's so hard to figure out which way to move after such a violent response—we shot rooftops, the RPG launch site, and the evil store. During the shootout someone hit a transformer behind us that sent electricity screaming down to the next one that blew up quite spectacularly above my head. It makes it crazy when you don't know exactly what is going on and you're getting showered with sparks.

We got the infantry moving down the right alley and apprehended their getaway car with seven RPGs and four launchers. They would have shot a lot more had our initial actions not terrified them. Okay, score! I go to get down on the ground, and rounds start zinging by me. Sh—. I jump back in the track. What was that … oh, that's 2d Platoon shooting out a light. Ricochets. I flip out. The XO flipped out real bad on them, so I got back into chill-out mode and started searching some houses in the local area. Adrenaline and stress are crazy high. We finish questioning some guys. They, of course, love America and want to help … since we have lots of guns pointed at them and they are terrified. We then have the Bradley that got shot at run over the getaway car. We take off the plates and find one of the guys' sandals. I want to conduct Operation CINDERELLA next for these a—holes. We roll back to the CP without issue. What a terrifying sound the RPG makes in a condensed city, it sounds like a M203 on crack! You just sit there flinching until you see it fly by. Then it's game on … crazy times.

8 October: Everyone was raving about our actions on contact. I am just pissed that the insurgents got away. They decided to let us go on the offensive now and start doing some raids. We performed the gun run without incident. We went down the route that provides the most standoff and fewest alleyways to take keyhole shots at us. I think we might just roll that way more often and fight them on our terms. Varying the route is good, but they are working interior lines on us and engaging us from the worst locations. If we role the easy route, one of two things happens: they don't engage us, or they engage us on our terms. It's like building an engagement area. The danger is IEDs and the ambush ... but that is happening on every route—might as well take the punches on our terms where we can engage them best.

We got back and had an informant give us the call for an on-call raid. I got the MPs, scouts, and a portion of Alpha Company attached to me ... I got everything outside the wire. The scouts mark the objective, and we move through the two buildings real quick and smooth. I start talking to the detainees, and they are not the right ones. They show us the guy's house. We hit that house and get four more males. They tell us another bad guy lives next door ... what the hell. We take that house too. We go through what we thought was a door, but it was a wall to their living room, and the family was sitting in there watching TV. Way scary for them. The lieutenant colonel is on pins and needles when we are operating out there. I think he thinks we are going to have an international incident ... we are just trying to detain every of-age male in Iraq. We get a couple of AKs and then pass the detainees off to the MPs. Turns out, the third and fourth houses have the bad guys. Good score, but battalion is a little edgy with how we just haphazardly enter houses down there. Sometimes, it's just Jerry Springer actions. You have to own the town, or they won't respect you. Squeeze them tight all the time is how you gain respect in this town. I have read all the hearts and minds literature; it won't work in Samarra. I wish it would, but it is a different mentality here.

We roll back. The next day we do our standard protect FOB STODDARD by patrolling along the riverbank looking for a red Suburban. Once the Apaches came on station, we got to chase every red car in the city. That night we have a simultaneous takedown with SF at 0300. We roll out at 0250. I have one platoon isolate the objective at 0310, and 1st Platoon goes in at 0315. We pull a Brad up to the wall, and the guys climb on top of it onto a roof. They start freezing the inner courtyard down while guys hop down to enter the house. The gate comes open; the men come out. I ask them their names ... score—they incriminate themselves. My flashlight broke, so I have been using my under-gun light to shine in their faces ... that is more intimidating. We process them and load them in one of the Brads. I have them cut one of the old men free ... we got our targets. We speed away 0325. The isolation platoon links up at 0330, and we roll to the CMOC [Civil-Military Operations Center] to drop them off. The SF guys are finishing their objective about the same time … damn, we are getting good. They have only twelve guys going in with nontactical vehicles. We got eighty guys moving around with all these Brads, and they are just a little bit faster than us. At 0340 we pass the prisoners off to the MPs and roll into the command post at 0350. The SF guys call me up and say we got their two targets. It was just one of those sweet operations that you are glad to be part of—more bad guys off the street. The offensive is so much better.

9 October: "Hey, do you like getting donked?"

"Hell no, I hate that noise."

"Yeah, me too."

It's always amazing to me how we deal with terrifying situations. We get RPGs launched at us from these narrow alleyways and fifteen minutes later we are joking about it, knowing we are going to get donked again. We had to patrol down some narrow streets during our daylight patrol. We are just cruising down the streets dodging low-hanging wires and trying to figure out how to clear through this sector. I am watching the infantry on the ground, and they are doing well. *Crack! Crack!* We are shooting around a corner. I am two Brads back from the squad shooting, and I can't see the target around a building. "Get the Brad out into the street to support the infantry," I yell. The problem is that part of the squad is shooting across the front deck, using it as cover. We got the Brads moving, and the squad starts running down some roads. I don't even know what we are shooting at yet, but we follow the infantry … it's a great squad.

Situation on the contact: RPG firer is in a white man-dress with face covering. We engaged him before he could get a shot off. We are getting better. Target acquisition is so hard, and the infantry was shooting at 150 meters from alternate firing positions around a corner … that's tough. We did the chase for awhile. All I am thinking is "please don't donk me, please don't donk me." I really don't want to hear that noise again.

We start pulling spider-web checkpoints around the area. I link up with the squad that fired, and we start walking the area. I have a fire team with me, and we move to the firing position. I try to feel where the shooter would go. We move down the alleyway and over toward a rooftop where they thought they saw him. I get up on the rooftop and spot an abandoned building. We start clearing it; I feel much better being in a stack clearing rooms than in a Bradley about to be donked.

The guys are good; they just fall in behind me, and it's one man, two man, etc., as we clear the building ... cache. We grab a bunch of AK–47s and magazines. I get back on the roof, and we start hopping buildings ... so Mogadishu. We reach an impassable area and clear down into someone's house. I love top-down attacks because you are coming down the stairs freezing all the homeowners down, and they freak out because you entered the house from other than the front door. I talk to them for a little while and then we move on; I have to go to the BUB. The general is there, so everyone is a little stressed. I guess the general just listened on the radio to our contact—he wants us to fight. It was a real good action. We don't realize the second- and third-order effects of our fighting these guys, but human intelligence has increased three times since we got here. I still don't want to get donked. The BUB proved pretty standard. I had to pick up a photographer for tonight's patrol. I gave him the "don't do anything stupid" brief and never be more than ten feet from a soldier. They don't realize how rough this town is ... I don't think anyone does. We head back to the CP and pick up the company for the night patrol. Standard OP dropoff (I think that OP is so worthless) and we put the infantry on the ground at Power Line Road. They clear the alleys while the tanks and Brads secure the field to the right. We get all the infantry loaded back up and start moving north. *Donk!* "Sh—!" *Boom!*

"What do we got?" I yell.

"Trail tank hit."

"Move to secure it."

"It's taking forever ... how bad hit?"

"I don't know. There's smoke coming out of it."

"Sh—, we need to start shooting now. Figure out where it came from and fire coax."

The tank blew a halon bottle, and no one could breath for a couple seconds. They come up on the net and say it was from the field to the south.

"Get on line and open up in that field." I crosstalk with our OP, and we fire a burst into the area where the contact came from—my coax jams but comes right back up. It's a pain in the butt because I have the computer right in front of the gun door, so I get squashed in the turret whenever I have to fix it with all my gear on. "Hey, are those rounds anywhere near you guys?" I check just to be sure. "No. You're good, sir." Okay, blast it. There is an all-out fusillade into the open area. We have another explosion to the north, and I send a platoon to check it out—it's not a donking, though. We work on the field area for a little while and check on the tank—no damage. That is really scary—we've had two tanks go down in this city to RPGs already. Not too comforting ... they are destructible. I don't think the reporter liked the patrol too much after the donk. The tankers think they might have hit something out in the field. I call the whole thing off, and we move back to the base. I hate this town.

I read a general's letter in the *Assembly* [the U.S. Military Academy alumni magazine] where he begrudges the "noise-ex"—firing at unknown targets to suppress the enemy. Let me tell you—I am a huge fan of the noise-ex. It ain't right on a live-fire range, but in combat it's a necessity to scare the sh— out of the enemy, build confidence in the men, and take the wind out of the enemy's sails. They shoot at us only once for a reason—the noise-ex. Prior to the arrival of our bullish tactics, we had multiple shots and reloads from the enemy in this city. Now they shoot and run ... fast. Shoot as much as fast as you can at the enemy regardless of straight-up target acquisition—if you saw him there before, shoot there and continue to look for him. Recon by fire—this is not a surgical operation. There is a time and place for that—it's called a raid—and we are very good at that. Controlled execution of a great deal of violence is the order of the day for the Bradleys. If you think you can argue against me on that point, then you haven't been there. Good luck, you'll lose.

11 October: I thought we were going to leave on 10 October, but they argued for us to stay here and guard the bank during the Iraqi currency exchange ... great. That's a definite way to get shot. Park your Brad next to a bank offloading a bunch of money. They don't want the money; they want to donk you, just read the graffiti. Our patrols during the day are pretty quick. I don't think anyone wants to mess around on the ground anymore. Everyone is on pins and needles. It doesn't take much to get violent with these guys. I don't blame them. The populace of this town is never going to like you, so they need to fear you.

The mortars continue to fall. The ADC-S came to visit our FOB. Right after the helicopters landed ... *Boom, Boom, Boom* ... 82-mm. mortars. I don't think he believed that could happen. We pushed down for the thunder run and split into multiple elements on different routes. I wanted to work the periphery of the city, where they had a lot of contact before. This time I put the tanks and Brads farther out of the city with a little standoff and let the infantry clear the alleyways. We worked a bunch of different areas simultaneously en route back. We are not supposed to patrol at night. I take half the battalion out with me every time we roll. No one donked us, so we felt pretty good as we headed back to the FOB.

We parked the Brads and then *Boom. Boom. Boom. Boom.* Mortar barrage. I got into the back of 65, and we shut the ramp. We were screaming for battalion to counterfire. Okay, they fired two rounds ... great job guys ... they fired twenty at us. It's almost like we don't want to win because that would mean we have to be violent. This town will never like you; they must fear you. We sent the platoon to man the bank. Yeah, they got donked with an RPG two hours into it. They returned fire with small arms and searched all the houses next to the alleyway. This place sucks. We need to just leave and let them screw up again and then reinvade properly—in a manner where all the RPGs don't just disappear into the countryside.

12 October: So they want to send us into Zone 8 for our last few days here. That's cool. It's the worst place, but we know how to fight it now. We keep the Brads and tanks on the outside of the city and let the infantry walk the streets. We keep a loose outer cordon with some decent standoff so they can't take keyhole shots at our vehicles. The system works pretty well. The infantry walked down, and the Brads kept their standoff to the east. We had a good system going on, and the infantry did very well. One platoon caught a guy burying AK–47s in his yard. I guess it's the town crop. We policed up that guy and his weapons while the other platoons continued to clear. We had a little separation on line as we moved through the city. The other two platoons reached the LOA [limit of advance] early, so we had them pulling local security as the other platoon moved down after securing the local bad guy.

I started getting antsy because we were sitting there a little longer than I wanted, but time moves so slow when you feel the pressure. I kept on pestering Blue to pick up the pace, but I feel pretty good about the standoff in the field. Suicide to attack from the open field to the south, and they would get tagged by the infantry trying to come out of the alleyways. *Donk!* "Sh—! RPG! Contact!" *Crack, Crack, Crack* goes the coax. Chaos until they report a red motorcycle moving north. We blast it. I try to establish a cordon with the Brads. The motorcycle screams down the gauntlet of infantry who blast it as we move the Brads north to cut them off. Two guys on the bike, one dead guy slumped across the back. We are tagging the bike with small arms, but you need to hit it with HE in order to stop it. I've extensively studied the effects of small arms on vehicles recently; our bullets just rip through them, causing less damage then one would think. Vehicles will travel for a while on flats and all shot up. We go on a red-motorcycle bloodlust for awhile—detaining every guy on a red motorcycle and running over his bike ... winning the hearts and minds ... not my job. Let the State Department do that. That goes on for about thirty minutes before I call the search off. He will either go to the hospital or bleed out. I talk to Staff Sergeant De Wolfe, whose track shot him. I was around the corner, so I couldn't see the engagement.

"Hey, did you hit the guy?" I ask.

"You know, sir, how in the Westerns where they have the shootout and the guy gets hit and flips over in the air ... yeah, that happens with coax too. The RPG hit the berm in front of us. It was actually kinda funny that they thought they could shoot us like that."

"So you hit him?"

"I'm 100 percent sure. His buddy put him on the back of the bike around the corner from us. My gunner said he is dead."

"Okay, good engagement. Let's roll."

We remount the Brads and roll north on Power Line Road with the tanks. The engagements are so fast. It's over in thirty seconds. They fire and flee. We fire and pursue. Unfortunately, they have every advantage in regards to hide and seek ... except when they try to run the infantry gauntlet ... bad route selection. The guys are getting much better at returning fire and pursuing immediately. I make the turn onto Albino Street. *Donk!* "Sh—! RPG! Contact right—they shot at the XO's track."

"Cunningham, turn the car around," I yell.

"Are you for real?"

"Yeah, let's go."

We reach the field just in time to see all of Blue Platoon screaming down the alleyway. That is an awesome sight. Brads move down Italian-style alleyways at forty-five miles an hour crushing everything in their path. We drop the ramp and grab some guy running from us. He has a motorcycle, a military build, and a bad attitude. They detain him. Wrong place, wrong time, wrong company, a—hole. You know who's shooting if it ain't you. He's going to the CMOC. He doesn't want to cooperate after the platoon tied him up.

Controlled violence. We don't mess with them once handcuffed. If they get roughed up in the detention process ... tough. We lack the Los Angeles Police Department's training in the use of less-than-violent detention means. If they are in the alley, they are spotting for the bad guys or firing. I hate the double donking. It's not even dark yet. We get back to the CP and AAR the contact. It was some good action. It is such an unnatural action to move toward the contact, but it's our reflex now ... muscle memory. I don't really have any improvement AAR comments. The company is on it. The city knows it too ... that's why we get more intelligence and only single RPG shots now. They know the fusillade cometh, and we always roll ten Brads deep with well-trained infantry on the ground. The platoons move so smooth in the city, soft-clearing all their sectors. You can tell these guys have been working together for awhile. It's not like everyone knows only what *they* need to do. They know what they need to do and what everyone else on the ground needs to do ... as well as what everyone in their platoon is doing at any given moment. Clear high, low, car, deep, doorways, high/low corners, Rolling T in the alleyways, left side covers right's deep high and vice versa, trail element picks up the rear, and Brads cordon off. It's a constant clearing drill, and they all know it. I guess it helps when you have the "in your face" impetus of a Somalia-type town complete with mini-shootouts to learn in.

15 October: Well, the HETs are coming tomorrow to take us back to our old area. I guess the LSA is under siege, and Lieutenant Colonel Sassaman wants to burn my old town to the ground—he just might do it. Plus they just don't have the facilities for us to stay in up here. We need to get out of the heat, sand, and dirt. So frustrating living in the worst living conditions in the division. I feel sorry for Aggressor Six [A/1-66 Armor commander]; he so wants to win and he always rolls with us. You just feel so lonely out there. We rolled out to test-fire the weapons prior to our day patrol ... last one up here. I looked over toward the ruins and figured ... company picture. Easy last day. We went down to the coliseum built during the twelfth caliph's reign. Pretty sweet. We got some good pictures and then rolled out for a quick patrol in Zone 6. We had some grids from the Q36 radar of mortar-firing locations that I wanted to check out. Chief Albreche, aka Radar, from the Q36 radar, wanted to come with us. He's an old guy with Somalia experience, and he loves infantry patrols. We hit the dropoff point; and five minutes later Red One, First Lieutenant Terrence, calls up ... we got a cache.

"Okay, how big?"

"Give me a minute and will send more info."

"Okay."

"A guy in a yellow number 22 soccer jersey ran from the cache site."

Five minutes goes by, and my dismount RTO Cutuca calls up in his thick Romanian accent, "Sir, I have number 22." Hilarious. Sweet action. We caught him trying to get into a taxi. I hop down and push security out. I know the donk is coming. We pull out 10 RPG launchers, 3 mortar tubes, 35 rockets, numerous small arms, and enough demo to bring down the Sears Tower ... with enough det cord to stretch from here to Baghdad and back. We grab up the shop owners, discuss the living conditions at Guantanamo Bay, and then have them stack all the stuff in the street. I get battalion to push the MPs and a 5-ton down to cart this stuff away. I don't have nearly enough space. This place. The MPs show up with the 5-ton and Mike, the interpreter. I love that guy. I think the feeling is mutual because he loves coming out with our company. We detained two uncooperative guys that definitely looked foreign, with the wahabi beards. We put them up against the wall blindfolded and flex-cuffed. I had the shop owners load the truck while we pulled security. I am all about employing the local populace in our endeavors to clean up their country. We get the stuff loaded.

Donk! "Sh—!" The XO and I slide back into the store and stare at the 5-ton with all the demolitions loaded on it in front of us ... I sure hope it doesn't hit there! Game on! We step out of the building and Blue's Bradleys are coaxing the RPG site 600 meters away. We start sprinting across the field.

The XO and I get the step on everyone, so we are way out front ... I sure hope they follow me. It's a Civil War charge across the field. I look over my shoulder, and everyone is running toward the contact. Good. The other Brads start roaring up as we continue to engage. My driver pulls up next to me ... it's kinda comical. I jump up on the Bradley and start doing the company commander thing as we roll. We cordon off the area and roll through ... lots of blood in the vicinity of the RPG alley. Destroyed car with blood in it, dead guys on the street ahead. We search the area for a little while, but these guys can just vanish it seems.

We continue the hunt when *Crack, crack, crack* go the small arms. We're in small-arms contact with a black BMW that tried to blow through our cordon—it's the same BMW we have seen at the other contacts. My wingman, the XO, heads south while I go north. There are abandoned motorcycles all over the streets ... time to win the hearts and minds with our motorcycle campaign. They really should just ban them; they use them at every contact. I hear a long burst of coax and then get talked onto my wingman's location. We pull up ... he found the car. Jimmy looks at me from up in the turret and just shakes his head. The car is smoked. I have no idea how it kept rolling, kudos to BMW. Our marksmanship is pretty good. I can say from the number of bullet holes in the car, but it just kept rolling on flats. The driver lived, but I am not sure how.

We got three more dead guys in the car ... lots of holes. The interesting thing is that they have bandages from previous wounds ... you have to wonder if these guys have donked you before. There is blood all over the seat and pieces of bone where the driver sat. We hunt him for awhile; he is bleeding bad. He must have gotten in another car because we lost the trail. The BMW is still running, playing Arabic music. We call up to have them check the hospital, but somehow the guys we shoot never go to the hospital. One of my future platoon leaders took a bullet or shrapnel to the leg, and we work the medevac for him as we simultaneously go after this guy. We block the road off, but some jackass wants to run on through. The guys are on edge since we are supposed to have a car bomb in the next few days, so they take his car down with M240. The wheels come off ... it's not a BMW. They move on the car and find it's clean, although we did shoot the dumb ass in the leg: 7.62-mm.... compound fracture. It's nasty looking, too—I tell the CLS to throw some gauze on it, and I recruit a local to take him to the hospital.

These people just don't take us seriously in this town. We so easily could have killed him. If I see two Bradleys blocking the street, an armed soldier signaling for me to turn around, and everyone else turning around, I would not try to squeeze by … taking Albino over Market Street just ain't that important. Okay, good action guys, keep moving. We police up the scene a bit, make sure the MPs got away and our medevac is good. We remount and head out. So much for a quiet day. The battalion is very pleased with the actions. Our guys are on it. We just can't find all the guys we shot, but we are hitting them. This stuff doesn't bother me until I think about it later, and then I realize how much this whole thing sucks. It could be so different for these people if they just accepted that it's over and they need to work with us to set up a new government. So much potential, so many a—holes.

We all get back to the CP, and I call everything up. Second Lieutenant Tumlinson is fine and will be returned to duty. Good. I hate that part. They asked me what I did with the bodies of the bad guys … I left them there. I don't have any bunk space where I am. Okay, we'll send the Iraqi police. We probably will have a riot now. I go to bed and tell the CQ to wake me at 0645. Crazy day. One of the tanks hit a mine going into its perpetual blocking position. I wonder why they put that mine there … is it because we go there every night? The night proves really quiet. The SF guys are getting lots of intelligence for future raids. We have definitely stirred up the hornet's nest, but it has caused people to fear us. Once they fear you, they try to cooperate with you more and then you can go quietly and get the bad guys instead of having a running gun battle through the middle of town each night. The guys did awesome in the actions, and we saved some American lives tonight by getting that cache off the streets. I just wonder how much sh— is still out there.

16 October: It will be good to be back in our old AO. At least they are only indirectly opposing us through mortars on ANACONDA and IEDs on the road. *Boom! Boom! Boom!* It's 0635 and we are getting mortared … up in the morning, out of the rack … greeted at dawn by a mortar attack. I hate this place. I roll out with a platoon to ANACONDA for a meeting with [Maj. Gen. Antonio M.] Taguba [then the deputy commanding general for Third Army, a colleague, friend, and neighbor of Captain Brown's parents]. I don't know who he is, but he seems real nice. Must be a friend of my parents. The aide kept asking me if I was the right Captain Brown, and I kept telling him I didn't know, but I was willing to go with the flow. The general was great. Real nice guy and talked about stuff we wanted to talk about. You don't get that very often. Felt so good to be back inside my big bunker with huge standoff. It will be nice to go for a run without mortars falling, foot-deep moon dust, or an ever-shrinking, claustrophobic perimeter. Turns out the guys we smoked today were involved in a plot for a suicidal car bombing. They may have been trying to recon our perimeter under contact for future operations. Suicide bombers terrify me. Well, he was half successful ... with the suicide part. Found out my plebe roommate, Jeff Sutton, died in a climbing accident in Alaska. Unreal.

18 October: We got back to the bunker and were to stand down for maintenance and a general refit after the previous craziness. In the midst of our stand-down, we get reintegrated into the battalion—as the main effort for three different missions over the next thirty-six hours. Cool. I just can't get any good sleep lately. Our first mission is site security for the Balad City elections. So funny going through Balad because they all love you there. I am still in the street-fight mode during all our leader recons, and I think I am freaking everyone out. You just can't relax. The elections prove a great feat. The locals respond extremely positively, and lots of people vote; some liked it so much they voted twice. It's hilarious explaining democracy to them. Sassaman keeps on telling them that they will follow the same voting rules as they did under Saddam when they elected him. I love the reactions from the locals. No violence at all. Amazing. If they held an election in Samarra, we would have an all-out civil war.

In the midst of the elections, I have to go run a raid on some wahabi extortionists. We call it the Red Rose Raid. Brigade assembled all this stuff for a Jerry Springer–type raid. We have an informant wearing a yellow shirt and ball cap who will make a money drop at the butcher shop. He must pay some wahabis for "protection." They have the fake money in a black trash bag. It proved total Matlock amateur hour. We put a squad in overwatch from an abandoned building and established an outer cordon with the Bradleys to go into effect on bag drop at high noon. Everything gets set in nice and smooth. We got eyes on, and everyone is in place ... except the wahabis never show. Everyone is shocked, except for us. We do these stupid single-source Jerry Springer raids all the time. The guy probably crashed someone's car and owes him money. We all had visions of a great takedown but knew that it would turn out as bad information.

After we called off that debacle, we headed back out to the election site to finish with the "vote must right to democrats always" election ... that's what their banners read. It ended well, and we moved right from there out into counterambush sites in the vicinity of the mortar firer's position. The night before they started lobbing these trash-can rockets at the LSA. They are huge and apparently pretty loud. They jerry-rig an initiation system, and they fly away ... no one knows how to aim them, so they go all over the place. With 15,000 people packed onto the airfield, though, the insurgents really don't need to aim the rockets. The LSA sustained four injuries. Well, nothing happened while we were out there, and it proved another really long night. The next morning we went to the Eagle Prayer Breakfast and then had the combat stress guys come out and talk to everyone. I finally got to sleep in my bunker. Hopefully, tomorrow will be a normal day.

24 October: We have had a couple decent days, but the randomness goes on and on. I have gone from one battalion commander who only acts on very specific information to a battalion commander who wants us to act on everything. We went into these shops located a kilometer from the "Snake" [LSA ANACONDA] and cleared them out prior to receiving a follow-on mission to find Saih Mohammed Huseen, a weapons dealer in our area who is hiding weapons in a well. The information smells very Jerry Springer. It's a double-house takedown, so we give a quick Frago and drive down the road. The TAC showed up with some reporters, and they interviewed me and the XO about the raid.

"Are you surprised that you didn't find anything here?" she asked.

"Hell no, we never find stuff when we are looking for it," the XO tells her.

She keeps on saying that she knows me and Jimmy from somewhere, and this is driving the S–3 crazy because he likes her.

We go on the raid, and the guy is not there. I work my Arabic with one of the locals and he shows us the well, the guy's house, the car, where he went, when he'll return, and everything else. Of course, battalion will not listen to what I am saying and we go on a clear-the-whole-block tirade, finding nothing ... except for a hole near the well where the weapons might have been. We have quite a traffic jam built up by the time I get to the road; the Air Force plans on dropping two 500-pound bombs, so we have to clear the area. I get bored with the random house clearings that we always go on; so I walk down the line of cars, spot the white Opel and green BMW. Bingo. I walk up to the car, hand the guy a piece of paper and pen and tell him to write down his full name. Yep, it's him. The Iraqis always think I am screwing around with them when I have them write stuff down in Arabic, but it's my JV attempt at being Matlock. I BS with the guy for a little while as I move a squad up to detain our target and the five guys from Baghdad with him. Everything in this country is so random … our successes, our failures, everything. We police those guys up and hand them over to the TAC and torment old Roy some more.

Staff Sgt. Cory Blackwell on a cordon and search operation

Raiding a house just outside Balad

The Air Force drops two 500-pound duds. Awesome. We just put 1,000 pounds of IED-making material into someone's backyard. We so talked up the event like it would be the greatest thing ever and really loud: 2,000 meters away ... nothing. We part ways with the TAC and head back to our CP. They move out with their circus of random people and vehicles. As we make the left to go onto ANACONDA, the TAC comes into contact ... three RPGs. I turn our formation around, and we start moving down the road to their action. Fortunately, nothing is hit. They return fire. It came from across the canal. I can't believe the TAC didn't hit anything with the amount of ammo expended. You know contact comes from that side of the canal, so three-fourths of the formation watches that side. We drop off the infantry and cross over a little footbridge to clear the field areas and houses around the area, finding nothing. It's so frustrating, and the lieutenant colonel and S–3 are pissed. You have to scan always, and we never let the gunners stand up outside the wire, especially at night.

I think everyone thought scanning while moving was kind of an NTC, OC-type deal [this expression refers to techniques stressed by observer-controllers supervising training at the National Training Center] until we went to Samarra. The open field contacts with your thermals up ... we were begging for that kind of easy contact in Samarra. We finished up there and left. I don't know why I was so frustrated with that contact; none of my guys even got shot at, and I really don't know what exactly happened. I just can't help but be critical of every failed engagement these days, and it seemed like such a perfect location to seal the deal. You don't get the wide-open field shots often. We never have. I think I am also frustrated because this area has not had a direct-fire contact in such a long time. You start to think it might be getting safer. It sure freaked out all those reporters.

29 October: Well, we continue to lie out in the field and wait for mortars to fire, but they don't fire when we are in the area. They have good intelligence, and we just keep the screws turned on them tight. I heard the report that Samarra lost two soldiers and had four wounded in a mortar attack. It's so sad, but they still won't counterfire. I think they should just call in all the leaders and lay it out for them. A mortar fires from the city, we will fire back at it. Clean up your city. We laid in 48-hour ambushes and then pulled out. An hour after we pulled the guys out, they called us and said they want us to go to 24-hour operations in our area. Great. Then after the 24-hour operation, we want you to lay in 48-hour ambushes, and we will minimize our presence during Ramadan. Okay, so minimize your presence but conduct continuous operations. I am really confused. My gunner and driver did get to go on leave. They both have newborn babies at home, so that's great. It sucks that we will get to send so few guys home. I am hoping for 20 percent, but we will see. Some days time can just drag by.

31 October: I have been delinquent in my efforts to remain up to date. I got "stuck" up at brigade for the great Cobb and Datray court-martial. It proved a comedy of errors, but the judge saw through the whole thing and sentenced Cobb to six-and-a-half years. That's a long time. I felt really bad for Cobb and talked to him about it afterward. He is going in at the age of eighteen and coming out at twenty-five. That period of life encompasses so much. Hopefully, he'll be able to turn things around while he is at Leavenworth. Well, brigade was good for me. It felt like R&R. They had these couches that we would sleep on and e-mail and phone access. They also had three outstanding hot meals a day in a wonderful dining facility. I know exactly how to lose touch with reality—move into ANACONDA. I don't know what reality is, though. Maybe I am the abnormal one living in an evil fantasyland outside the wire. The vast majority of people in Iraq do not make it outside the wire on a daily or even weekly basis. After a few days it started getting really weird being up there … no sense of mission, purpose, or hope.

They had the pictures of the M1A2 that got blown up across the river. Not reassuring. Total catastrophic kill with the turret thrown 100 feet. One guy lived. That is not supposed to happen to main battle tanks. It is the first ever catastrophic kill by the enemy on an M1. All the other incidents have been chalked up to friendly fire or just not catastrophic. Needless to say, it terrifies us all, since a Bradley weighs as much as the M1's turret.

Everyone tends to find fault with the person that got blown up. I think it is a defense mechanism to keep you going. They were briefing that the reason they got blown up stemmed from them continually going to guard this pump house. Well, that's their mission. The pump house did not leave, and there is only one dirt road to get up to it. Fixed-site security is a no-go: it makes you predictable and enables the bad guys to bury a 500-pound IED in the trail you have to use. We are basically doing fixed-site security around the towns for Ramadan. I continually try to get out of it, and we vary our positions. There are only so many places you can go though without entering the city. It's all about minimizing yourself as a target. Patrolling exposes you to more terrain that in turn exposes you to more hazards, but not patrolling emboldens the enemy and allows him to attack LOGPAC convoys and support areas. I can't figure it out.

We had to pick up two *New York Times* reporters and head back to the base after the trial. As I finish talking to the brigade commander, I hear from the brigade XO that I have a Bradley on fire. He starts in on me and demands why I have a Bradley 200 meters north of Lion FOB. I look over at the colonel incredulously, and he looks back at me the same and nods.

"That's where I live, sir."

"Well, how long have you lived there?" he asks, trying to save face in front of the colonel.

"Oh, since we got to Balad 125 days ago."

"Oh, I didn't realize that." The XO backs down … good situational awareness.

My first sergeant comes across the net and says it's over for the Bradley. We keep on reporting its status every twenty minutes … like something has changed. The rounds are cooking off, and TOW missiles are flying. Fortunately, we got everyone out of there in time. I can't move down the road, so we go around the north side and take Route Ginger. Quite a fireworks display. The official report reads something like this:

B32 and B33 had LOGPAC security on 30 October. As they returned from this duty, they smelled raw fuel and decided to stop at the UMCP en route back to our CP at Lion FOB. Sgt. Jacobs, the company mechanic, diagnosed a leak in the fuel line and replaced this line. The track worked without incident, and the crew fueled up at the FTCP [Field Trains Command Post] since they were low on fuel from the mission—not the leak. The track worked without incident until it arrived 200 meters shy of Lion FOB. The track stalled. The crew restarted the engine and heard a loud pop. S.Sgt. Zawisza, the BC, directed the driver, Pvt. Santiago, to open the engine access panel. Flames shot out of the engine and the sides. The BC directed the driver to drop ramp, and he ran to the back and fought the fire with fire extinguishers. The driver's compartment had flames on the floorboards, and they all got off the track. After using all B32's fire extinguishers, the crew got more from B33 and started pulling sensitive items off the track. They pulled the halon bottles but to no effect since the hatches had all been opened. By this time, the hull was engulfed in smoke and flames, and they could not retrieve the CLU or any more sensitive items, though they tried desperately. The BC succumbed to smoke inhalation and the B33 BC made the call to evacuate the immediate area, get S.Sgt. Zawisza to the medics, and avoid the round cookoff that followed shortly thereafter (2 x TOWs, 2 x AT4s, 1,200 7.62-mm., 120 AP non-DU, and 230 HE). LION TOC sent their QRF to cordon off the area and designated the "safe" perimeter. They evacuated all personnel behind this line, and Lion 6 took charge of the overall situation. S.Sgt. Zawisza received oxygen from the Bravo Company medics prior to a command-directed evaluation at 21st CASH.

It made for an extremely painful night. No one wants to believe that a Bradley is just imploding. The next morning we dragged it off the road so al Jazeera couldn't film it. Everyone was freaking out about some reporters seeing it. The irony is the *New York Times* guys were in the backseat and took zero interest in the whole thing. Lieutenant Colonel Sassaman was real cool about it and just yelled at me for some guys taking their Kevlars off. "I don't give a rip about the Bradley burning to the ground, but I do care about guys taking stupid, needless risks with their uniforms outside the wire." I agree. The next day folks descended on the scene and wanted assessments.

"If you drive a car 250,000 miles and one day it catches on fire out on the highway … do you really ask yourself how it happened?" I understand all the safety implications; but I also understand that we drove 530 kilometers on the Bradleys last week and that was pretty much a normal week. The high

The end of B32

end is often 700 kilometers in a week. We'll see how this one turns out. I am sure somewhere along the line it will be my fault. The next morning we had a raid up in Alpha Company's sector. I swear they pull us into these things so they can be the main effort. That's cool, though. It allows us to put 100 kilometers on our Bradleys. Yeah, we had two Bradleys go down on that movement. Recovering the Bradleys is so painful, but the XO is the one that really has to suffer through it. The raid/clearance goes pretty well. We had a bunch of reporters with us and, fortunately, no bad guys.

Most of the entertainment came from the girls' school we went into. The kids are so beautiful. We played chalkboard games for awhile before calling off the search. We do a lot of these unactionable-intelligence clearance drills, but it's good to go on the offensive, and it keeps the guys sharp. After finishing the recovery of the Bradleys, we moved back across the river and headed home to take a nap and shoot at the range.

The next day we went up to the TOC for a meeting and to watch the Ghazani tribe for Halloween. Their tribe jams stuff into their bodies to celebrate events. Apparently, we arrested their leader and were going to release him when he offered to eat the long fluorescent light bulb in return for his release. Well, he did it and cut his mouth to shreds. So we invited the tribe back to celebrate Halloween, and they pierced their body in all kinds of ways I never thought imaginable. They jammed knives into their heads. Crazy. This explains a lot about their ability to get away from us after being shot. Sassaman called off the event before they started shooting each other in the love handles with pistols. I have never seen so many freaks on Halloween. Unreal.

"Contact" comes across the battalion net. No grid, no call sign. We are trying to figure it all out. Everyone starts calling their units, and we get an "up" from all elements. We continue to try to figure it out.

"We need a medevac. We have limbs everywhere," a frantic call comes across the net. It has to be the brigade commander's Humvee convoy. All elements start moving onto Route LINDA to find the element in contact. I call Red 4 [1st Platoon sergeant] and tell him to move west on LINDA until he comes in contact. Red 4 gets moving and finds the brigade commander's convoy. He reports up the grid.

"Hey Sergeant First Class Berg, you are in charge of the scene. Secure the site and work the medevac piece. Put tourniquets on the guys and move them to the CASH. You are only ten minutes away," I instruct Red 4. He calls back and reports on the situation. We have three BRT soldiers wounded, but they have no CLS bag, no litter, no commo, no grid, no security; any one of those mistakes in B/1-8 IN would have afforded you the opportunity to improve your stomach muscles through a mnemonic we call the flutter kick.

"Hey Berg, you are the man down there."

"Yeah sir, tell me something I didn't already know," he replies cockily. He is great, and his cocksure attitude makes us all calm down. First Lieutenant Frank, my old FSO, now in the BRT, gets on the scene, so I start feeling a lot better knowing we got two solid guys down there. They get the security situation under control, and the bird comes in with no more issues. I feel so bad for those guys. I know exactly what they are going through under their first contact. It always goes badly your first time around, and you beat yourself up for it over and over again. Return fire, establish security, treat and evacuate your casualties. Easier said than done. It sucks because I have to roll back through that area tonight. We leave the TOC for the white-knuckle ride down LINDA.

"Hey sir, it's Frank on your company net," Frank calls up as we roll by.

"Yeah Frank, sounds like it was a rough one tonight."

"Yeah, it didn't go according to plan. Berg and Red Platoon were great, though."

"I know. I felt so much better once you two came up on the net. I knew you'd know what to do."

"Exact same circumstances as the one we had back in July."

"Sure sounded like it. Tough trying to figure it all out, isn't it?"

"We just took the same actions we did back then, but this time I was in charge … treating casualties, controlling aircraft, providing security," Frank said.

"Well, I knew you would do it well. You the man."

"Hey, sir."

"Yeah, Frank."

"I am real glad I was in Bravo Company."

"Me too, man, me too."

NOVEMBER

November was a particularly bloody month for coalition forces in Iraq. In the deadliest single attack on U.S. forces since the fall of Baghdad, sixteen soldiers died when their Chinook helicopter was shot down outside Fallujah. A few days later an RPG attack brought down a Black Hawk helicopter, killing another six soldiers. On 12 November a car bomb struck the Italian military police headquarters in Nasiriya, well outside the Sunni areas previously considered dangerous, and killed twenty-five. Two days of convoy raids by anticoalition forces in Samarra left twelve coalition casualties and forty-six Iraqis dead.

Captain Brown's company, now back in its familiar haunts around LSA ANACONDA, similarly experienced an upsurge in violence and casualties, including direct-fire ambushes in areas where they had not occurred for awhile. In addition to fighting back with often overwhelming firepower, his battalion totally isolated the troublesome town of Abu Hishma, surrounded it with barbed wire, and methodically identified and processed every "of-age" male they found. Those of legitimate local origin were given an identification card and were subject to surveillance; those from out of town were incarcerated or expelled. These draconian measures ultimately yielded salutary, albeit imperfect, results. They also got the battalion unfavorable coverage in a number of American newspapers and invidious comparison with Israeli tactics it was alleged to emulate. Curiously enough, the locals in Abu Hishma seem to have been pleased with, rather than offended by, their shiny new identity cards. Unfortunately, similar measures for population control in Fallujah, Ramadi, or Samarra seemed beyond the coalition's means at the time.

In Washington, D.C., the upsurge in Iraqi violence and the increasingly occupation-like behavior of U.S. forces lent renewed urgency to administration efforts to map a way out. Paul Bremer returned to Washington for consultations on 12 November, and on 14 November the United States committed itself to transfer power to an interim Iraqi government in 2004. Ten days earlier President Bush had secured Senate approval for $87.5 billion to sustain the continuing costs of Operation IRAQI FREEDOM.

Pundits at the time were fond of making comparisons with the Vietnam War. At the strategic and operational levels most of these were specious but at the tactical level perhaps less so. With minimal adaptation, Captain Brown's combat narratives could have described any of a dozen American counterinsurgencies in *the twentieth century. Such emotions as his grief when S.Sgt. Dale Panchot died were, of course, timeless.*

---

5 November: The days continue to pass by, and we continue to train at our ranges and watch over Abu Hishma 24/7. That sucks. Third Platoon was moving around at 2300 when *Boom.* They hit a land mine, knocking the track off one of their Brads. We rolled all available Brads up to secure the site and brought out the M88. Mines are straight-up terrifying because you can't fight them and they can be everywhere, especially on the spider trails. The most heavily traveled areas don't have the mines because of all the other vehicles; the least-traveled areas don't have them because they are not good targets. It's the medium-traveled dirt routes you have to watch carefully. It was an Italian plastique mine, best we can tell. I hate this place. We took the M88 out there and recovered the vehicle and the blown-off track and then had to deal with the tirade on the net. Somehow it's your fault that they hit a mine.

The mission sucks, and there is no way to vary it. When you have 24-hour presence around a five-kilometer town, the only variety you can really figure out is not to have 24-hour presence. No one realizes that the guy that wants to hit the mine the least is the guy driving the vehicle. Emotions were high on the net. The LSA hasn't gotten anything shot at it, but we've been getting 60-mm. mortars and mines. We have become the target … and no one wants to provide any support or suggestions on how to get through it. I am out of ideas, and everyone acts like you screwed up somehow when you get attacked. No one looks at the fact that the LSA hasn't been hit since we returned to the region three weeks ago … longest streak yet. Oh well, I have twelve more Bradleys that I can destroy trying to protect 15,000 people that walk around like they are back on the block, choosing not to wear their Kevlars and body armor. Brads are the only thing I am willing to destroy, however. So frustrating. I wish someone would tell me how to win this war. All my Bradleys are falling apart; we need to go to surge operations and not 24-hour guard. I continue to improve on the range and shoot with anyone that comes down, whenever 1-68 AR TOC isn't acting like range control. It's my solace, and we are getting much more proficient at MOUT. Hilarious to listen to the specialists and junior E–5s, who last month didn't have a clue about sectors, talking to the privates and new shooters like they had been doing this for years. I love that. A little knowledge makes them want to lead.

11 November: We've had a couple of groundhog days. Things were actually going quite well, with us doing surge operations instead of 24-hour guard. I had to send a platoon back up to Samarra to help them with their force protection requirements. That sucks. Fortunately, they don't ever have to go into the city. With them gone and 3d Platoon in services, Jimmy and I had to man the OP with our Brads at night. We were staging at H7 when *Donk, donk, donk.* I called up battalion to see if anyone reported mortars firing or if I was just hearing water bottles blow up in the fire. Unfortunately, I have the capability of identifying mortars, and the hunt was on for the Mad Mortarman of Balad. They counterfired, but we couldn't do BDA since it was so dark. Fortunately, the mortars really didn't land close to anything, and I think I was one of the few people to hear them of the 15,000 getting shot at. We set up a checkpoint to detain any suspects, but it proved quite fruitless. I was just glad I was out there, as the battalion commander went on a tirade about wanting to win and firing his mortars. They counterfired with the howitzers, and our battalion mortars did not fire. He was hot. It lasted for quite some time. We then rolled back to our FOB. The next morning, we went to the weekly commander's meeting at the TOC. It started at 1300 and went to 2000. The only real break we took was when they mortared us. They hit the city instead, so the meeting continued.

The brigade commander came out, and we talked about some "foreign affairs" strategic-level fight. I just want hot water for our shower. He asked me what I thought of the situation. We are trying to apply a Western-style national organization on a tribal people. It just doesn't work. We are an American tribe that interacts with all these other tribes, and the attacks have reached homeostasis. The Iraqis just don't grasp it. There is a reason Saddam ruled the way he did. You have to brutally motivate these people into cooperation. They don't understand teamwork, and they blow up their own stuff more often than they blow up ours. Crazy. Not a good meeting. I think we are all a bit disenchanted. Happy Veterans' Day.

12 November: I am tasked to the max. I have a platoon in Samarra, a platoon in services, FOB security, and 24-hour presence in Tu-Pac. Insane. We had to cancel LOGPAC today because we had no one to get it and no one to enjoy it. No fuel, no food, no mail. Sad face. It was kind of fun playing "Joe Rifleman," though. The first sergeant and I had tower guard. No one asks you any questions or really bothers you when you're on guard. You just sit up there and look out into the darkness and hope some insurgent ain't trying to sneak up on you. Jimmy and I also pulled six hours up in Tu-Pac.

We rolled out to FOB BEAST and talked to Paliwoda for a while and just sat chilling out there.

"Contact CP 2A," a frantic voice calls over the net as gunfire sounds in the background. I hate that phrase. Every time I hear it, I always try to think of some excuse to stay where I am and "develop" the situation … no excuse. We are out the door and rolling west on LINDA before the initial report is finished.

"We have action to the north and several guys running into the orchards," comes the next report as we roar down the road. The locals aren't used to seeing Brads out here since it's the engineer companies' AO. The traffic seems to cooperate with us rather well, though. There is something about a 33-ton vehicle moving down a tiny road at fifty mph that convinces the locals to yield and drive rather defensively. We arrive within five minutes and are the first reinforcements on the scene. We start actioning in the direction the engineers point us. They hit the LOGPAC convoy … damn, it's fajita day. They have sappers on the ground clearing the orchard area, but I really think they initiated the contact from the south. We rapidly clear north, not gaining any contact except with all the trees as they smash into me. I call off our chase after about fifteen minutes and head back to the scene to help secure the site. More reinforcements show up, and we secure one slightly wounded soldier. We check out the scene as the medic finishes up with him, and then we escort him to the aid station back at the LSA as the engineer company takes over the scene. We flew back to ANACONDA and dropped off the casualty, then we ate some fajitas. Definitely made the time fly by, and the kid turned out fine. So frustrating, though—everything in this country is an ambush.

17 November: When I woke up this morning, S.Sgt. Dale Panchot was already dead. He died in the back of B23 as an RPG penetrated the hull, went through his body, and buried itself in the far side. The entire battalion converged on the scene of the RPG ambush, and we began to lay havoc with Apaches and indirect. We started clearing toward the ever-present L6– L7 ambush berm. I linked up with Lieutenant Colonel Sassaman, and he assigned us sectors to clear.

Donk! Donk! Donk! "Incoming," we yelled. These guys have some serious balls. They started engaging us with mortars as we cleared the field. All my guys ran for cover, and we dropped ramp on the tracks to load the infantry and start moving to the contact. For some reason, Alpha Company charged right at the exploding rounds—not a good idea to attack indirect fire. I was totally confused and started yelling at them to stop. The lieutenant colonel and I saw some smoke coming from the wood line and started moving on it. We had the right direction but the wrong house. The Q36 picked up the acquisition; and then we hammered it with our 120-mm. mortars; the Apaches fired 30-mm. and Hellfire missiles into the area as well. It shook the earth as they hit 1,200 meters away. After a good, long barrage, we moved the infantry onto the grid. About this time a car ran Alpha Company's checkpoint ... a onetime mistake, as they destroyed it. My infantry found a large cache of 120-mm., 82-mm., 60-mm., and RPG rounds. We couldn't move it, so we just blew it all in place. Another nice explosion for the Abu Hishma tribe. We cleared the houses of the field's owner and then got the armored combat earthmovers and bulldozers into action leveling the berm. They pushed the dirt right into the canal and reduced the enemy's engagement area. We also imposed a 1700–0800 curfew and blocked the exits to the town with a dozer. I am trying to figure out how to destroy this town without violating the ROE. Now they have only one entrance; we are running a checkpoint with ICDC and police spotting all nonlocals, but it's the locals that are bad.

I can't believe Panchot was killed. I have such a huge feeling of vulnerability, followed by guilt, followed by some random abstract thought that I should not be thinking since he is dead ... like what will we do with his stuff, etc. None of it really makes much sense to me. He was a good soldier and a good person. It's so hard to keep going on. We visited the two guys that were wounded in the action. They suffered minor wounds, but the psychological ones are much deeper. Total mess. Total bad day. I would never have guessed that this would happen the way it did, in the place it did, to the vehicles it did. Just unfathomable, how they are trying to attack the Bradleys. After an all-day Abu Hishma affair, we went to get some chow. We were starving, and all they had was bad fish for dinner. There is so much crap we have to do, and everyone is stepping forward to help out. The escort officer was identified, briefed, and arrived in less than twenty minutes. Everyone was helping out with the whole notification process, etc. We swung by the UMCP and fixed my batteries and then headed back to the CP. Awful day. I got all the leaders together and we AARed the whole action. We then had a moment of silence and said the Eagle Prayer ... that will break you. We will be back out in the AO at 0330 tomorrow. Get back up on the horse, as if we don't have enough to think about. This is what I said at the memorial service:

I possess neither the eloquence nor the stoicism to provide the eulogy Staff Sergeant Dale Panchot deserves. He served as the 3d Squad leader, for 2d Platoon, Bravo Company, 1-8 IN ... and he loved what he did. Staff Sergeant Panchot was a very quiet, tall soldier with an easygoing, infectious grin characteristic of folks that have suffered through the long harsh winters of Minnesota. Dale didn't like a lot of attention and would have been a bit embarrassed about all these people gathered here for him. He was twenty-six years old, a model squad leader and a fabulous soldier. You could tell that's what he wanted to do and was designed to do from birth. He didn't sit around pontificating on military matters, he just liked shooting guns and hanging out. He was always tinkering with and cleaning weapons both American and foreign. I have a picture of him embedded in my mind sitting on the back of B22, hands all dirty, cleaning his coax, and just smiling. He loved what he did.

We had just moved Staff Sergeant Panchot from the BC's position to 3d Squad Leader, and insomuch as fate plays a role in all that we do, I'll always bear those scars, and that sense of guilt. As a BC he was extremely aggressive, never afraid to action on contact or hop off his track to help the infantry. He loved going on missions and only very reluctantly gave up his track to me in Samarra when mine broke and he had suffered a mild concussion from an IED. I on the other hand would have looked for any excuse to not go into that particular town at night. I remember the marked contrast between his Bradley and mine. I loved BCing 22. I did not have to deal with the terribly placed Blue Force Tracker computer, and he kept the turret immaculate. As I opened the doors to the coax to test-fire before patrol, it provided me with a snapshot of what a phenomenal soldier he truly was. The gun was immaculate despite the two-foot-deep moon dust plaguing Camp Daniels. He cleaned it that day ... for me, and the zero was absolutely dialed on. That night, we were ambushed by RPGs while the infantry were clearing forward, and we returned fire with coax. It fired like a dream, and the contact ended on our terms. During my tenure in B22, I managed to accidentally run into a wall head on, knock off a whole panel and side skirt, break the ramp, and wedge a large fender into the side paneling. Each time I returned after breaking his track, Dale just smiled away and helped fix it. We would laugh about my attempts to break his track, and he would figure out ways to go on the missions in other tracks. He was a fighter amongst fighters.

I take some solace knowing that this great soldier died a soldier's death, scrambling to get out of the track and into the gunfight. He was born and raised in a very close family from Minnesota, and he died amidst a very close family here in Iraq. Soldiers aren't friends. They are comrades. "Friend" does not quite encompass the bond that develops amongst men under fire, living at close proximity day in and day out for seven and half months. It is a bond and a necessity for survival. On November 17, we lost a great comrade. I'll miss Dale's sheepish grin, his can-do attitude, and his good nature. I know that he is in a better place now watching over us ... tinkering with some sort of gun waiting to go hunting. God Speed, Dale, and rest in peace.

19 November: We pulled out of the town tonight to prep for the memorial service. After three days we need a break. I now don't have to deal with range hot times. We are running some phenomenal live fires in the area where they ambushed us. It's a react-to-contact play out at Panchot Point, and we have a couple of houses we now use for live-fire training. We rehearse our actions and build the engagement area with crossing sites for the infantry across the canals and identified routes for the Brads to get on the north side. The actions are great for training and rebuilding confidence. I just have to continuously talk 2d Platoon's 25-mm. rounds down and prevent them from sailing north. I am pretty sure that Jimmy and I are the only ones who still give a rip about that stuff. We absolutely hammer the area with 155-mm. artillery and 120-mm. mortars several times a day. The people on ANACONDA think it's a WWI battle out there. Especially since they started pushing joint direct-attack munitions down to us … the 500- and 1,000-pound bombs … yeah, real loud. We targeted an abandoned house along the road that they had been using to plan attacks; I couldn't find it in the dark. As the sun came up I found it … all over the road. Incredibly impressive seeing as how the barn out back remained unscathed while you couldn't even tell there had been a house there. Amazing. We started laying wire around the town today. It's about five miles worth of triple-strand across the crazy orchards. Not fun, but we have to fight them every day. We were just getting ready to start the project.

Construction of the finest gated community in Abu Hishma. We surrounded the town with concertina wire after numerous attacks on American forces.

Boom! "Contact north." The TAC was hit by an IED. The coax and 25-mm. started firing, and they have targets—sweet. We all start rolling west toward the contact.

"Yeah, I got ol' boy," Roy drawled across the net. He was the trail Brad and "skinned ol' boy up with some 25 HE." I got there as they secured the guy, who was stable but a little heavy on the shrapnel side of the house. I didn't bother gloving up to treat him, and we let one of the new guys practice on him. They interrogated him for awhile as we planned out the wire-laying task, and then we sent a section to take him to the CASH. They are so stupid. If they just didn't attack us, their lives would improve so much. Oh well, we started the monumental task of laying all the wire for the day.

We were just finishing tying down the wire when I heard this swish, thud, small boom, and saw a puff of smoke seventy-five meters away. I thought someone had an accidental discharge with the 25-mm. or maybe they fired an RPG at my track—I was on the ground. I started looking around at the barrels to see who had it when the Q36 keyed in and gave us the grid to mortar fire—I think it was a dud ... yeah, blast it. We fired about fifty rounds of white phosphorus at the grid and then went down there for a cursory search of the smoking area. I'm more interested in firing mortars at them than looking for mortars in the dark. We headed back to the FOB to prep for the memorial service and listened to CP ROCK call in a medevac for someone that got hit out on Route 1. The casualty did not sound like he was in good shape ... there is no military solution to this place.

26 November: It's been a whirlwind of activity the past few days. We had a very nice memorial for Staff Sergeant Panchot, completed the wire-laying around the town of Abu Hishma, and began the registration process for the endless supply of males who live in the town. We made IDs for all the of-age males, but everyone wanted a card. It was pretty funny. The 85-year-old blind sheik demanded that he get one as well. The cattle can't walk along their normal migratory routes, so they have to come through the checkpoint. I directed that we register a couple male "baqaras" [bovines] for good measure. The people appreciated my sense of humor, although the cows did not. We have done a pretty good job with the psyops campaign: we are fencing off your city and registering you for your protection against the Saddam Fedayeen, instead of we are fencing off your city because you are a tumorous growth that we must isolate so that the body can continue to grow. These guys love status, and ID cards are just that ... status. The registration campaign is really quite painful, but now we have a great live-fire area since they are not allowed south of the fence line. The 1-68 AR lost a soldier in a vehicular accident as their Humvee rolled into a canal and the kid drowned. Tragedy. We really had a rough week. They did a great memorial; we are becoming far too proficient at these services.

The next morning we launched Operation EAGLE PANCHOT, in which we rounded up about twenty guys whom informants had given up as bad guys. The operation kicked off at 0100, and we had ten different houses to hit. The downpour of cold rain kicked off at midnight, so it proved a real party for all those involved. We policed up a bunch of targets, and Staff Sergeant Reagan brought me some blind ninety-year-old man and a dude missing his hand. The questioning proved pretty funny, and I cut them free and made fun of Reagan for bringing them down. The old guy had no clue where he was, so I assigned the guy missing his hand the task of escorting him back home. The night finally ended at 0500, with us rolling back into our FOB cold, wet, and tired. It was good to go on the offensive, but we were kind of JV out in the rain. It made for a painful night.

The next day we just kind of lay around and prepped for the great Thanksgiving feast. The mortars fired on ANACONDA, and the brigade fired back with artillery. Unfortunately, they had 24-knot winds and the rounds fell 500 meters short. They landed on a house, killing a lady and two kids. This place is so sad. They rounded up all the people from those houses for questioning. Now they seem to be helping us … until we let them go and they attack us in revenge—the rule of five hamza (if you attack someone, it is the responsibility of five bloodlines over to attack you in return). I am glad that I wasn't on the cleanup crew for that action. Sassaman told them that Saddam Fedayeen caused it all. You have to lie; it's the locals' way. Never admit to anything. I guess he got in trouble with brigade, but they really don't understand how you must deal with the locals. Admit to nothing because then everything is your fault—things here are simply different than in America and we have to adapt in order to make any progress. Sometimes you just have to take the "in shaa' Allaah" approach to dealing with bad problems with the locals … God willed it. That way no one is at fault, and you can carry on with the task at hand— I read that in a book, so I am certainly not making it up. So incredibly sad, but in reality the Saddam Fedayeen did cause it. I have learned to rationalize everything. We got reactive armor put onto the Brads; unfortunately, it's reactive in more ways than one—we are reacting to losing so many soldiers in the Bradleys. The armor was just sitting down in Kuwait all this time—that really pisses me off.

27 November: Thanksgiving in Iraq. The best day in the Army is always Thanksgiving. I went for a run in the rain and mud. It felt great. However, I came back to no water in our shower trailer. Great—it's 50 degrees outside, and I get to use the "berserker," the outdoor gravity shower. That will wake you up. I think everyone heard me scream when the ice water hit … it was 40-degree water. It made me hungry though, and they put on a huge spread for us to celebrate Thanksgiving. Outstanding chow, and we kept the mermites [containers for keeping food warm] for second helpings later on. Turkey makes me so tired. We got over on the VIP visits. Lieutenant Colonel Sassaman was our only visitor, and he came pretty late in the day. No need to hold up chow waiting for someone you don't know to come talk to your guys who just want food. I am being a bit harsh, but the rewind message we get time after time does grow old.

When we first got here, we dug a hole to pee in. It's six by two feet wide. Unfortunately, the water table remains about three feet down, so we developed quite the piss pit, since piss tubes wouldn't work. There is nothing quite like the pit after five months of people peeing in it and throwing random objects into it. I throw rocks into it all the time for entertainment. The smell of ammonia is quite sensational, as the wind passes over it and wafts it in your direction. I have had more than one nightmare in which I fall into the pit and keep sliding back down the mud as I attempt to get out. We have had countless conversations as to exactly what it would take to get you to drink an entire canteen cup full or lay in it for thirty minutes. The fantasy prizes have included one month of leave, $50,000, Britney Spears, Batman's outfit with belt, etc. Needless to say, the availability of prizes has limited our drinkers to zero.

There are all kinds of floating things in the pit. A "Code Red" Mountain Dew with Staff Sergeant Panchot's name on it was floating in there for at least three months, but I haven't seen it since 17 November. I wonder if that is symbolism. Sassaman also lost a small soccer ball into the pit back in August, and we talk often about retrieving that ball. He always asks me to get it out for him, but that is five months' worth of urine I cannot deal with. Well, Sassaman came down for a little turkey visit, and I showed him how I got his soccer ball out of the pit; the rain flooded our pit and erupted the contents. Now we have a giant piss pond with every object we threw into the pit outside of the pit. This place is so disgusting. The rain and the desert just don't match. I hope it stops raining soon because if that pond flows over the road … I'm out of here. Some days entertainment is rock bottom.

30 November: We continue with the registration of the Abu Hishma tribe. It has become groundhog day up at the school. Sometimes I entertain myself by attending the English classes. They love interacting with someone other than their teacher. We did the Arabic/English alphabet, and the kids are learning it pretty well. They just try to write it backward. The schools are so poor. The teachers have two pieces of chalk that they must keep on them at all times. They just don't have enough supplies. I think I got some of the boys in trouble during recess; they all lined up and had their hands hit with a switch. Education will breed out the hatred, and the victories the military could not achieve, MTV will. It's the key to the West.

I don't think anyone realized what a monumental task registering all these people would turn out to be. It's pretty easy to wave your hand and say do this—totally different when you are trying to figure out how. It's taking forever, but they do love their ID cards. We haven't been getting any mail lately because a mail plane got shot and had to crash land. They are doing a big investigation into why it got shot. It's pretty easy from where I sit … you flew over Iraq, you got shot. What are your questions? Fly low and fast next time—or really high. The day I fly out of here, I am going to fire all my ammunition at Abu Hishma, set the fields on fire for smoke, give the pilot a twenty, and tell him to bank hard left and climb fast.

DECEMBER

BACKGROUND

On 11 December 2003, troops of the 4th Infantry Division (Mechanized) literally unearthed Saddam Hussein, who had been cowering in a hole about the size of a refrigerator not far from his ancestral home of Tikrit. Within hours stunned audiences around the world witnessed the pathetic remnant of a dictator meekly submitting to dental examination and further processing by his captors. His successful apprehension capped one of the most thoughtful manhunts in history. For months Maj. Gen. Ray Odierno, commander of the 4th Infantry Division, and others had constructed elaborate matrices of colleagues, known associates, and relatives by apprehending one person who, when questioned, led them to another. Bit by bit, an intelligence picture was refined over time to bring the Americans ever closer to their elusive nemesis.

The shock troops in this hunt for intelligence were soldiers such as those Captain Brown led. Given a name or address and generally accompanied by an informant or an interpreter, they would break into buildings during the dead of night, apprehend the adult males, and cart them off for questioning. Most, adjudged innocent or harmless, were returned to their families with apologies and recompense for physical damage done. A unit's daily battle rhythm could include a midnight raid, payment negotiations for destruction wrought in earlier raids, tea with a newly rehabilitated returnee following incarceration, and logistical support to local schools. By December coalition forces averaged 1,690 patrols, 20 raids, and 108 anticoalition suspects captured per day. This carrot-and-stick approach was successful by at least one tangible measure: by the time Hussein was captured only 13 of the 55 Ba'athist leaders most sought after by the coalition were still at large.

The capture of Saddam Hussein coincided with an interphase in operations in Iraq. The restoration of the Hussein regime was now clearly impossible, and the morale of those seeking such an outcome correspondingly deflated. Coalition fatalities dropped from 105 in November to 48 in December, and reported daily attacks on U.S. troops had declined steadily from a high of 50 in September to 15 in December. U.S. troops were becoming more savvy, their uniformed Iraqi allies more numerous and perhaps more capable. In the summer U.S. soldiers had discovered only 10–15 percent of the ubiquitous improvised explosive devices before they exploded, whereas by December they were discovering as many as 75 percent in advance. Iraqi police climbed in number from the 9,000 who still stood by their posts in May to 72,000 in December; whereas the Iraqi Civil Defense Corps, Border Patrol, and Facilities Protection Services climbed from nonexistence to 15,200, 12,900, and 65,200, respectively. The pace for restoration of the Iraqi Army itself was more disappointing, with as few as 400 soldiers considered available and capable by that time. Perhaps more important, a massive rehabilitation effort had cleared more than 16,000 kilometers (out of 20,000 kilometers) of irrigation canals and the supply of potable water had leaped from approximately 13 million liters before the war to over 21 million liters in November. These measures enormously improved the posture of the agricultural sector, with the so-called Marsh Arabs of southern Iraq being a particular beneficiary. The countryside never became much of a platform for resistance to coalition forces. Resistance increasingly centered in such urban areas as Baghdad, Samarra, and Fallujah, where unemployment exceeded 50 percent.

Not all the trends reported in the afterglow of the capture of Saddam Hussein were favorable. Urban unemployment remained disturbingly high. Oil production and electrical generation were improving much more slowly than hoped, in part because of the nagging persistence of theft, vandalism, and sabotage. Hussein loyalists might have been passing from the scene, but an inchoate neo-Ba'athist Sunni resistance remained. Mass casualty car bombings and suicide bombings, widely considered a hallmark of foreign or international terrorists, tripled from November to December; the resulting casualties rose from 198 to 287. Criminal violence remained high, and a simmering feud with Muqtada al-Sadr's Mahdi militia remained unresolved. Perhaps most disturbing was the ability of anticoalition forces to replace losses. Since May the coalition had killed or captured an average of 1,000 suspected insurgents a month, with a spike of 3,000 in November. By December 10,000 losses had been inflicted on a resistance estimated at 5,000 active participants nationwide. For Captain Brown's soldiers the capture of Saddam Hussein was a positive development that changed the nature and perhaps the capacity of their adversary. But it certainly did not end the continuing rigors of their operations in a war zone.

---

8 December: The registration of the tribe is complete. We have a checkpoint that the ICDC runs in conjunction with the police twenty-four hours a day … or at least when we are there. The fence has blocked off the feeding routes for all the livestock that live in the city, so we constantly have herders moving all their cattle through the serpentine checkpoint. Great picture. I wanted them to register the male cows. The police love our interviews of the baqara for their identification cards; unfortunately, I think sometimes the cattle understand me more than the cops do. The police had a difficult go at understanding the concept of the checkpoint; but the more police we threw in jail, the closer they got to perfecting their checkpoint operations. In Iraq, nothing works to break through to understanding like a little jail time. The sheiks are all in the slammer, so it makes my job much easier as far as the city council meetings are concerned. We are going to release them to the new Stryker Brigade when we head north for an operation.

Cattle passing through our serpentine checkpoint at Abu Hishma

Samarra is a rough place where they are still fighting with a degree of organization—not as much as the press would assess, though. There are just a lot of bad dudes up there. I got some real heroes coming out of an engagement we had up there last week. Sergeant First Class Berg, my 1st Platoon sergeant, got blown up by an IED, took all kinds of shrapnel, and rejoined the fight … yeah, they awarded him a brigade coin and a Purple Heart. No one wants to admit how bad a town Samarra has become, so we go real cheap on the awards. Well, a lot of the bad guys are gone and the rest are intimidated … 120-mm. HE makes quite the statement. The town has gone south, and the CG has taken a keen interest in turning it around.

The next few weeks should prove interesting. We have a division operation coming soon, but no one is asking how to fight in the city. I saw an initial cut at a plan … they are planning in a vacuum. It is a corporal's war. I learn how to fight the company from how the team leaders and squad leaders fight. It's small-unit leadership at the focal point and then pile on the combat power. During the great Samarra shootout, my guys took over the rooftops, and the squad leaders assigned alleyways as sectors of responsibility and then picked off RPG/AK firers. Just like at our MOUT range. Unfortunately, not too many people understand that fight, and they think the MOUT fight is won through Civil Affairs projects. It's really tough to rebuild a city under direct and indirect fire while the locals destroy and loot every project you start. It's amazing that the enemy will fire mortars at you inside their own city. Fortunately, they missed us, but they destroyed all kinds of their own. Of course, they will blame the Americans, and we will give them all kinds of money, when we should just lay siege to Fallujah, Tikrit, and Samarra. No one in, no one out ... clear everything, break the insurgents' backs. It is all about isolation, and we know the major weapon hubs: Samarra and Fallujah. So bring the hammer down. Isolate and clear the entire town, bring in outside Iraqi police, and turn the city over to them—and we can go home. Let them figure out their own government.

Governments evolve just like creatures. When a society can have a democracy they eventually will, but it has to come about because they want it. We can't force our way of life onto them. De Tocqueville laid it all out in *Democracy in America*: A definitive set of conditions exists at a particular time that will cause a community to organize itself in the most appropriate manner given its natural resources, quality of populace, and proclivity to defend itself. I don't think we understand that those conditions do not exist everywhere ... democracy does not work in mental institutions.

9 December: We were sitting around talking about contacts, and some of the guys from a different company, who have been here awhile, were saying they just wanted to make contact to see how they would react. I was quite incredulous ... one, that they hadn't been in contact and two, that they would want to. I guess I am beyond all that. At one point, I wanted to see if I "had it," but now I know what happens and I explained it. The first thing is you get absolutely terrified because fighting is incredibly loud. Then you get really angry because someone is shooting at you, so you start shooting back. Then you get really confused as to where exactly the targets are and you start maneuvering forces to isolate and destroy the bad guys. After that, you leave and become really tired from all the adrenaline. Then you lie down and can't sleep because you are nervous and worried from the engagement. So fear, anger, confusion, and weariness are the order of emotions ... none of which have a positive connotation to them and all of which I could do without.

10 December: They brought us a bunch of mouse glue. The basic concept is to place a piece of food in the middle of a Styrofoam plate surrounded by a sea of glue. Mr. Jingles ventures forth to get the niblet of food and becomes stuck in the quagmire of sticky glue. He then starts squawking up a storm until you put him out of his misery. It works quite well for keeping the rodent population down. The other morning we heard a new, hissing sound on the trap. It turns out the mouse got stuck, and then Mr. Snake followed him onto the plate and got trapped in the glue. Classic scene as the snake just hisses and rears back on his haunches trying to get the mouse. He was furious with the glue. Staff Sergeant Guidry pushed the snake's head down onto the plate, so Mr. Snake became a permanent fixture on the glue plate. I'm worried that one morning we might wake up to a kid stuck to the plate screaming. The days continue to roll by as we prepare for the division operation in Samarra. We are assigned the worst zone and are leading the division into the city — lead element for the main-effort battalion of the main-effort brigade of the main-effort division of the main-effort corps in Iraq. It's funny because all of these division assets key off of the Bravo Company LD. I guess that is a vote of confidence for the company, although I have zero desire to go to Samarra in general and to Zone 7 in specific. We have already been involved in several shootouts in that zone — not a good place. We test-fired the weapons, conducted rehearsals, built the door breaches, cleaned weapons, back briefed, and re–back briefed. We have had lots of experience in the city and lots of training in urban operations. It is still extremely nerve-racking.

Outer cordon in Samarra

12 December: We got a tip on one of the shooters from Abu Hishma ... game on. I gave guidance to our newly attached engineers on a demolitions breach to go into the house. I had to link up with them at Checkpoint Six. I checked on the charge ... more C4 than I had expected ... five pounds. We talked about the initiation system and the standoff required for about thirty seconds and then moved into the city. Outstanding movement techniques and the guys looked great.

They just reported capturing Saddam Hussein five miles up the road from me next to a place I lived at for a month. Sweet! Now maybe I don't have to go to Zone 7. We had members of the Stryker Brigade consisting of a bunch of ex-Rangers. I ran forward with the breach team, inspected the site, and gave the go-ahead as the gate was set back from the wall providing us with cover. We pulled out thirty feet of shock tube, looked down the line at Lieutenant Colonel Sassaman and the Strykers and said this is going to be loud.... *Kawoom!* We were covered in the dust cloud and cordite. The lead squad rushed by me and the engineers. Awesome sight. We should have filmed it. I followed the platoon leader in, and we hit the house hard. The bad guys just freaked out and lay there. Every window in the house was shattered. Hard demolition breaches in MOUT. Nothing quite like it exists. I moved back to the breach site and looked for the large iron gate. I found where it was attached on one side, but the gate and wall were gone. Okay, we went a little heavy on the C4, but it definitely made a statement. It had to be the coolest raid I have done. We got half the shooters, which is outstanding for these types of actions. The Bradleys moved forward to establish an outer cordon; we policed up six prisoners, passed them off to the fighting TAC, and left. The lieutenant colonel called me on the radio as we drove away.

"What was that?"

"Brazier breach tamped, sir."

"That was really loud."

"Was it too much?"

"No, that's exactly what I wanted."

"Yeah, it's designed to go through a wall, but apparently it works on gates pretty well."

"Yeah, gates and any glass in a 500-mile radius."

Well, the Strykers liked it.

14 December: So I am sitting in line waiting to use one of the five porta-johns we have for the 900 soldiers of Task Force EAGLE up here in Samarra, when the brigade commander comes up.

"Hey Todd, I have a question for you on your eighteen targets in Samarra."

"Shoot, sir."

"How many are you planning on knocking on the door, and how many are you planning on kicking in the door?"

I thought he was setting me up. I have been to well over 500 houses and have never knocked on the door. That's a great way to get shot. I am squirming, trying to figure out how to answer this one as I look over to all the engineers building our fifty-plus door and wall demolition breach charges. Wow, I didn't realize the disparity of views on raids in Samarra. I think you have to go in hard or else you accept a huge risk for our soldiers ... I am not willing to have one of my guys walk up to a door, knock on it, and ask suspected terrorists to come outside. That is crazy! I guess Lieutenant Colonel Sassaman and Colonel Rudesheim haven't been talking about these things. Well, I'm not knocking on any doors; that's how that battalion commander of the 101st was shot and killed. Don't send me to the house if you don't expect me to breach, and demolition breaches are much less intrusive than Bradley breaches—trust me, I've done both.

"Well, how have you been entering the houses in Abu Hishma?"

"Uh, we have been kicking in the doors ... *or following five pounds of C4.*"

I linked up with Sassaman and told him about the conversation. I accused him of setting me up for a face shot. The plan remains demolition breaches tonight, but the two colonels definitely need to talk.

23 December: We had a two-day delay in offensive operations due to the capture of Saddam. Of course, we could not just delay for two days, so they sent us into the city to tip our hands for a big upcoming operation. I got punked on the patrol matrix, and we ended up patrolling at night in the freezing rain. One of the tracks died at 0200 when we were coming back to the FOB. Dropping prop shafts on a bridge in the cold rain … rough. Charlie Company did manage to catch Kai Sadam—one of the big financiers of the region, and they dragged in seventy-three other guys who were hanging out with him around Isaki. Charlie Company is an area weapon: send them to get one guy and they bring you seventy-three. Good mission, and hopefully that will improve conditions along Route 1. I really think that the gangsters are mad at us out there because we keep interfering with their truck-heisting operations. We can't want a better life for them; they have to want it for themselves.

The operation is a go, and we are all ready. Hit time is 0200. No one can get any sleep as we check and recheck weapons and plans. Hopefully, the intelligence doesn't lead us on a wild goose chase. We roll south of the city and stage at the old FOB STODDARD. On call we move into the city, queuing the division operation. My first target is on Mosque Road in the absolute worst section of town. We are surrounded by six-story buildings that offer easy top-down shots on the Bradleys. It's nerve-racking, and the intelligence leads us to an apartment complex that would take twenty-four hours to clear.

"Bag that target. Let's move onto 281," I tell Blue Platoon.

"Roger sir, we are moving south at this time."

Everyone is pretty keyed up and nervous as we move down the alleyways.

"Six. This is Five. Red has HVT 111," comes across the radio.

"Roger, good job." Already more successful than I would have initially guessed.

We move south across the street and identify the house. The breach team comes forward. We use tamped tent peg charges to minimize the amount of damage and demolitions required. The team places the charge, and I get the press back behind cover. Staff Sergeant Moyer initiates the charge … *Piff.* It sounds like a loud match.

"Sh—, bad M81 initiation system, sir."

"Okay, go again."

Piff.

"Let's go in manually."

"Wait one."

Kaboom. The gate swings open and the platoon flows in through the breach. We let them get the foothold and then head into the courtyard—these missions look awesome. They bring all the people out of the house … no males. I have an interpreter this time, but I can't stop speaking pigeon Arabic. It's pretty funny. All the males are in Mosul. Very strange. We search the elegant (by Iraqi standards) house and find it's clear. Okay, get a picture and move on. The press loves the demolitions breaches … great "bad" story. We head south down the back alleyways, and the guys are moving well. We get to target S0045 and prep the gate. The background explosions from Alpha Company and my other platoons make us all a little jumpy. We figured out the M81 seals aren't connecting with the shock tube because the wax melted the connection point closed sometime this past summer. That's good to know and easily fixable. We run down a trash-strewn, muddy alley whose stench causes you to question just exactly what you stepped in. It's layered with that dark, slippery, bubbly, oozy mud characteristic of open sewer systems … maybe that's why it stinks so bad. We move stealthily to the door and set the charge.

Kaboom. The gate flies open.

"Hey sir, we got two locked steel doors."

"Roger, go ahead and breach. Make sure everyone's behind good cover."

KABOOM. The overhang of the balcony caused a much louder explosion since the energy from the charge had nowhere to go. The house got rocked. We move in and nab the males, who lead us on a Jerry Springer chase after more bad neighbors. Oh well, I am not going anywhere for awhile. We police up those guys and load them into the XO's trailer. It's our trailer caged up and dragged behind the XO in which we load all the prisoners. It is not a real fun ride, and normally when they shoot RPGs at us they go behind the track. We have made countless jokes about the XO being on CNN dragging a burning trailer loaded with detainees behind his track. After that house, I hopped in the back of one of Blue's tracks and they drove me across town to Red's houses and the other tracks. I got onto my track to get a better picture of the other platoon's actions as the early morning wore on. We had our backs to the giant water tower, and you just couldn't help but envision someone launching something at you from 300 feet up.

Red finished their actions, and we uploaded the detainees and headed north of the minaret traffic circle to stage for Operation INDUSTRIAL CLEAN UP, part two. We passed off the detainees to the CMOC, and Jimmy breathed a sigh of relief with regard to his potential "trailer" infamy. We waited on Charlie Company to set the outer cordon and then moved down to commence lock-breaking and seemingly hooligan actions to clear the area of caches. This is the area from which we carted out five flat racks' worth of weapons and ammunition … more than a light infantry battalion's MTOE. I don't think the press really understood what we are doing, and the caches we find really don't support the operation … a couple of RPG launchers and rounds and about twenty AK–47s and other small arms. Not as fruitful as we hoped, but we got seven more RPGs off the street. The town proved quiet with a siege mentality, and we continued with a 24/7 presence throughout the area.

The next morning we drove around with one of the informants and a mistaken detainee on a series of raids made famous by Nick Robertson and CNN.

Minaret at Samarra, aka OP Insurgent. Spotters used this tower to communicate our movements and adjust fire accordingly until we prevented them from climbing it.

We ended up getting three more bad guys for the THT teams to work with and thirty minutes of fame. I am sure I will get counseled about being a poster boy for political incorrectness. I guess the CG had a meeting with the battalion commanders and told Colonel Rudesheim he was getting an A+ for his dealings with the press but that Lieutenant Colonel Sassaman was getting a low C. "Hey sir, a C is passing," Sassaman told him—I guess the CG loved it.

Oh well, I am comfortable with retiring as a captain. What are you going to do, send me to Iraq? I think it's important to tell the right story and not some fantasy. The funny thing is pretty much everyone operating in the city, including the Iraqis themselves, agrees with what I say. The mayor of Balad gave a class to Sassaman on how to work in Samarra. However, nontyrannical societies don't really condone the mayor's methods. The town has calmed down significantly since we dropped the hammer, and the people are starting to wave and smile at us. Our interactions have drastically improved since we introduced them to the smackdown, and they seem to love us now. I think they really just want someone to restore peace and demonstrate authority. The Stryker Brigade continues to cut its teeth over on the east side of the city. They had their series of rookie mistakes and left some AT–4s lying around. Fortunately, my cash-for-weapons program came into full swing, and we recovered them for $40.

I have initiated a repatriation program for detainees who have served their time. We take them down to the family and read them the riot act prior to sitting down to tea and a pleasant conversation. I have quite a rapport with the seventy-year-old fat Iraqi women in the region—they love "Bono Brown." It's part of my win-the-hearts-and-minds campaign. It also helps me with my raids. I can go down and tell the family to have the guy show up at the CMOC within forty-eight hours, and he does. I have to threaten them with an exaggerated amount of violence, but that's part of the culture. We have gotten several guys that way. Now if I could just get Alpha Company to stop harassing my informants and to start using proper charges, we would ∙ be good. I guess they used an improper charge and killed a guy; I told them what charge to use.

We ran over some wire at one of the traffic circles going into the city, and we stopped while two of the tracks cut the wire out of their road wheels. I had my guys set up a hasty checkpoint with the THT teams watching the guys we pull out of the cars. Bingo, we nab one of the head financiers of the cells operating in Samarra. Sweet deal. He was en route to Syria with $1,400 in cash and a bunch of fake 10,000-dinar notes. That is a bit of money for these parts. We police ol' boy up and move into the city for some more raids and questioning. Standard day in Samarra. We pay off one of the houses that we damaged during a breach and conduct a repatriation operation. Everyone in the house just starts crying and reciting the "Mister, I love you" routine. The ADC-M [assistant division commander for maneuver] and brigade commander show up, and we walk them right down Mosque Road through all our contacts. Way too many people walking down one street, especially this one. I always make my guys move as if they are under contact on this street. We finished that patrol, did some test-firing of the Brads, and hung out. The city is much better now than the past two months. It's quite amazing.

24 December: Christmas Eve day proved tragic as a convoy from the 5th Engineers got smoked by an IED. They share the warehouse next to ours. They were heading south on Route 1 in three soft-skin Humvees when they got hit by a 155-mm. shell in a trashcan full of .5-inch-diameter ball bearings. They didn't stand a chance—killed their battalion S–3 and two others immediately. Charlie Company had to secure the site and medevac. It just pisses you off. No wonder guys have zero love lost when dealing with the Iraqis. They also got some ICDC guys and U.S. contractors, who showed up in our bay all shot up. We got the scoop on the action from them and then tried to hunt down the drive-by artists … no luck. Five contacts on Christmas Eve on our stretch of road. Those guys out there in the soft-skin Humvees and white Suburbans are just asking for trouble. You either go covert or overt with lots of combat power, and then when you make contact you just unleash an incredible amount of firepower and detain everyone because they all know something.

We had gate guard duty that night, and my guys had been passing off security of one of the dead Iraqis from shift to shift. About 0200 Sergeant Hays calls up, "Yeah, we still have a dead guy here at the front gate." Battalion came back that they would handle it, so we just let it go. Sassaman and a bunch of the TOC guys went out there to get the body, but the guy was really big and stiff. It turned into a *Weekend at Bernie's*–type event as they tried to fit this 250-pound rigor mortis corpse into an SUV. They kept trying to bend parts to fit him in, but they couldn't find the dude's knees once they put him in the body bag and he kept falling out. Sassaman kept referencing the swing set he had to assemble on Christmas a few years back as being much harder than fitting the corpse into the car. It was one of those surreal comical scenarios where the guys involved are asking what are we doing with this dead guy on Christmas morning, but it's not really funny and it's not really Christmas.

26 December: Christmas was actually pretty fun. We had a battalion candlelight service and sang Christmas carols ... with the interpreters. I don't know if they got the whole deal. We had pork chops for dinner ... cultural awareness. The meal proved outstanding, and they came up with some pretty funny Iraqi adaptations of the twelve days of Christmas.

The eight-hour patrols in the city continue to drag by. Especially at night— you just sit out there if you don't have any raid information. Fortunately, "Doctor" Alex Williams, the S–2, has pushed us a lot of targets, probably more than our fair share. We roll around with detainees-turned-informants with bags over their heads to conceal their identity. They drag us on some wild goose chases because they will give you any sort of information to get out of the pen. Apparently, they don't appreciate the lifestyle and psychological games. Or maybe they do, and that is why they give us all these targets. Regardless, we roll around the city policing up more targets. I used to feel guilty about the *Clockwork Orange*/Orwellian role America plays here in Iraq, but a populace that doesn't want to find peace or prosperity forces us into it. They want to thrive on vice and graft, so we bash in their houses and imprison them in order to force them to accept self-government and freedom of choice. Does anyone find this ironic? I know the intellectuals will all say

Discussion with an informant on a nighttime raid. Toward the end we wouldn't do raids unless we had talked to the informant ourselves, and most of the time we brought him along.

that it's a hearts and minds campaign and come up with all kinds of grandiose solutions to our situation in Iraq. From where I sit, none of that will work. You have to establish authority and gap the insurgency [separate insurgents from the population]. Prove that you are in charge—not by money but by action. You have to run the city.

31 December: "Yo Cunningham, where you going?" I ask my five-foot-two-inch driver who has never left his hatch outside the wire.

"Sir, I can't take it no more," Cunningham says as he walks behind the destroyed building at FOB DANIELS ... toilet paper in hand.

"Man, this is the first time you have ever left that hatch."

"You know it, Sir."

"Hey Sergeant Cummins, throw me an MRE," I yell up to my gunner as the platoon leaders move over for a quick planning session.

"No way, man. I can't do another chicken breast. Give me something better," I protest.

"Here's a spaghetti." He tosses it down—violating the you-get-what-you-grab rule.

Boom! sounds off in the distance. "Did you hear that?" I nervously ask.

"Yeah, let's move into the busted-up building."

KABOOOMMM.

"Oh sh—, that was really, really loud. Let's get back on the tracks—we have incoming!"

Boom!

I hear the launch as I attempt to mount the Bradley with all my gear on over the cumbersome reactive armor. Great, we got rounds in the air and I am attempting to pirouette onto the front slope. I clumsily hop into my hatch.

KABOOOMMM.

"What the hell is that? They aren't mortars—or else they have the giant siege train mortar," I think to myself.

"Get 100 percent accountability and start driving south to the soccer field where they have launched mortars before," I command over the net.

"Cunningham, let's go!" There is a pause.

"Cunningham, let's go!" No answer. I see this little fella running back toward the track under my NODs, just cursing up a storm. He jumps from the ground into his seat, and I start laughing as I realize his predicament. He cranks up the track and heads into the city.

"Hey Cunningham, I bet you won't ever get out of the track again."

"Hell naw, I am going to keep a garbage bag up here now. What the hell is that?" he replies in a funny, breathless panic.

"I don't know just yet."

The gunner and I start laughing as battalion gets the Q36 radar grid and calls it down. I plot it on the computer and realize it's seven-and-a-half kilometers away. I clear indirect and simultaneously figure out it ain't 82-mm. mortars we're after. Higher denies counterfire … big surprise … shoot the guns—it's farmland out there. Maybe I take it too personally when they shoot at us. We move to the grid and start firing illumination and searching for clues. The bad guys have long since disappeared, but we can always hope to find their cache. We get to the grid and search around with two platoons while I send one on a "meet the locals of the area" patrol. The 1st Platoon grabs some guys who say they heard nothing "Yeah, right, a—hole."

"Okay, you have ten seconds to start telling me the truth or I will ram this tank into your living room."

"Oh yes, we heard two explosions."

"Where?"

"Mister, I don't know."

"Okay, the satellite showed me that it fired from around here. That same satellite will send a ray down here to melt your house to the ground unless you take me to the exact spot you heard them fire."

"Mister, come in my car, I show you the canyon."

Now we are talking. We follow this guy toward the canyon that my Blue Platoon was already searching.

"Hey sir, we got the sight," Ben Tumlinson calls over the radio.

"Sweet, what is it?"

"Rockets."

"Great ... now they are lobbing these trashcan rockets at us."

We get on the ground and take a look at the dud rockets. It's crazy. They just lay these rockets against a berm, aim them with a compass, and launch them with a det cord fuse. Totally inaccurate, but totally loud and terrifying. We blast the rockets with 25 HE until they catch on fire, and then move back to FOB BRASSFIELD MORA. Just when you thought things were getting better!

JANUARY

The capture of Saddam Hussein changed the nature of the war in Iraq but certainly did not end it. Tough Sunni towns like Fallujah and Samarra continued as focal points for armed hostility. Captain Brown's soldiers continued their battle rhythm of patrols, raids, cache destruction, and counterambush response at about the same pace as before the Iraqi dictator was plucked out of the ground. On 17 January the total number of U.S. personnel killed during Operation IRAQI FREEDOM climbed to 500, of which 346 were combat deaths. The next day a suicide bomber outside the U.S. headquarters in Baghdad killed 20 and wounded over 100, virtually all Iraqi.

Saddam's capture seems to have emboldened the Shia to greater assertiveness. For so long cowed and brutalized by the dictator, they had largely cooperated with the Coalition Provisional Authority and the direction it was taking the country. With Hussein clearly gone for good, perhaps they could secure a better deal than the coalition was currently offering. In particular, they thought the complex American plan for regional caucuses to select an interim government diluted advantages they, constituting 60 percent of the Iraqi people, could gain through direct elections. After considerable give-and-take, Grand Ayatollah Sistani openly rejected the American plan and demanded direct elections. Within days tens of thousands of Shiites took to the streets to march in protests around the country. By and large these were peaceful, but the atmosphere of crisis and confrontation reinforced the inclination of such firebrands as Muqtada al-Sadr toward violence. This would become more of a problem later.

On 28 January David Kay, the former chief U.S. weapons inspector, told the Senate that prewar intelligence concerning weapons of mass destruction in Iraq was wrong and thus that particular logic for IRAQI FREEDOM was misguided. This was not a new charge, but timing and the nature of the witness persuaded President Bush to initiate a formal third-party investigation before he had one forced on him. As visible as all this was in the media, there is no mention of it in Captain Brown's journal. He and his soldiers had more pressing problems of a rather different nature.

---

4 January: Well, higher denied our illumination mission for 2359 and 2400 New Year's Eve ... I don't even think they got the joke. It's not like we have a shortage of ammunition out here. I know I need to write for the cathartic nature, but I sure don't feel like it right now ... so there I was, up at the little gym using the stair-stepper machine (since we can't run here) and starting up with a little squat workout. I wasn't lifting crazy or anything like that, just doing a normal routine at 1629 in the afternoon. Meanwhile, FOB EAGLE is taking incoming rounds. I head over to the Internet—which is in a tent inside our makeshift gym—to log on to e-mail. As I stand in line at the tent, an 82-mm. mortar round bounces off the inside Texas barrier (big Jersey barrier) of the Engineer connex and blows. I sit impatiently waiting for my name and putting my clothes back on. They call my name and I sit down at the computer, complaining under my breath how slow it is. At EAGLE FOB, the second round of the barrage blows and a small piece of shrapnel comes hurtling out. Yahoo finally opens up for me. The piece of shrapnel cuts through the air and into Eric Paliwoda's side, collapsing both his lungs. I get my e-mail open. They get the medevac bird in the air and en route. Sometimes this e-mail thing seems more painful than it is worth. I struggle to send a message as the doctors struggle to intubate Eric, "the Giant." I get off one message during my thirty-minute tenure at the computer, close out the web page, and walk away pissed off. The dustoff lands at the 21st Combat Support Hospital at 1714, where Eric is pronounced dead upon arrival. I knew him for over ten years.

"Hey sir, they want you over at the TOC. They had mortar rounds at EAGLE FOB and had two critically injured and four returned to duty."

"Who is it?" I ask the first sergeant.

"Captain Paliwoda and Staff Sergeant Moyer were the criticals," he replies, already knowing that he was dead.

"Sh—, I wonder if he is going to be able to go with the commanders to Qatar on R&R ... we had been planning that for awhile," I think to myself— amazed that is what pops into my head. I had already been through this before with Eric when he got the giant gash in his head out at BEAST FOB back in September. We couldn't get an accurate report on him over the battalion net, and I feared the worst. They made it sound terrible. He was released the next day and had to wear a turban bandage on his cranium. We immediately started with "look at the size of that Iraqi" jokes. He was a Swedish giant with fair skin and looked nothing like an Arab. That is what made it so funny. I worry too about Moyer, he is my attached engineer squad leader and a great, tough soldier. I run over to the TOC for no real particular reason. I am not very worried at all at this point. Eric is way too big to really get hurt by a mortar, and the initial report is always a little off. We'll still go to Qatar together; it will be great to hang out. We haven't had a lot of chill time together for awhile. I think it's a three-beer limit—I wonder if they have a bonus ration for giants.

I enter the TOC and sit down in my seat. Everyone is talking, and there is a flurry of activity. The XO walks in, and everyone gets quiet.

"At 1629 today they had a 60-mm. mortar attack on EAGLE FOB." I write down 1629 and 60-mm. MRTS in my notebook.

"There were six injuries, four return to duty and two critical—Staff Sergeant Moyer and Eric Paliwoda. Beast Six, Eric, died at the CASH fifteen minutes ago." I drop everything and stare at Tim Knoth in absolute disbelief ... he was just sitting in the chair across the table a few days ago.

"Tim Knoth will escort the body and we need to get him out of here ASAP." I am listening but not hearing. I write KIA next to his name and walk out to brief the company and lock them down from the phones and Internet. I am in a state of shock. Still am.

Everything rushes back to me. I remember him out on the river in the boats for PENINSULA STRIKE—huge guy, totally sunburned, piloting the boats up and down the river and us laughing at him from the shore. I remember the Air Force football game out at Colorado, where he got totally sunburned drinking beers. I remember the harassing visits as cadets where he would come in throwing stuff and wrestling while I was in crunch time on projects. His size would always break me, but I would always get a good choke to make him remember the thrashing—then we would all laugh and I would be that much further behind in my work but grateful for the friendship. I remember the terrible haircut I gave him down in Kuwait when somehow he got the idea that I knew how to cut hair, even after I had butchered so many others. I remember him digging the first piss tube I ever saw and giving the staffers a class on how to use it. I remember him playing center on our captains vs. lieutenants football team, and the intimidation his size offered. I remember him always waiting impatiently at the TOC for me to finish my business so he could have Bradley escort or ride in the back of my Brad during the white-knuckle trips down Route LINDA. I remember him showing up with medics and security after our July IED, when I treated the injured scouts from my soft-skin Humvee. I remember how glad I was to see him out there with his company because we were so very alone that night. We discussed how bad this place had become ... how little did we know. I remember hanging out in his CP when we shared presence patrols down in Abu Hishma doing joint targets and raids. I think we were the only companies to share target information together. I remember the time the IED went off on his LOGPAC and the wide-eyed expression on his face as we raced out to the tracks. I got down there first, and Jimmy and I started working the area. We returned to the scene and I remember seeing the Giant out in the street with his M4—it looked so small when he carried it. We policed up his wounded guys in the Brad and moved out. We shared so many bad experiences together, but we had a great friendship ... through shared pain and suffering.

Eric was a giant of a man in more ways than just size. Six-foot-seven and 250 pounds. He would always accost me with his big burly voice. Our conversations would start out with such antagonism until we couldn't take it anymore, and we would start laughing before having a real conversation. I guess that's what soldiers do. I'll wait for you for an hour to eat dinner and that way we can make fun of each other for thirty minutes ... wouldn't want you to feel too good about yourself. Eric was in his element as a company commander. We called him the doctrine monster, and he truly knew it inside and out. On the FM updates he would always smoke us on the doctrine trivia ... I don't think he ever got a question from that category wrong. I remember numerous conversations and scheming to keep us from moving our FOBs. I was supposed to move to his FOB and he to the TOC. Our lynchpin argument stemmed from the containers at EAGLE FOB not being mortar proof and ready for his guys to move in while his FOB could not support my numbers. In the end we moved up to Samarra, and they got the containers good and surrounded to protect them from mortars. The irony that he died in one of those containers will never be lost on me. I remember countless arguments on not moving. The second we turned over BEAST FOB to the ICDC, the locals overran it.

I remember at Fort Hood living in an eight-mile trailer park with Eric. After our night on the town, John Hancher showed us how he ran over a curb earlier in the day as we stood outside watching. John drove the rental car over the curb but didn't stop in time and the front end went straight into the irrigation ditch. I was lying in the parking lot laughing hysterically as the car's trunk hung up in the air.

"Bring out the Giant, he can get the car out," we all agreed and got Paliwoda the wookie up and retrieved the car. Such a stupid, hilarious scene. I can go on and on with fun times I had with Eric, but the end state remains constant … he is gone … forever. He won't marry his fiancé; he won't teach geography at West Point; he won't go to Qatar on R&R; and I can't have him as a friend anymore. God chooses his angels, and I know we have a giant one watching over us now.

5 January: We had some more Jerry Springer action, but I am just not in the mood for it. We just haul in detainees now and wait for them to tell us the truth. It takes some time, but eventually they start talking. This place is really starting to wear on us all … Josh, Kevin, Jeff, Panchot, Brian, Eric … when you start putting names with the numbers, it just ain't worth it anymore. Lieutenant Colonel Sassaman is not doing well with it at all. The Stryker Brigade won't clear fires down there, so the enemy mortarmen just get bolder and bolder. I don't know the answer, but shooting back certainly makes you feel better and makes the populace respect and cooperate with you more. EAGLE FOB and our old AO are getting pummeled right now. Our shift work has gotten pretty dull, so we have taken to bringing targets out to the test-fire area north of the city and training. We cleared some farmhouses to the north, and then went to the "range" to shoot.

"Hey sir, can we shoot 203?"

"Roger, go ahead."

Donk … Boom.

"Good shot. Let me see it. Hey, where is the leaf sight?"

"I had to choose between the under-gun light or the sight, so we just Kentucky windage it."

"Okay."

Donk … "Wow … uh … " *Boom.* I sailed one deep over the berm.

"Well, I guess we better go check out what's on the other side of the test-fire berm."

We drive up there to confirm that no one has moved into the live-fire area and allay my conscience.

"Eagle Six, we got a HET that went over the side of the bridge."

Disgusted cursing follows, and I get the company moving toward the eighty-foot-high bridge over the Tigris—fearing the worst. The TOC calls in the 9-Line medevac, and we race to the bridge. The HET hit the guardrail and was hanging over the side of the bridge. Wowsers! Minor injuries to the driver. We got lucky today. I spent the next four hours directing traffic and recovering the vehicle in a comedy of errors that one can find only here in Iraq. We finally got out of there, thankful that the vehicle stopped where it did. They got so lucky today!

6 January: An informant gave us the skinny on a cache and a bad guy house. We moved down the alleyways dismounted and cordoned it off with infantry. The source moves forward and points to the house as we move Brads forward to blocking positions. The platoon enters the house and clears it, finding only women and the overhead space supposedly packed with weapons—but no dice. We break out the metal detectors and search the vacant chicken lot next door as they talk to the women. We dig up a small cache of AK–47 ammunition and then, bingo! We find the meat locker full of RPGs, rounds, mortars, and IED material. Good score! I guess the source is doing all right. It takes us about two hours to dig it up and get the 5-ton down to move it. Eagle Three [1-8 IN operations officer] brings it down, and we redecorate the walled compound with the Bradley to allow easier access. It's

Sergeants Kapheim and Adcock entering a building on the outskirts of Samarra

a decent score, but the press was with us that day and had a field day making it seem like the largest cache ever. Pretty funny, and we got the Division Play of the Day for our efforts—a new thing.

7 January: We decide to patrol Zone 10 from west to east with the Bradleys, staging off of the southern boundary of the city. As the platoons reach the LOA with the infantry, I push the Bradleys forward to them.

"Machine Six, Red One, we have reached the LOA."

"Roger, move your Bradleys forward to link up." Red rolls past the headquarters Bradleys, and they link up with their infantry.

"Machine Six, White One, we have reached the LOA."

"Roger, do the same thing and we will follow your Brads out in a minute." I swap my Kevlar for my CVC to get ready to move out.

Donk ... Kaboom ... Donk ... Kaboom.

"Oh sh—," I swallow deep and tell the driver to floor it. We got contact.

"Gunner scan for targets on your right," I command. I hate the adrenaline, danger, what-the-hell-just-happened feeling. I can see White's Brads firing 25-mm. down the street to my front, but I have no target. Good that they are shooting back, but it makes me even more nervous because I can't see all of them or what is going on. Black smoke starts rising from the vicinity where one of the Brads disappeared from view ... I fear the worst. As I round a berm, I see their three Bradleys and start moving them to set up a perimeter as smoke from a diesel fire rages.

"White Four, push east down the road and the headquarters will cover the west side. We need infantry down here bad." I roll past three cars that are smoked. The locals are moving one of the cars out of the street, and we don't have the infantry to stop them—just five Brads.

"Everyone move toward the fire. We need all elements here now." Red shows up with his infantry and makes me feel a whole lot better. EAGLE TAC starts doing their "where are you at" routine that makes command and control for the companies impossible. Eventually, I can't take it anymore and get on the ground to get a feel for the street and C2 from the manpack radio. Let the XO handle that one. We move some Iraqis over to put out the fire, and I start selecting guys to question with White Platoon. I get infantry up on the rooftops providing overwatch and cordon off the area. It happens pretty much instantaneously. The platoon leaders know exactly what to do on the ground. We get the medics treating the nonshooters and start questioning everyone else. It's crazy down here, but they shot at the wrong unit today. I talk to Staff Sergeant Legendre, and he confirms the blue taxi was the one he saw the RPG come out of. That's good because it is split in half and totally stripped of all its contents—I don't think it went too well for them. Three of the five cars involved will never move again. I am certain they are foreigners because the locals seem to know not to attack.

EAGLE TAC shows up with Colonel Rudesheim. The Iraqi police arrive at the scene, as does the ambulance and fire department. It's actually pretty cool seeing the Iraqis try to work it. Rudesheim is incredulous that they fired at us—"Are you sure they fired RPGs?" "Yes sir, that's number 106 I've heard." The battalion commander is shaking hands and promising awards. Every action that ends on our terms brings us closer to winning. Apparently, the division commander feels the same as Lieutenant Colonel Sassaman, as he awards us the Division Play of the Day. We did hit two innocent bystanders but smoked the RPG team—that is how it goes in the city fight. What are you going to do, not shoot back? That's why the city is the way it is now.

8 January: We went to Eric's memorial service. It was outstanding, and Sassaman spoke extremely well. It just breaks you down. It proved a long day in the saddle riding down to LION FOB and back. Our FOB was overtaken by mice—not good. The accelerator pedal on one of the Bradleys broke, and they built a system with 550 cord where the driver had to pull on the cord to get it to go. It was a bit of a smoker for that guy. Sad face, but now his left bicep is incredibly strong.

The days take on a pretty standard routine: go work out, go to the BUB, and then patrol ... repeat. The THTs love us because we action on just about anything since we have to patrol for time ... eight-hour-long shifts. We had an Iraqi Easter egg hunt with one of the informants who showed us an RPG round, then two RPGs, and then a bunch of dirt mounds that were supposedly RPGs. We did some metal detector work and found 137 82-mm. mortar rounds in various caches. We called EOD [Explosive Ordnance Disposal] out to blow it up. They showed up on the brigade command net. Apparently, brigade won't let them blow this stuff at night. That's cool because the brigade S–3's vehicle came out with us.

"Striker 3, Machine Six." I call our Brigade S–3.

"This is Striker TAC. Last calling station identify yourself," a familiar voice comes across the net.

"This is Bravo 1-8. We have a large cache and want to blow it in place now. Otherwise, I'll have to upload it on the brigade S–3's track to transport it."

"Yeah, this is Eagle Six filling in for Striker 3 at Striker TAC. Go ahead and upload it in his vehicle."

"Yeah, roger. I'll upload it and keep all our Bradleys 300 meters away from it." It's straight comedy as we upload his vehicle. Eagle Six is dying laughing, and we move them out with EOD and a tank section. We can barely fit all the rounds in the vehicle. Too funny. It's a huge mobile bomb. I see Major Perry, the brigade S–3, later, and we share a good laugh about that whole scene. They launched two rockets at us last night. I was outside the wire and watched the rounds sail through the air — so pretty, so deadly. No counterfire. We must fire back if we want them to stop.

16 January: So the SF team in town calls us up to help them on a raid. We are supposed to link up at noon, but we got a late start. As we roll through Huwaish, I see a group of thirteen Iraqis sitting on the railroad tracks.

"Hey, keep an eye on those guys. They are up to no good."

"Yeah, roger. I see them. No good."

We link up at the ODA [Operational Detachment A] house at 1230 and head in for the mission brief. They are a really good SF team and love having the infantry. The target is a gas station on the southeast corner of Samarra, with a followup mission on a fish store and a pool gallery.

"Hey, I got extra room in the headquarters Bradleys if you guys want to roll up there in those. No one is going to run from the gas station. It's too wide open," I observe.

"No, we will take our SUV and the two gun jeeps," Kelly, the team chief, replies.

"Okay. Do you want me to lead and put you guys in the middle?"

"No, we will drive right up to the gas station and you guys pull outer security and search the area around the gas station for weapons."

"Too easy. What time do you want to roll?"

"1315."

"What route do you want to take?"

"Well, Market Street has less IEDs but more traffic. Power Line has IEDs but is quicker. We'll take Power Line because it is more open," Kelly replies with a half grin.

"Okay, just go a little slow so the tanks can keep up," I tell them.

"Roger, are all those vehicles going?"

"Yep, we like to roll deep … you know we have the capacity to take out an entire street if they shoot at us." It's their raid, so I just kinda back off and let them give me task and purpose. I give the platoon leaders the plan, and we head out to our vehicles staged at the CMOC traffic circle. We hit the gas station really quick. We form the cordon and start searching the area.

"Machine Six, Borderman 92. We got the target. He is going to take us to his house once this action is finished."

"Roger, I'll link up with you guys." I walk over to the gas station, and we look at the map with the informant and the interpreter.

"Okay, the guy lives on an alleyway off of Power Line."

"Okay, we'll put a section of tanks and a platoon of infantry on either side of the alleyway that you go down and then move in on the target dismounted. Do you want me to lead?"

"No, we'll be up front with the target. Just follow us to the alleyway," Kelly replies. I head back to my Brad, not knowing the next time I saw him would be very, very different.

I hop up top and move the tanks and Brads over to South Park Road while the SF team finishes up with the detainee. We creep forward until they catch up. They come zipping around with the SUV and two Humvees. We follow them. I drive by an alleyway and see a guy on a black motorcycle turn around. Totally suspect.

"Hey, watch this guy on the motorcycle," I call back as we speed by.

Boom. The SF guys floor their vehicles, and there is dust everywhere.

"Machine Six, we just hit an IED," Josh comes over the net, real calm. It doesn't sound bad since all the vehicles roll through the dust cloud and I barely even heard it.

"Hey, shoot that motorcycle if anyone can see it." No one can.

"Machine Six, we got one wounded," Josh calls up from the SF team very calmly.

"Sh—, how bad?"

"We need security up here now, and an aerial medevac," Josh comes over more urgently.

This is just getting worse. I push the tanks forward, but we don't have a good feel for where they stopped. We find them and get the cordon set around them. The 18D [Special Forces medic] is here, so we'll execute the medevac bird here. It's 1415.

"White Platoon, you have local security with the tanks. Red, you have HLZ setup and security. Five, call in this grid to battalion and get the bird in the air now. HLZ will have VS–17 panel [a bright orange panel used to clearly signal friendly forces in daylight], and it is secure. I am getting on the ground real fast to get an assessment." I see the tanks and Brads cordon off the area; the junior leaders know what to do. I run up to where Josh is and see the damage.

My memory of the event flows through a series of snapshots. It's not like a movie where one thing happens after another in real time. I see pictures of the events flashed in front of my face. I see Josh standing with one leg in the Humvee with the hand mike up to his ear, trying to talk to battalion. I see the Toyota SUV with two fist-size holes through the windshield on the passenger's side, otherwise undamaged. I see Kelly lying in a pool of blood, with the right side of his scalp peeled back ... and I know I am watching him die. I run over there and see the 18D [Special Forces medic] start working on him. I see him attempt to intubate Kelly through the mouth and then immediately go for a tracheotomy. I think to myself ... I just watched a guy perform a tracheotomy on dusty, nasty, South Park Road in Samarra. This place never ceases to amaze me. I watch Kelly breath through the tube. He has respirations of 12–14. That is normal. Maybe it looks worse than it is. I snap back into it and grab the hand mike.

"Hey Five, is the bird in the air?"

"Battalion got the message and will call once it flies," Andy replies.

"Roger, go to single channel plain text 33.550 once it flies and talk to the aircraft. I am running over to see what Red has for the HLZ." I just feel like I've got to do something. We got a soccer field to the south, and it looks good. I run back over to see Josh and plan how to move Kelly down there. I call a fire team over, but they find a route they can drive over there. I ask Josh to borrow his interpreter and then walk back to White Platoon and the trail tanks. The HLZ is secure, the medics are working, local security is established, the medevac bird is en route, and Five has their net.

What am I missing? I know how long the flight takes and also how helpless you are to change that. I also know that you can go absolutely crazy in that timeframe. I walk down with the interpreter and head for the house closest to the site. I point at the house with the terp and the platoon reads my mind and stacks on the door. I think they know that I am going in there. I am so pissed. We bash through the door and I go looking for someone to take my aggression out on. The place is packed with women and children. That is good because I would have throttled someone if it had been a military-age male. My anger drops from about 98 to 50 as we move to the next house. I don't even remember some of the stuff I was saying, but the rage went on for awhile and the people on Power Line probably won't forget how pissed off

I was. They do cooperate more with people that lose it on them, so I don't feel bad. The helicopter finally lands at 1452 and I head back to my track … thirty-seven minutes. That is the fastest Samarra has seen from incident to evacuation … I am nauseated.

"What's your assessment?" I ask the medic.

"Sir, it looked worse than it is, I think."

"Okay, let's take the team back to the house. You will follow the tanks. I can't take anything else right now."

We load up and take them back to the house. Their Intel chief still wants to hit the market and pool hall, so we get the plan together. I guess you just got to keep moving. We move to the road south of the pool hall and fish market and drop the infantry. They rush the two objectives, and police up all of-age males. We do onsite interrogation, but the fish market proved empty, save one fish on the counter. I think it was a carp. We police up all the non-ID-cardholders and anyone that looks suspicious; however, it seems like a definite dry hole. The SF guys want to take them back for questioning, but we don't have room in the Brads. I go over to the barber shop where I spot a guy with a nice big ol' pickup truck, and he agrees to chauffeur all the detainees down once he finishes with his haircut.

All we can really think about is Kelly. It looked really bad. It feels like someone is going to come down and say cease work, we got a change of mission. Then we can do an AAR and go back and do this thing differently without any casualties. We drop the detainees off at the CMOC and then roll back to the FOB. We pass by Alpha Company and pull over to the side of the road to let them pass in Huwaish. *Boom*. Alpha Company hits a landmine, right where those thirteen suspicious-looking guys were hanging out earlier today. I just can't take this place anymore. One of my tankers took shrapnel to the face but nothing serious. That is twice today I didn't trust my instincts when I should have. As we roll into the gate Eagle Five [1-8 IN executive officer] comes across the net and informs us that Kelly is still breathing but medically retired. Doesn't sound good.

20 January: The next few days just drag by. We take the THT on some recons, and the guys have a couple of shops they want to check out. Sounds good, pay heed to everyone's instincts these days. As we cart the informant around, White Platoon uncovers a weapons cache of fifteen RPGs and IED material in one of the stores. Great, grab the store owner. They police up some guy, and when I show up he is scared sh—less.

"I didn't know there were fifteen RPGs in my [ten-by-ten-foot] shop."

"Yeah, bullsh—! Who do you work for?"

I think he knows it is time to tell the truth, and he starts telling us all about this guy on 1-66 AR's city council. Great. We detain him after some more questioning, and I make the call to blow the homemade fertilizer bombs in place … I certainly am not going to move this stuff. I get our engineer and we go over the charge … three sticks of C4 with all the doors tamped. I have the interpreter explain to all the locals that I am crazy when I see RPGs and that they need to collect all their valuables and leave the area because we are going to blow up the shop with all the explosives. We tamp the door with a desk, generator, and sofa. I have him set the charge for three minutes, and he pulls it.

"Hey, help me with this desk," I ask as we prop it up. It's such a weird scene knowing that the time fuse is ticking down, and this thing is just going to blow up here shortly as we struggle to prop up this desk and couch. We finally get it set and run back 100 meters.

Kaboom! The walls blow out, and the fertilizer catches on fire … as well as the store next door. Oh well, their fault for allowing RPGs in the neighborhood. I fill out some claim sheets for the guy with the shop next door, and everyone seems appreciative of the action. This is what some of the higher-ups do not understand. The locals want to see the bad people punished—there are cultural differences that just don't make sense unless you spend every day with these guys. It makes them feel safer to see the Americans taking charge. We get the brand-new fire department up there to put out the fertilizer fire. We turn it into a great exercise, and it will end up being a huge IO [information operations] piece. They now know there are consequences for harboring illegal weapons, and they have a revived faith in their fire department. I spend an hour talking to the people about it and let them know how upset I am. The leaders all come out, and we work through a lot of issues. We roll back to the FOB, and I report the whole action up to higher—no issues. One of the TOC guys hands me the new CJTF [Coalition Joint Task Force] 7 policy letter on how we are winning the war and need to tone down all our interactions/actions with the locals and press. Oops! The irony of it all. I ask for $1,000 for the damage for the friendly shop owner … it's way more than the store was worth. He calls brigade TOC, and they freak out about the damage. Just give me the money and let me fight the fight. We know what we are doing.

21 January: We go back to the street the next day, and the locals are all waving and thumbs up. I get off the track to talk to them and ask the owner to give me a week to work the issue. They love it and invite us over for tea and dinner. I tell them tomorrow, tomorrow—after I pay for the store. It is very important that I do that before we enjoy ourselves. They agree and appreciate that. Kelly is still breathing: they took him off the ventilator at the request of his family. We conduct a couple of checkpoint and dismounted patrols but nothing significant going on. We head out to the test-fire area and fire off a couple of AT–4s and the 25-mm. Tomorrow I head down to the LSA for the Cobb and Datray trial.

22 January: We drive the two hours down for the trial. Balad seems so much nicer than Samarra. We end up staying in brigade HQ because our FTCP is jumping. Wowsers. You can shower with hot water for as long as you like. You can talk on the phone with crystal-clear communication for hours at a time. There is no line to get on the Internet, and it is incredibly fast. All the soldiers there hate it—my guys are in hog heaven. I go for a run in brown T-shirt and shorts and get stopped by a senior NCO for being out of uniform, but we don't have PT tops. Such a different perspective down here. Soft caps, three hot meals a day, omelets to order, and ice cream. It's R&R down here compared to Samarra. If I stayed down here with the three hot meals a day, all-you-can-take hot showers, indoor living, no patrolling, MWR tents, and lots of TV, I wouldn't understand why someone is blowing up a cache in a store in Samarra either … this place is so peaceful, so nice. I need to check on the pool hours.

24 January: The trial went well for the prosecution. Datray got ten years in the slammer for his antics. He proved absolutely flip and cocky about the whole deal. Cobb came back and sold him down the river. I talked to Cobb for a little bit, and he is the true sob story. Datray is the punk of the group. He continues to blame all his woes on everyone else. He will have a long time to think about that one. We went down to the FOB and sifted through all the mouse droppings to get out some more gear for our ever-increasing stay in Samarra. The brigade is in the midst of doing some redeployment transfer of authority rock drill. A bunch of my captain buddies were on block leave while I was there. That is pretty cool. None of the officers at battalion have gotten that luxury. They are miserable up there, though. The time goes so slow for them.

26 January: We continue to perform our checkpoints on Route 1 and the "I can't wait to get back to the FOB" six-hour patrols with no real mission. We have been checking in with the ICDC and trying to gain intelligence, but no one has anything. They continue to yo-yo us back and forth on our redeployment to Balad. Our tracks continue to break down since we are now at fifty days without focused maintenance. We try to entertain ourselves with the ICDC, police, fire station, hospital, etc. We have been into the hospital a couple of times, and it looks pretty bleak. I ask the doctors for a list of the equipment they need and turn it into battalion but know that no one will action on that. Everyone is so focused on going home.

28 January: "Hey, are we going to get some water over here?" I ask the CP.

"Yes sir, we just need to get a Humvee and talk to the dining facility," they reply.

"Okay, well, we don't have any Humvees, so drive a Bradley over there and load it up. I don't want to run out of water." I go back and start playing Connect Four—about seven games.

"Hey sir, a civilian car just crashed into the Bradley that went to get water."

"Son of a b—, where are they?"

"Right out the front gate."

"Okay, I'm moving."

Bad scene. They had five civilians in the car, and they were driving about eighty mph when they hit. Two of them died instantly, and there was no way to pry them out of the car. I called for the field ambulance and a 10-ton wrecker and set up the Bradley in an overwatch position. We got the guys out of the backseat, and I started telling the medics which ones to treat. One looked pretty stable and the other two were breathing, albeit poorly. It was disgusting getting them out of the vehicle, and I really hated seeing it. We unfolded the car with a Bradley and 10-ton wrecker. The bodies were smashed to bits and stuck in the car, so it just sucked. We proved pretty much callous to the whole event; but I am sick of seeing dead people. They were traveling from Mosul and were Christians. They had a picture of Mary and rosaries hanging from the mirror. That made me even sadder. We spent a good two hours pulling the car apart and medevacking them to higher care. I had the joint operations center call for the civilian ambulance and police to pick up the pieces. We loaded the three guys into the ambulance and moved them back to the battalion aid station. Two of them died on the table, and we sent the third one to the CASH. Just a really bad day.

31 January: "Hey sir, they said Nathem al Marsoumi was in a car crash and is at the hospital."

"Well, move ICDC there and we'll link up with them and take a look."

We all rush out the gate and head to the hospital. We are greeted with a scene from some bad seventies movie staged in Colombia with the ICDC all wearing mismatched uniforms and equipped with AK–47s. Their leader has a revolver that he carries over his head, and he wears some crazy-looking armor vest with whacky-looking *Top Gun* sunglasses. They move through the hospital with about twenty guys clumped together looking in all the wards. It's a crazy scene. I keep all our guys away from them. Their intentions are good, but the training level just ain't there yet. We clear the hospital but cannot find the number one gangster, Marsoumi. The ICDC wants him and the car bombers just as badly as we do, so it is a pretty good working relationship. Our patrols center more and more around interacting with the public. The city is still quite scary, but the VIPs all want to come walk through the center of it. If they only knew how quickly the "coolness" of the artifacts can change. The police are a different story from the ICDC. They are hired through the Iraqis and are straight-up connected lazy dudes. When we ask the ICDC what they need, it's always weapons and trucks. The police want blankets for their beds. They just come to the station and go to sleep. I have caught a bunch of them napping, so we mostly empower the ICDC.

FEBRUARY

By February 2004 the realization that fighting in Iraq would not end soon had crystallized into the determination to sustain over 120,000 U.S. soldiers and marines in Iraq for the foreseeable future. Army Chief of Staff General Peter J. Schoomaker, following up on initiatives of former Secretary of the Army Thomas E. White and former Army Chief of Staff General Eric K. Shinseki, had directed a unit-manning system wherein fully manned units would train, operate, deploy, and redeploy as a whole. This revived concepts associated with regimental systems of the nineteenth century and set aside the individual replacement system that had sustained the Army in its overseas campaigns since 1907. It also set in train the largest single rotation of integral U.S. ground combat units ever and the largest discrete movement of such units since World War II.

The wisdom of sustaining high force levels in Iraq was underscored by the continuing violence. On 1 February suicide bombers killed 106 and wounded 247 at the headquarters of two major Kurdish parties in Irbil. A few days later Ayatollah Sistani narrowly evaded an assassination attempt near his office in Najaf. Further suicide attacks marred the rest of the month, with some evidence that the targeting was intended to foment sectarian strife among the major ethnic groups. On 19 February UN Secretary-General Kofe Annan announced that elections could not be held in Iraq before the 30 June target date for a transfer of authority but asserted that a transfer of sovereignty to a transitional government should nevertheless occur on that date. Clearly, it would be some time before an Iraqi government legitimated by elections was on hand to facilitate coalition objectives.

Despite these frustrations, the pace and nature of operations seem to have mellowed a bit. Captain Brown's men were seasoned veterans familiar with the territory, and that territory was becoming more manageable and less risky than before. They were familiar with enough of the locals to get things done, and they were getting useful albeit intermittent help from the Iraqi Civil Defense Corps. During their second tour in Samarra, they found themselves being shot at once a week rather than several times a day.

For the 1st Battalion of the 8th Infantry, its time in Iraq—this tour—was coming to a close. The continuing violence dictated sustained operations, even as the unit as a whole prepared to rotate back to the United States. These twin imperatives *were daunting, when juxtaposed almost surreal. In Captain Brown's words the unit was "to police up as many bad guys as possible in the final weeks while maintaining all the OPs, cleaning all the gear, trying to make Re-up mission, and writing all the AARs." Also in his words, "They have made leaving here so hard that you almost want to stay."*

---

11 February: Working for two battalions is a double-edged sword. You get pummeled by both and minimal support from either. However, the nice thing is you get written off from a lot of extra duties and details. We finally got out of Samarra on 8 February, after running countless patrols with 1-66 AR. I had mixed feelings about leaving the place. I had a huge base built within the city and pretty much ran the show.

We did have a couple guys decide to celebrate with some whiskey, and it turned into a really bad scene. I hate punishing guys who have been over here suffering for so long, but I guess it's the price of good order and discipline. Some of the guys have serious emotional scars and demons to exorcise from the killing and death that we have been involved with over here. It's really quite sad, and they will not get real help for awhile. Too much to do. It was nice moving back down to the bunker, but the mission down here sucks.

15 February: Now I have 24-hour mandated OPs around the LSA. Very unimaginative and totally defensive; we are on our heels. Fortunately, we built up seventy-two targets during our time away, and we will work off them. We got the worst area on these crazy canal roads that just weren't designed for Bradleys. It's absolutely terrifying driving those things at 0100, all tilting to the side over the freezing, fast-moving canal water. The dust also makes for poor visibility, and I recall why I never went down that way at night. We did find a homemade rocket launcher complete with cigarette lighter and wooden handle. It looked quite crazy, but the ingenuity is very frightening.

17 February: The *Newsweek* photographer and *Stern* magazine guy found the FOB again. I am still trying to recover from the last piece. The brigade commander was furious about it; I haven't seen him in a month so hopefully he has forgotten. I guess Lieutenant Colonel Sassaman took the brunt of the ass chewing and pissed him off even more. They are constantly fighting, which puts the company commanders in some awkward predicaments.

20 February: We had two nights of raids that proved quite fruitful, capturing grenades and machine guns. The open farm fields make target identification so much easier than the crazy streets of Samarra. We are actually batting over 50 percent on our intelligence, which I haven't seen yet in this war. I think the intent is to police up as many bad guys as possible in the final weeks while maintaining all the OPs, cleaning all the gear, trying to make our reenlistment mission, and writing all the AARs that no one will read. We just have an incredible amount of stuff to do and no respite. When we got back to LION FOB I felt like I could stand on my head for two weeks doing stupid stuff, but now I feel like all the blood is in my head and I'm going to pass out. We did get the Abu Hishma road started. Now the gated community will have a new road and a police helicopter on 1 April ... yeah, right.

Sgt. Enea Cutuca. In the background is a controlled explosion of about 10,000 pounds of ordnance we had collected over time.

24 February: Today we found and destroyed two IEDs and got the B-Bag connex (metal container that carries all our nonessential gear) through Customs. It should represent a huge accomplishment, but the IEDs were a kilometer from the ten-digit grid for the OP, so we got smacked down for not sitting at the overt OP and patrolling instead. You have to patrol. If the IED went off, you would be the jackass who let it go off in your area. This place is just a no-win situation. Just give me a task and purpose. I am way too close to the flagpole, and both sides benefit when I am farther away from the flagpole. We did get some really good pictures and I got a sweet rug from the PX, but I think I got ripped off. Oh well. It's Iraq. They have made leaving here so hard that you almost want to stay.

25 February: The OPs continue to suck the life out of the platoons. It is a really boring mission as a commander, but that is really good. The platoons just sit out there on the OPs, and I drive around talking to them until I get bored. I went from a 250,000 city in which no one monitored what I did or checked on me, to a village of 250 outside the LSA where my every move is monitored and someone is always telling me how to do it better. The village is dirt poor, but they are getting more money working on the LSA as ICDC. I try to talk to them a couple times a week. They know me as Abu Baqara, the father of the cow. I appointed Sergeant First Class Harkness the supreme allied commander of Latif Shakur and renamed him Abu Dejaja, the father of chickens. They really liked that and gave us some bread and chai. They are pretty friendly and enjoy talking. Very poor, though.

26 February: My town is getting a little crazy. They started throwing grenades at one another. It's just my luck that I get a town that I could throw a baseball across that hasn't had any trouble this entire war, and the second I get control of it they start a mini civil war. The grenade blew a big hole in the mud hut but caused no injuries—it's the fourth attack this week. The owner of the house started his ICDC training that day. He is a private, day one. Welcome to ICDC, get a job working with the Americans and have grenades thrown at your house. They were pretty happy to see Abu Baqara but really wanted to see Abu Dejaja, who was off shift. They asked me if he was flying the helicopters overhead. Yeah, roger, he's flying the helicopter. You've really got to wonder what these people think about us. I got the ICDC leadership of the town together, and we worked out the battle drill for them receiving contact. Whenever there is an explosion each man grabs his AK–47, puts on his ICDC ball cap, and runs to his assigned street to capture Ali Babba. The lieutenant cracks the chem light and moves to the road to link up with the Americans coming to investigate. Bottom line is we are steering clear of that place if these guys start shooting at each other. Converging Iraqi forces is one of those actions you don't want to partake in—way too scary.

27 February: The big talk right now is about the Shiite celebration of Ashura, in which they whip themselves silly in order to gain spiritual energy. It basically commemorates the death of Husayn in 680, I think. I tried to figure it out with the locals. Muhammed is the prophet. Ali is his cousin that he wanted to succeed him; but they swindled him, and three caliphs gained power before Ali finally got it. Husayn, the sixth caliph, was Ali's grandson and was killed in Karbala when he maneuvered to seize total control of both the caliph and imam titles. They had a ten-day standoff and then he got killed by a superior force. It basically established the whole Shiite acceptance of suffering and martyrdom as their lot in life. Then we got to discussing the twelfth caliph, whom no one really saw—he just sent messengers. I drank way too much overly sweet "diabetes" tea and really couldn't concentrate, so I ended up confused about the whole ordeal. I just know some dudes are going to start whipping and cutting themselves sometime this week. We'll have to get a picture.

29 February: Well, the whole ICDC react-to-contact drill proved a great failure. As I took off my boots to lounge around, I got the call that we had contact in the north. Great. My crew was up at LION talking on the phone, so I grabbed Cooper and moved up there as we tried to get better information on the squad in contact. Cooper nearly snapped my spine turning the Bradley around, but we found Cunningham and Sergeant Cummins and got out the gate quickly and to the squad in contact. By the time I got there, the platoon had assembled on the northern OP and detained ten guys. I had them start marking the houses they came from on their hands and did some limited questioning. I walked the area of contact with the squad while we waited for the interpreter coming up with White Platoon. Once the interpreter arrived, we started working the guys for intelligence.

We started talking to one of the guys, and he gave us this big line about how he was ICDC and had chased off Ali Babba that very night. I asked him how the whole thing went down. He walked us over to his house and showed me where he shot from. The front of the house got all shot up during the contact. He told me that he fired at ol' Ali Babba from the roof. The squad leader confirmed what I was thinking. They had chased two guys violating the curfew down the alleyway. The ICDC heard those two messing around in his yard and started firing on them—understandable since the multiple grenade attacks on the ICDC this past week in this village. The squad, thinking ol' boy shot at them, mowed the guy's house. Thankfully, the Bradleys couldn't get into the fray and everyone's night marksmanship could use some work … although the house was definitely suppressed. The guy recognized me as Abu Baqara, and he had a note from me telling him he was allowed to shoot at anyone throwing a grenade at him—I love reading some of the notes I write these guys. I have been trying desperately to get these guys to take action and defend themselves against the "bombers." I guess the irony is their first really good action is against us.

Well, it looks like ICDC has this village under control, so we definitely won't make dismounted nighttime forays down here anymore. No need to get shot at by our allies. It proved a really good action on both sides, although they should have both shot at the two guys prowling around after curfew rather than at each other. This place is just way too confusing, with far too many variables. We messed around with trying to gain intelligence on the grenade throwers for a little while and then headed back to the FOB about 0100. Happy Leap Year Day!

MARCH

*C*aptain Brown arrived home at Fort Carson, Colorado, on 19 March 2004. The war in Iraq was temporarily over for the soldiers of the 1st Battalion, 8th Infantry, but certainly not for the U.S. Army. Indeed, events in March precipitated some of the bloodiest fighting of the war. Some argue that the large-scale rotation of American units caused a loss of traction, as new units took up the fight without the experience, personal connections, and intelligence appreciation of those they had replaced. Several days, or even weeks, of transition could not make up for a year's worth of combat operations in Iraq.

On 28 March the Coalition Provisional Authority forced the closing of Muqtada al-Sadr's newspaper Al Hawaz for its persistent anticoalition stance and its support for anticoalition activities. Within a week al-Sadr's Mahdi militia launched attacks on coalition forces and their Iraqi allies in Kufa, Karbala, Najaf, al-Kut, and the Baghdad suburb of Sadr City. The most disturbing aspect of these widespread attacks was that they occurred in the theretofore largely quiescent Shia areas of Iraq.

Not to be outdone, a Sunni mob in Fallujah killed and mutilated four U.S. contractors, hanging their charred bodies from a bridge in a scene grimly reminiscent of Mogadishu a decade earlier. Anticoalition attacks within the Sunni Triangle continued unabated.

Not all attacks were directed against the coalition. On 2 March, the holiest feast day of Shia Islam, suicide bombers in Karbala killed more than 180 Shia pilgrims and wounded over 500. The attack seems to have been intended to increase tensions between the Sunnis and Shia, just as similar attacks in February seem to have been designed to foment unrest among the Kurds.

Not everything associated with the unit rotational period was bad news. On 1 March the Iraqi Governing Council announced the results of weeks of hard bargaining, to include agreements that Islam would be a basis rather than a source of civil law, that 25 percent of transitional assembly seats would be set aside for women, that endorsed federalism, and that endorsed a continuation of the then-current Kurdish government. Several weeks later it signed an interim constitution after negotiations that again resolved points of contention among the involved parties. Whatever the ebb and flow of events on the battlefield, *only the emergence of effective Iraqi governance would allow U.S. forces to withdraw successfully.*

---

2 March: The shower down here has deteriorated into a no-win situation. If the heater works, we run out of water. If we have full water tanks, the heater breaks. I have reverted to the solar shower since returning from Samarra. I have a little routine of putting the shower out when I first get up and letting it warm up until midday. I then heat up water in the coffeepot—one pot for days over 65 degrees and two pots for days under 65. It's really a foolproof system because the coffeepot must always work. I have found there really ain't nothing quite like an Avian coffee-flavored shower after running and shooting. Tomorrow Red Platoon moves into the Corps Tactical Assembly Area for redeployment.

Since our combat power has started dwindling, I had to take the first sergeant and our guys out to the promotion board at EAGLE TOC. I brought my book and planned on just chilling out while I waited for our meeting to start at 1400. I logged onto e-mail in the S–3's office and was stealing some of his chow. I called home and was talking to my parents.

Whoom! Whoom! Whoom! Great, we had incoming 120-mm. mortars ... and those are really loud. I ran into the TOC and listened to all the chatter. I don't know the area real well, so I kinda watch as the ten-digit from the Q36 comes in, the mortars lay onto it and fire, and then I take my section and follow the scouts to the point of origin. I am used to my sector, so it was weird chasing bad guys someplace else. We followed the Kiowa helicopters onto the point of origin. The white phosphorus was still burning when we pulled up, and Sergeant First Class Bolyard and I started running through the orchards. It was getting hot again. We found a 120 firing point but no mortar. I spotted a possible cache, but when we dug we found nothing. Lieutenant Colonel Sassaman had his interpreter, but no help from the locals today. I had flashbacks to the summer, sweating through my Kevlar helmet. We fired some more counterfire for area denial, but it proved another fruitless game of cat and mouse. The rest of the day we spent in the meeting and waiting for the board to finish. Sassaman and I were sitting out on the front porch talking about things.

Wham! A rocket lands right out in front of the perimeter—so much for an easy day. Everyone ran to positions, and we left back to our FOB. What a nightmare of a day, just getting bombed. The Q36 didn't pick up anything, so it was most likely one of the 57-mm. rockets fired indirect. We have to move up to the LSA tomorrow. I guess it's one of the steps along the way, but it will be tough moving onto post with all the rules, rockets, and general stupidity.

5 March: The lieutenant colonel came down for an Article 15 for one of the guys who drank all the Iraqi whiskey. The move to ANACONDA and closing of LION FOB proved long but not too trying. The lifestyle has definitely improved in the realm of e-mail, showers, and toilets. Very nice. They have hired Filipinos to clean and service all the showers so that they actually work—well. We all lined up inside Kevin Ryan's connex hut to do the UCMJ [Uniform Code of Military Justice].

Kaboom!

Great, a rocket landed 400 meters to our south. We were supposed to do an Air Force bomb drop at 2100, so we all just assumed that it was the repercussions from said event, until we saw all the dust and dudes running to the bunker. Sassaman and I ran over to my CP and started talking on the radio with the Kiowas. The point of origin was to the south, exactly where we don't have any OPs. LION moved their QRF there, and we pushed the Kiowas over to their net. I had my guys set out checkpoints, but I knew we couldn't get over to that side of the LSA in time to do anything. They didn't counterfire, so we just got worked over … I hate getting sucker punched over and over again up here. We then went back to the Article 15 and finished that action. There is nothing quite like doing UCMJ during a rocket attack.

6 March: The chow hall has come a long way since we moved up here. My stomach shrank from the MRE diet, so I can really eat only two meals a day. I normally eat a powerbar and work out in the morning, so by the time lunch hits I'm starving. As more people move into the LSA, the lines get more and more out of control. I was standing in line chilling out talking when we heard some explosions on the north side of the airfield. I didn't think much of it until I heard the 155-mm. cracking away. No one in line did anything … even flinch. I ran into the chow hall and got all my guys out onto the Bradleys. The CP called up the grid to the rocket launch. It's from the all-too-familiar Abu Hishma orchard. My White Platoon moved to the area while I waited at the gate for a wingman. The Kiowas came on station and started searching. About ten minutes into the search, they spotted the rockets from the air. It was an incredible find from a helicopter. They also spotted the getaway truck with a flat next to the launch site and confirmed that no one was in it. I pulled into the orchard right as they found the truck and gave them permission to destroy it with rockets once they confirmed that the Bradleys weren't in the gun target line.

"Yeah, just do a south to north gun run and ensure none of the tracks are inside the danger zone. Take the commands from my White element. I don't know exactly where this truck is located," I instructed.

"Dragoon 26, White One. We are cleared," Amick told him.

"Yeah, there is one track that's a little close, but we'll hit it from an angle," Dragoon 26 told us. The birds looped around and flew straight by my track, popped up for the rocket launch, and hammered the truck ... right next to my Bradley—I was the track that was a little close. Wowsers! That was really close, as I look at the hood fifty meters away. They fired off eight rockets and then went to refuel while we prepared to demo the 89-mm. rocket they spotted. The adrenaline was quite high as we watched the rockets zing by. It was pretty close and pretty awesome. Not too many people get to clear helicopter rocket fire in their AO, but I guess I got that luxury. We conducted a clearance by fire of the orchard area and then cleared the rest of it with infantry. Nothing there but date trees and angry cattle.

The scouts brought out some demolition with the BC, and we blew the rocket in place with about ten sticks of C4 ... nine more than necessary, but we have to get rid of the ammunition somehow. We nominated the grid for a 2,000-pound Air Force bomb drop, and then I headed out to the TOC for some chow and a transfer of authority meeting with 1-77 IN. I am totally famished. The meeting was really long, and my guys went over to drop mortar rounds for H&I fires. I guess it freaked out Red Platoon. They couldn't get commo with us, so they moved to the TOC because they thought we were in contact. It worked out because now we have five tracks to run the Route LINDA gauntlet with the 1-77 IN guys.

8 March: I spent the day with my replacement, taking him around to all the towns and showing him the various haunts and leaders. They were asking how we keep the people away from us. I think they were a bit shocked when we walked straight into the town with the whole pied-piper mob, drinking tea and eating bread. They were concerned that the tea was poisoned. That seemed pretty funny to me after all the stuff we have eaten and drunk over here at the houses. I guess our TTP and methods on patrol would probably shock most people. We had the whole Abu Baqara mob scene going. The father of the cows can't really walk the town in peace. It is entertainment to say the least; too bad we didn't have the real interpreter. He is on leave.

10 March: The 1-26 IN guys had just finished getting their reactive armor on right when I heard the BC going crazy on the net. We all thought someone was in contact, but it turned out to be one of my OPs sunbathing up on the bluff … what a group of morons. I thought for sure he was going to fire them. Complacency is such a killer. These static OPs are killing us. The platoon sergeant was on the OP and really didn't get it. I can't believe how much babysitting is required. It's the same guys that got ambushed 100 meters from there. Dumb a—es! Well, now I have to take them all out to the TOC for a screaming. It worked out decently since I already had to take the 1-26 guys out there and show them Route LINDA and the police station. Of course, right when we go into the session we take rockets at the FOB. What is up with all the firing? We spent the next hour and a half chasing phantoms since the Q36 didn't acquire the rocket. We finally got the meeting over with but had to push the bomb drop back to 2130. We also had the sample raid with the new guys on the south side of the canal right after. Red had the Air Force liaison element, and we pulled up to the site at 2129.

"We got three minutes until the drop."

"Roger." About thirty seconds later they call: we have forty seconds until impact. About ten seconds later we get the *Kaboom!* and shockwave. The flash is pretty damn big and right on target. A 2,000-pound bomb from 1,000 meters away is pretty awesome. Crazy days! I link up with the platoon leader for the hit, and we decide to do it light infantry style, not wanting to take the Bradleys across the canals. The two battalion staffs and onlookers outnumbered the raid force by about two to one. It's a good thing this guy isn't a super legitimate target. The raid goes down, and we get one of the HVTs from our battalion list. We cleared about five houses and had their squad leaders clear one of the houses. One of the guys we detained was a Guz Gazani—the guys that eat glass, shoot themselves, and pierce body parts as a part of their religious ceremonies. We released the ol' boy since he was part of the performance last Halloween and we like those guys.

13 March: Well, we are inside the wire. We just sit here trying not to go crazy. Our days revolve around PT and food. Lieutenant Colonel Sassaman and Matt Cunningham went up to Tikrit today for their General Officer Article 15 over the Alpha Company drowning incident. Basically, a platoon from Alpha company forced two guys into the water near the Samarra Dam as punishment for violating curfew (an incredibly stupid if not illegal decision on the platoon's part). The platoon leader claimed that he saw the guys get out of the river and start walking back toward town. Their relatives claimed that they had drowned and demanded the $2,000 death gratuity from the Americans. Sassaman demanded to see the body before he would pay the gratuity, and the Iraqi relatives brought him some body that they dug up from the cemetery. Sassaman didn't really need to play CSI Miami to understand that they were trying to pull a fast one on him and get some money out of the deal. A higher-level criminal investigation was launched into the whole ordeal, and Sassaman told the soldiers involved to not talk to the investigators about the water. He wanted to handle the punishments in house since he did not trust his chain of command.

All this of course came out in the investigation, and Sassaman ended up getting punished for the cover-up. It was so stupid that Sassaman took the fall over this one. He is such a great leader. I am just sitting here wondering if he is still the battalion commander; it's a killer after all we have been through over here. Sassaman really shouldn't have tried to defend those guys. It's all so stupid and will cause us to leave here with an incredibly bitter taste in our mouths. The irony Sassaman faces on the other side of the Article 15 table is replete. I wrote a character statement:

Dear Major General Odierno:
I am not certain of the Division's open door policy, but I felt the necessity to serve as a write-in character witness for Lt. Col. Sassaman's Article 15. I have known Nate Sassaman since I was nine years old. We used to vie for his autograph at Army Football games, and my respect and super status for the man hasn't really wavered over the past nineteen years. As a kid I unknowingly watched him turn around a terrible football team into a bowl-quality organization. As an adult I watched him systematically take a battalion with the absolute worst command climate I have seen and turn it into the best command climate I have witnessed to date. He is the best fighter in the battalion, the kind of soldier who would be the best squad leader in the company or the best commander in the army at any level. I know his tough, passionate leadership inspired me to stay in the Army when I was definitely getting out. He is the most gifted leader I know.

The irony of seeing my boss get an Article 15 is not lost upon me. We have dealt with the infractions of the soldiers in our microcosm and know the incredible pain of

punishing those that have done such phenomenal jobs over this past terrible yea
I know we didn't want to punish them, but we understood the need of zero defec
for certain sins. Lt. Col. Sassaman has spoken to me of the decision he mad
and he has mentally abused himself for this poor split-second decision. A poc
decision made against the backdrop of thousands of good ones that undoubted
saved soldiers' lives.

The Iraqi populace that we deal with daily connives and distorts the truth to gai
money and privileges, which causes you to approach every allegation with a b
of incredulousness. Our opinion of the Iraqis following the death of Capt. Er
Paliwoda was at an all-time low, and no one in the battalion had the right frame
mind following that event. It didn't help that we had a particularly gruesome RP
contact earlier that day in which Eagle Six personally came to reinforce us ...
and help place the bad guys in body bags. At the time of the infraction, I think w
were all just trying to move on after a particularly bad month whose repercussion
continue to follow us.

Our battalion operates on a higher level because of the incredible loyalty we fe
towards the Battalion Commander. I really haven't seen this degree of loyalty i
any organization I have served. He can get soldiers to reenlist just by personall
asking them. This loyalty runs both ways and serves as the Shakespearian trag
flaw in this story. His desire to protect the junior leaders, in a case where the burde
of proof rested on the accused, has caused all his current personal trouble.

In many ways, the morale and esprit de corps of this battalion following this bitte
year of fighting will be determined tomorrow. The five members of this comman
who know of the Article 15 will anxiously await and pray for the results wit
the full realization that all things happen for a reason. The greatest complimer
in our profession a senior can pay to a subordinate is to have his son serve i
the subordinate's command. I know my father wished that for me and Lt. Co
Sassaman, and I never regretted a moment of it. Our faith in Lt. Col. Sassaman
and your leadership remains unshaken regardless of the outcome. We all hop
to be in Col. Sassaman's Brigade but realize the unenviable position you hold i
regards to this matter. Our thoughts and prayers will be with you both tomorro
as you deal with this daunting task. Thank you for your outstanding leadershi
this year and your consideration in this matter.

Oh well, it will probably all backfire. The Army has an uncanny way o
chasing off talented leaders, and Sassaman is certainly one of those. Waitin
is so painful—waiting for the HETs, waiting for the planes, and waitin
on this decision. Of course, there are about 10,000 changes ... and all th
changes are in the wrong direction—keeping us here in Iraq longer.

I have gotten to swim the past two days and to take guys rug shopping. Of course, the owner was so happy that I brought guys to his store that he wanted to sell me another rug at cost. The tractor beam of Persian carpets simply engulfs me. I guess we all have our hobbies and vices. Life inside the wire is so different. I just can't believe we are finally getting to just sit around. I think it's a plot for us to decompress. Hopefully, tomorrow we will have HETs, planes, and our BC.

15 March: Well, the lieutenant colonel made it through the whole hearing, but he won't see a brigade. He is pretty torn up about the whole ordeal. He has great plans for a book, which should prove interesting. The past few days have just confirmed our need to get out of here. Guys are starting to put the pounds back on, and we are having to deal with the other side ... the "three hot meals/never left the wire" type. We had a private first class female tell one of the platoon leaders that he needed to hurry up and eat so her friend could sit at the table. That didn't work out too well. Let's see, girl who has been in theater for eight days versus table full of infantry officers with over eleven months. She tried to get mouthy with them but got the entire rank structure explained to her in no uncertain terms from the position of attention. Very comical. All the equal opportunity representatives came over to our table to "defuse" the situation and protect everyone's "rights." We had a little discussion about following orders and respecting rank and experience. Eventually, they all saw the light, and I realized the difference between my FOB and the corps support area. I was pretty pissed about the whole thing but realized that the only solution for us is to leave ... and that's not just the LSA. Our squad leaders would have killed someone in there.

We are supposed to fly tomorrow. Good, because the Family Readiness Group is driving Kris crazy. I can't wait to take on that organization. I guess that tells you a little bit about our level of action. We have gone from the street fight to the domestic fight. Other than that, the days have consisted of reading, running, lifting, and eating. Between transit and sitting around talking, we spend about four hours on our two chow hall meals. We are doing a little ceremony for our interpreter, which will prove a significant emotional event. He loves us and wants to go to America. It is kinda nice having nothing to do but work out and BS. It really reminds me of Camp Buckner in the desert. A bunch of dudes sitting around watching planes fly with nothing to do but get anxious about going home.

Well, it happens at breakneck speed. We went over to the airfield in-processing site at 0400, got word our plane would land two hours early, and had to hustle through the whole Customs, Central Issue Facility, briefing line. A brigade plane got bumped, and they tried to hustle our flight, but we quickly shut that down. All the briefings went well and Customs was a breeze, except they had the Customs officials plant a bunch of 5.56-mm. rounds in my gear and make a big stink about it. It proved pretty funny when they finally told me it was a prank ... we even filled out some make-believe paperwork. Matt Cunningham totally got me on that one.

The plane landed and whisked us out of Balad. We held our breath for seven minutes—our estimation for the completion of the spiral—and then kicked back until Turkey. We had a ton of anxiety built up as to how long we would wait playing planes, trains, and automobiles. We got off the plane in Incirlik, Turkey, after waiting for a bus because of lightning. I thought it would prove a huge nut roll. They whisked us away, gave us a roast beef (but we were in Turkey) sandwich, and threw us on a civilian plane. We flew to Rhein-Main and then to Bangor, Maine. The Veterans of Foreign Wars and all the old-timers were out at the airport at midnight cheering for us all—what a wonderful community. They had pictures hanging up of all the dead as you got off the plane ... very sobering—I know way too many of them. After twenty hours of lounging in first class we landed at the Colorado Springs Jet Center. We got off the plane at 0400, walked through the "McDonalds" tent, and headed to the gym to turn in weapons and paperwork. Way too easy, and we beat half the guys that left before us back. The garrison sergeant major policed me up and told me about my responsibilities as the plane load commander for the ceremony; then we grabbed our bags. We walked into the emotionally charged events center listening to Toby Keith's "Angry American." It was a great goose-bumpy feeling seeing Kris for the first time in a year. The general said about two words, I dismissed the troops, and ten minutes later the events center was deserted.

We went through all the drama of the culture shock and reintegration. It's a lot easier stepping into the twenty-first century versus the eighteenth. I still freak out about trash on the side of the road and loud noises, but otherwise it's all going really well. Had a beer with the neighbors and found out that the intelligence chief we worked with in Samarra blew himself away in Colorado Springs after a domestic flare-up ... yet another casualty of the war.

"So was it all worth it?"

"I don't know ... I don't know what we gained—I only know what we lost."

APPENDIX A

COMMAND AND CONTROL AT THE BRIGADE AND BELOW

Captain Brown has laced his narrative with references to command and control features that may not be familiar to the general reader. His journal begins while he is serving as an assistant brigade S–3 (operations officer) and concludes while he is a company commander. The leadership of soldiers and the means to carry it out dominate his daily life.

Within a Bradley company, a squad consists of nine soldiers who fight on foot and are equipped with a mix of small arms. The squad is led by a squad leader, ideally a staff sergeant (E–6). It can be divided further into two fire teams, each led by a sergeant (E–5) to facilitate overwatch and maneuver. Two squads and four Bradley Fighting Vehicles, each with a three-man crew, make up a platoon, led by a platoon leader (PL), a lieutenant assisted by a seasoned platoon sergeant, ideally a sergeant first class (E–7). When moving mounted, the squads are distributed throughout the passenger compartments of the Bradleys while the crews drive the vehicles and man the turrets. When the squads dismount for such infantry missions as close assault or clearing buildings or terrain, the Bradleys provide fire support and cover. The infantrymen on the ground are engaged in the close-quarters battle (CQB), and the nature of their opposition will dictate their individual movement techniques (IMT). By the virtue of after-action reviews (AARs) and lessons learned, units consistently refine their inventory of tactics, techniques, and procedures (TTP).

A Bradley company consists of three Bradley platoons and a small headquarters and support element. Key leaders include the company commander (CO), ordinarily a captain; the executive officer (XO), a seasoned lieutenant; and the first sergeant, an E–8 and the most experienced man in the company. Customary but heavily overlapping divisions of labor are for the company commander to focus on mission, tactical disposition, and collective training; for the executive officer to focus on logistics and maintenance; and for the first sergeant to focus on sustaining individual standards and the welfare of the men. All three can and often do serve as alter egos for each other in each of these roles. The commander and the executive officer are Bradley vehicle commanders, and one normally accompanies the dismounted fight while the other sustains communications higher from his Bradley. The first sergeant rides in a Humvee in most circumstances and in an M113 personnel carrier in combat. The company commander is ultimately responsible for all that happens or fails to happen in his company.

Battlefield leaders can use voice commands and hand signals to control combat over short distances and pyrotechnics over longer distances when their meaning has been agreed upon in advance. Platoons and companies by and large coordinate their operations by radio. The frequency-hopping SINCGARS (Single-Channel Ground and Airborne Radio System) is now in general use. Parties on the same "fill"—i.e., primed to frequency hop at precisely the same sequence—can talk to each other without fear of interruption or interception. In this they are greatly assisted by an evolved lexicon of terse, guttural nouns, verbs, and call signs most likely to be heard and understood amidst the din of battle. The First Platoon is "Red," the Second "White," and the Third "Blue." Red One is the First Platoon leader, White One the Second, and Blue One the Third. Captain Brown, the commander of Company B, 1-8 Infantry, was Machine Six, and Lieutenant Colonel Sassaman, the commander of 1-8 Infantry, Eagle Six. Other key players similarly had call signs consisting of a word and number. In his journal Captain Brown also speaks of Striker Six, his brigade commander, and Iron Horse Six, the division commander. Machine Five was his executive officer and Machine Seven his first sergeant.

A Bradley battalion consists of three line companies and a headquarters company. It might well have a tank company (three platoons of four tanks each, plus two tanks in the company headquarters) attached. If so, it might attach tank platoons to Bradley companies, and vice versa. It might also have one of its own Bradley companies attached to a sister tank battalion, as was the case with Captain Brown's company during his first tour in Samarra. Bradley platoons and companies have the flexibility to fight mounted or dismounted; tank platoons and companies have much more firepower and crew protection. A mix of tank and Bradley platoons under a company commander is a company team, and a mix of tank and Bradley companies under a battalion commander is a battalion task force. A heavy brigade consists of some mix of tanks and Bradley battalions, most often three all told. A heavy brigade combat team adds some mix of artillery, engineers, air defense, and other combat and combat support troops in contingents of company or battalion size.

Battalions and brigades are larger and more complex than companies, so their leadership cadre is more complex as well. Battalion and brigade commanders are lieutenant colonels and colonels, respectively, assisted by a specialized staff. An executive officer supervises the staff, and a command sergeant major fulfills a role analogous to that of the company first sergeant but with more attention to the career progression of subordinate NCOs. Primary staff officers include an S–1, personnel officer; S–2, intelligence officer; S–3, operations and training officer; and S–4, logistics officer. There may also be a fire support officer (FSO) controlling indirect fires; a signal officer; a battalion maintenance officer (BMO); an air liaison officer (ALO); a civil affairs officer; and a public affairs officer. The brigade executive officer is ordinarily a lieutenant colonel and most of his immediate staff subordinates majors. The battalion executive officer is normally a major, his S–3 a major reporting directly to the battalion commander, and the majority of his immediate staff subordinates captains.

More complex organization at the battalion and the brigade levels dictates more elaborate command and control nodes. The lion's share of tactical design and coordination occurs at the Tactical Operations Center (TOC), normally the haunt of the XO, S–2, S–3, FSO, ALO, signal officer, and their subordinates and other staff. In a heavy brigade, the working area of the TOC consists of four to eight M577 Command Tracks pushed back to back with tent extensions from them integrated into a common cover. The S–1, S–4, and other logisticians man a similar but somewhat smaller Administration and Logistics Operation Center (ALOC). A much smaller and nimbler Bradley-mounted Tactical Actions Center (TAC) allows the commander himself to speed around the battlefield and quickly establish or reestablish communications as the fight progresses. Even more austere variations on this theme are the Assault Command Post (Assault CP) or the Air Assault Command and Control (A2C2) "bird." As Captain Brown's narrative begins, he is the officer responsible for the brigade TAC, sustaining its readiness to support the personal leadership of the brigade commander anywhere on the battlefield. When battles are echeloned, the TAC, Assault CP, or A2C2 bird will be well forward; the TOC will be comfortably out of direct-fire range, and the ALOC will be clear of most indirect fire.

The ALOC is generally located amid the aggregated cluster of all the units' logistical assets, collectively called the field trains. Within the area of the field trains there might well be a Field Trains Command Post (FTCP) to manage the area itself, a Unit Maintenance Collection Point (UMCP) to handle the organizational maintenance effort, a Forward Aid Station (FAS) to deal with medical emergencies, and a Civil-Military Operations Center

(CMOC) to handle relationships with the local population. The UMCP, FAS, or CMOC might be pushed forward to the combat trains, a smaller collection of logistical assets focused on fuel, ammunition, maintenance, and medical assets of immediate necessity in sustaining the fight. They also might be separately located to accommodate circumstances, but to do so requires an increase in the manpower committed to secure them.

Battalions and brigades do not operate alone, so their facilities may collocate with those of a higher headquarters. Battalions, brigades, and even larger units may gather in a Tactical Assembly Area (TAA) preliminary to a major operation. For much of its tour, Captain Brown's company was attempting to secure the sprawling corps' designated Logical Support Area (LSA) ANACONDA, where many of the brigade facilities were situated at times. He also makes occasional reference to the 21st Corps Area Support Hospital (21st CASH), a destination of choice for the seriously injured. He lived at various Forward Operating Bases (FOBs), which headquarters designated as semipermanent facilities. FOBs were very useful when pushed close enough to support combat operations in such unpleasant areas as Samarra. All the facilities discussed thus far anticipate helicopter resupply and heliborne visitors and thus designate a helicopter landing zone (HLZ). When temporary, these were hastily marked in daylight with colorful, highly visible VS–17 panels.

Complex operations require elaborate procedures. Troop-leading procedures begin with the receipt of a mission, at which time a battalion or brigade staff undertakes an intense hour—time permitting—of mission analysis (MA) to assure the troops fully understand what will be required of them. At the same time the staff sends a warning order (WARNO) to subordinate units to alert them of the nature of the pending mission. When briefed on the results of the mission analysis, the commander gives guidance that shapes various courses of action that are developed, compared, and perhaps even war-gamed should time permit. Given the results of these deliberations, the commander decides on the course of action they will follow. The staff hastens to flesh out this decision in an operations plan (OPLAN) if the time—or even the likelihood—of execution is unknown or in an operations order (Op Order) if the time of execution is set. From time to time during this process, fragmentary orders (FRAGOs) are sent to subordinate headquarters to enable them to prepare in as parallel a fashion as possible.

Army doctrine elaborated by unit tactical standard operating procedures (TACSOPs) prescribes a host of control measures customarily applied to maps or graphics shared by all participants. Captain Brown speaks of BPs (battle positions to defend, block, or delay from) and LDs (lines of departure from which units initiate tactical operations). LD is often used as a verb; one can speak of a unit as having "LDed." Observation posts (OPs) and listening posts (LPs) facilitate early warning and intelligence gathering. Checkpoints (CPs) were once points on a map or route that provided a frame of reference for friendly locations, much as target reference points (TRPs) do for enemy locations. Usage of the term in the Balkans and Iraq has increasingly gravitated toward the manned checkpoint, a small contingent of troops positioned to intercept and control traffic along a particular route. In the aftermath of an incident, a unit can hastily throw out spider-web checkpoints positioned to entrap perpetrators leaving the scene. A limit of advance (LOA) may be specified to control the forward progress of units, and unit boundaries can fill the same purpose laterally. The former extensive use of phase lines and other graphic measures to track movement has proved less necessary in an era of global positioning systems (GPS) and Blue Force Tracker (BFT), a system that automatically forwards vehicle locations through secure satellite communications to produce a shared picture of the battlefield on screens or consoles in command centers or aboard command vehicles.

Units prepare for pending operations in as comprehensive a manner as possible. The orders process occurs at every level, albeit with less complexity as one descends through the levels of command. Pre-combat checks (PCCs) of troops, vehicles, and equipment guarantee that all are committed to combat in the best possible condition. If time permits, a somewhat more elaborate pre-combat inspection (PCI) involves several layers of the chain of command at once. Rehearsals on comparable terrain are invaluable in coordinating efforts, particularly in the case of offensive operations. Ideally, these would involve all participants of all ranks in a comprehensive combined arms rehearsal (CAR). Of course, the ideal is not always achieved, time can be pressing, and squads can flow quickly from one urgent event to another. In such cases, troops fall back on their training and the tactics, techniques, and procedures that they have developed over time.

Conventional wisdom holds that no plan survives the first round fired by the enemy intact. Leaders at every level must demonstrate initiative and flexibility to deal with changing or unforeseen circumstances. Radios crackle, FRAGOs flow freely, and the "push to talk" phase of combat supersedes the deliberate orders process. Within each TOC, TAC, and ALOC, a single "battle captain" oversees all traffic in and out and guarantees that the staff and branch particular cells are fully mindful of each other's activities. This may not be much of a problem if actions are brief and everyone is paying attention at the same time. In the case of prolonged operations it becomes necessary to pull shifts and pass responsibilities from one unit to another. The battle update brief (BUB) is a key mechanism in sustaining a collective picture as key players change out or become so absorbed in their own responsibilities that they lose visibility of those of others. The battle captain draws on all available communications, to include SINCGARS, BFT, tactical satellite (TACSAT), Small Extension Node (SEN), Secure Mobile Antijam Reliable Tactical Terminal (SMART-T), Secure Internet Protocol Router Network (SIPRNET); Nonsecure Internet Protocol Router Network (NIPRNET), and land lines. The radio-telephone operator (RTO) accompanying a platoon leader or company commander might well find himself out of range or in terrain defilade, both of which preclude effective communications. To work around such possibilities, the most critical frequencies can be received and retransmitted at retrans stations committed to that purpose.

TACSOPs specify an array of formatted reports to force the flow of information in a repeatable manner least likely to be misunderstood. The 1-8 Infantry relied most heavily on the Green 2 Report, which accounted for men, weapons, and equipment not less than twice a day. The steady flow of information is intended to sustain a common appreciation of what is going on and also to set up such key decisions as whether or when to commit the Quick Reaction Force (QRF) or where and when to send the logistical packages (LOGPACs) necessary to sustain troops in combat. Command and control has succeeded if the soldiers know what they are supposed to do and have the means to achieve it.

APPENDIX B

There was a merchant in Baghdad who sent his servant to market to buy provisions and in a little while the servant came back, white and trembling, and said, Master, just now when I was in the market-place I was jostled by a woman in the crowd and when I turned I saw it was Death that jostled me. She looked at me and made a threatening gesture; now, lend me your horse, and I will ride away from this city and avoid my fate. I will go to Samarra and there Death will not find me. The merchant lent him his horse, and the servant mounted it, and he dug his spurs in its flanks and as fast as the horse could gallop he went. Then the merchant went down to the market-place and he saw me standing in the crowd and he came to me and said, Why did you make a threatening gesture to my servant when you saw him this morning? That was not a threatening gesture, I said, it was only a start of surprise. I was astonished to see him in Baghdad for I had an appointment with him tonight in Samarra.

—W. Somerset Maugham

This paper depicts the experiences of B/1-8 IN (Company B, 1st Battalion, 8th Infantry) during its tenure in Samarra from 28 September to 14 October 2003. We were to conduct operations for seven to ten days. Our mission was to increase the amount of infantry conducting dismounted patrols and establish a presence within the city while maintaining the southern observation post (OP) to protect FOB STODDARD from mortar attacks (a task my 2d Platoon assumed for two weeks prior to our arrival). We learned a great deal during our time in Samarra and received tremendous support from our parent unit, 1-66 AR (1st Battalion, 66th Armor). In this paper I will provide a brief background of Samarra; discussion of our tactics, techniques, and procedures (TTP)/contacts; and lessons learned. This paper is intended to aid those fighting in Samarra and does not represent a volunteering or desire to ever return—I enjoy my 120-mm.-proof bunker down at LION FOB (Forward Operating Base) and the great standoff our FOB has to offer.

SAMARRA

The ruins of Samarra date to the twelfth century. The minaret, coliseum, and mosque were built during the reigns of the tenth and eleventh caliphs, whose remains are in the mosque. This makes the city a huge tourist (terrorist) site for Shiite Muslims. Although they represent 5 percent of the population, their buildings represent 100 percent of anything worth saving culturally. With twenty-one large tribes, the locals are fighting one another as much as they are fighting you. Legend has it that Saddam Hussein did not attempt to subdue Samarra, rather to just buy it off. This makes sense when you note the parity in relative wealth of the city, the Wild West attitude, and general anti-Western and anti-Semitic ideals. While 5 percent of the city actively opposes you, 90 percent of the city dislikes you and 5 percent of the city sees an opportunity to get Western dollars, power, and support.

The youth look very militaristic and fit. The Arnold Schwarzenegger gym speaks volumes to their tough-guy bravado and fighting spirit. Their general desire to fistfight with you when you attempt to detain them perplexed me initially, and we were forced to play "hacky sack" (get in a fistfight) with more than one of the guys we simply wanted to question. The physical aspects of the city demonstrate the classic urban sprawl discussed in Army field manuals. The old part of the city has a very European flavor to it with regard to alleyways, shops, random turns, and a general lack of traffic organization as it came into being prior to the automobile. As you move out of the downtown sections of Market Street and Zone 7, you find a street pattern developing that supports vehicular movement and the street movement techniques we found useful.

What We Knew and Thought

Our company's urban movement evolved throughout our Iraqi experience, but the classic Mogadishu lessons learned never rang more true for me than in the streets of Samarra. The alleyways, rooftops, crowds, and multitude of different buildings and shops create a nightmare of keyhole shots and in-your-face engagements that tanks and Brads just aren't designed for. We knew and understood this going in. You have to walk the streets, and the infantry must get out front. Brads scan deep and look at rooftops while the infantry covers doors, windows, and alleyways. When in contact, the Brads move forward to suppress and provide cover for the infantry to move across the streets and down the alleys. The infantry moves out front, continually working its sectors and soft-clearing everything. The guys must know: gun in every door and every window; rooftops, long security; right side cover; left side high and deep (and vice versa); Rolling T; high-low clearance of alleys; travel off the walls to avoid bullet corridors; clear cars; and always know exactly where the next piece of cover will come from. Everything you see in the street can also see you and subsequently engage you. Moving down the streets is an exhausting exercise in paranoia, and the men figure it out real quick with the rocket-propelled grenade (RPG) and small-arms attacks as a teaching mechanism. We never had issues with clearing rooms: we trained at our shoot house quite extensively and everyone knew their role clearing a room inside and out. However, you fight and die in the streets—all the leaders knew and understood that. The safest place in Samarra is entering a building and clearing a room on a planned raid late at night.

Our first night in Samarra my 2d Platoon came back to me from being attached to A/1-66 AR. We still had responsibility for manning the southern OP to protect FOB STODDARD. They would travel down with a tank section going to another blocking position while the rest of the company got settled into the foot-deep moon dust of FOB DANIELS. They traveled on Route RATTLER and took RPG fire on the south side of Zone 9. A quick map check will show you that the enemy uses interior lines on that route. They spot you coming around the north side, drive to the south side, and set up their RPG ambushes.

It took us getting ambushed on the north side of RATTLER with the enemy using their TTP in reverse to figure this out. I didn't claim to be smart, just trainable; stupid does hurt. The initial volley had two RPGs. The unit attempted to regain contact with the infantry and tanks. The Brads pushed out a little ways when the platoon leader (First Lieutenant Jiminez) and his gunner (Hansen) identified an RPG firer aiming and firing. They engaged with 25-mm. HE (high explosive) in a classic shootout. The RPG missed ... the platoon leader did not. We had a terrorist split in half with a smoking RPG launcher in his hand. I sent a platoon down there with a tank section since we didn't know the city and it was night. My Blue Platoon detained seven bad guys who had all suffered injuries in the shootout. The Alpha tank company commander, Captain Deponai, was with the tanks and directed the fight; we were just guns for hire. This proved our only multiple RPG shootout, although they had a plethora of multiple RPG contacts prior to our arrival. While we did engage victoriously, I think we were a bit hesitant to start shooting without a known target.

Observer-controllers and commanders will beat you up on live-fire ranges for the "noise-ex" and collateral damage. However, it's necessary to start shooting here to save Americans ... even at inanimate objects if you don't have definitive targets. It throws the enemy off balance, so they flee the scene after a single shot or they do something incredibly suicidal. The reason for returning fire immediately is twofold. The "donk" of the RPG terrifies and freezes trained professional soldiers from the company commander down to the new private, and you must get them moving again with confidence in their weapons. Second, our firepower against bush-league terrorists terrorizes them much more than their donk does us. I continually give my gunner inanimate objects, mitigating collateral damage, to shoot if we take contact in a given area. One can argue the hearts-and-minds campaign all day on this point; but they will lose ... especially among those of us who have been donked. Firepower breeds fear in the enemy and local populace. Samarra will never like you, so they must fear you. Fear coupled with our general target discrimination and efforts to limit collateral damage associated with just being American soldiers will breed respect, and that's the best you can hope for here. Bottom line: return fire immediately even if it's out into an open trash field. It will throw the enemy off and continually remind the populace that we will fight. I know it works because human-intelligence reporting skyrocketed after our most violent contacts. I am not trying to justify my TTP or violent responses. It is war—get used to it.

CONTACTS AND LEARNING

Our early-day presence patrols proved uneventful. We always rolled ten Brads deep with the associated infantry on the ground clearing forward. I figured mass coupled with seeing the infantry on the ground would deter any attack. It did for awhile. We went on the offensive with an operation called INDUSTRY CLEAN UP in which the company seized fourteen caches and filled up five 5-ton trucks worth of improvised explosive devices (IEDs), RPGs, mortars, small arms, ammunition, etc. I thought we had them on the run and scared of us. We got out into the town and walked, talking to the locals and passing out candy to the kids. No worries.

The next night we came back on Route RATTLER south to north when my internal commo went out. I had created an 800-meter break in contact by the time I got the XO briefed on my troubles and my wingman came forward to guide us back. The enemy, thinking the vehicle in front of me was the last vehicle, engaged it. This quickly turned into a real bad Reserve Officer Training Corps/Ranger School leadership lane ... you can't talk to anyone, your new platoon leader is getting shot at, and you have a giant gap in your formation. Take action, cadet! We really didn't have a good fix on what happened, and I got to the scene after the fleeing took place.

Fortunately, the platoon leader knew to dismount and assault. The infantry engaged a vehicle, but it escaped.

That night we discovered the ephemeral nature of contact in the city and the necessity for immediate application of controlled violence. I also learned that rolling ten deep doesn't make you immune ... maybe if we had infantry on the ground. We'll start working a section of the city each night en route back from the OP gun run. We were all very frustrated at the nature of the elusive enemy and our inability to regain contact ... especially the commander, whose sole situational awareness due to commo problems was the donk. We must have infantry on the ground in the places we are most likely to make contact, but it's a commander's call where that is going to happen. You can't walk the entire city every night.

The day patrols proved uneventful. It's Dr. Jekyll and Mr. Hyde, seemingly. This OP in the south is really starting to aggravate me because of the numerous mine strikes in areas we return to, but we have to keep STODDARD safe from the mortars. Unfortunately, there are only so many places you can go down by the river. I decide to walk Market Street on the way back from the gun-run OP insertion. This is my first night not rolling a tank section with the Brads. We dismount the infantry and start walking the street. The Brads are targets when they move this slowly, but we rely on the infantry to protect them down here. My 2d Platoon leader points out the building where he received eight RPGs one morning. It's a bad neighborhood. My wingman and I are the lead Brads, which isn't a good spot for the commander, so I start moving a platoon to assume the lead.

As they move forward ... *Donk! Crack! Crack! Crack!* The RPG flies by just like a hot Roman candle—you instinctively stare at it while it cruises by your head with the rush of heat—and the AK–47s crack down the street. The sound and "pretty" light paralyze you. My first instinct is to jump off the track and assault dismounted since I treat the Bradley like a big Humvee; however, I fight that urge and start yelling for everyone to open up on where they think the contact came from. My gunner starts shooting an abandoned shed in the completely wrong direction, so I take control of the gun and point him in the right direction and we lay down a huge base of fire with the infantry and Brads on the area where the enemy fired. We hit a transformer with one of the ricochets, causing a huge light show. The lead squad calls it up as an IED, so we have a little confusion. We move to cordon off the area and get the infantry moving down the right alley. Bingo, we nab their getaway car with seven RPGs and launchers in it. The Brads cordon off the alley, and we start clearing houses. The locals tell me about the incident … vast improvement in cooperation since we started shooting. Of course, they will report to the Civil-Military Operations Center (CMOC) tomorrow and file an outrageous claim, but I am willing to trade money for information. I was certain we had casualties with the amount of contact we had and seeing the infantrymen knocked off their feet from the blast. However, we were all knocked around, shaken, but complete … what a command and control nightmare.

That night the RPG roared down the street everyone had the opportunity to see it go by and learn the initial terror and paralysis that we all experience with contact. It seems like forever before you regain your wits and react. In reality we were firing before the secondary explosion of the RPG. Our efforts proved fruitful as we got the opportunity to "disable" a terrorist car and police up seven RPGs and a bad guy's sandal. Launch Operation CINDERELLA! Our reaction must be a battle drill. Return fire and seek cover. Know that close urban contact is straight-up terrifying and confusing, so junior leaders must move rapidly and break the seal on the live fire. Otherwise, you just have a company commander's Bradley shooting at an abandoned "enemy" shed because he's pissed off. We also learned that the bad guys are scared and make their own JV mistakes under fire, so shoot.

I realized that you don't have to roll Market Street, Elm Street, or 60th Street to make contact. Those are the most populated, densely packed areas in the city. We continue to roll en masse but along the more open urban areas like 50th Street and RATTLER. I have come to the conclusion they will come to you, so make contact on your terms. Build your engagement area. I know rolling the same routes makes you susceptible to IEDs, but there isn't an area in the city from which we haven't taken IEDs or RPGs. That's a known risk and one you mitigate by driving name tape defilade—or lower (keeping the Bradley commanders low in the turret to avoid their taking shrapnel—it limits your situational awareness but prevents you from getting killed). I want to force them out of the alleyways and engage them on the periphery of the city. We start working 50th Street extensively with the infantry clearing while the Brads move with the field to their backs. It works well, and we load the infantry in the Brads for the easy trip up through Zone 2.

Donk. Contact south. *Boom.* Trail tank is hit and smoking. "Sh—!" We start moving south to secure the tank and gain contact with the enemy. No one saw the contact except for the trail tank. Fortunately, the smoke we see is a combination of halon bottles and RPG remnants. They return fire with the coax out into the open field, and we get everyone on line and just mow it. Cease fire! Scan for heat signatures. I finally get the report from the tankers and they come up on company net. Superficial damage and they shot hot spots out in the field. I don't have time to look for bodies tonight. We've been downtown too long, so I call off the chase. The nice thing about 7.62-mm. is that they have to check into the hospital and we can find them that way. Tonight confirmed that they hunt us too. You get ambushed ... where you are ... so always build your engagement area and choose where you make contact wisely.

I couldn't believe they would shoot at us from the field. Not a good move on their part, and they suffered the consequences. The confusion of having a vehicle hit doubles the chaos with returning fire. That coupled with the southern OP made fire control difficult tonight, but we had good crosstalk with our OP who was actually able to walk us onto the RPG flash while the tankers got their breath back after the halon. The key to fighting these guys is to be everywhere at once with standoff and redundant, interlocking fields of fire. I should have had infantry with the trail vehicle and more people scanning south into the field ... it doesn't always come from the alleys. These contacts are like *Defense of Duffers Drift* (a book in which a commander fights the same engagement over and over again, improving each time), always revamping our tactics. We deal with a tenacious enemy, not a particularly smart one.

The daylight patrols enable us to see the city and press the flesh while working our street movement. To succeed, everyone can't just know exactly what they must do—they must know exactly what they must do, exactly what their buddies must do, and exactly what everyone else is doing. We start spreading out during the day with multiple clearance axes that can rapidly move to mutually support. Infantry out front. We clear some alleys and start moving south on Elm Street. *Crack! Crack! Crack!* We are shooting. I am fifty feet back and see my lead squad shooting up the street at a target I can't see. It looks like they are playing around shooting at coke cans or something because they are so calm and moving so smoothly. We got a man in a white man-dress attempting to engage us from the rear with an RPG as we turn on Elm. Sweet. We are dictating the contact. Get the Brads out in the road, and let's start moving. I jump down and join in the dismounted hunt. We bounce around some rooftops and do some top-down clearing.

You've got to love leading a stack down a stairwell and freezing down the terrified occupants of the house with under-gun lights ... I've got to do that more often.

We find a cache of five AK–47s hidden in an abandoned house with lots of ammunition. *They hide their stuff in abandoned houses and side stores. Rarely will you find anything in their homes.* You must search all stores and abandoned houses. We didn't tag the guy, but the action was on our terms. Classic example of decide, act, and report. Specialist Villegas pulling north security as the Brads made the turn, saw the enemy, and opened up. His team leader moved to him with the SAW (squad automatic weapon) gunner and they built a base of fire while the squad leader bounded his other team. The platoon leader gets the Brads in the hunt, and it's a chase; he reports to the commander who could have just taken the day off—the platoons are on it.

Shooting from alternate firing positions at ranges greater than 150 meters under that stress is difficult. We work our marksmanship program extensively and shoot daily at our FOB, but sometimes you just miss. The real triumph and lesson learned of the contact was that the Army gave you the weapon and the authority to use it, and we are getting that point across. Specialist Villegas saved a Bradley from an ass shot by his aggressive attitude and his flawless application of decide, act, and report ... and tanks and Brads are not standing up to the RPGs as briefed. We have plenty of holes in both to tell otherwise. Leaders can't withhold the authority to engage. Privates and specialists must have and feel they have the authority to shoot bad guys immediately.

It's our first daylight engagement. However, we have fixed-site security for the banks tomorrow, which is a definite way to get shot. No Americans in the Sunni Triangle should ever pull fixed-site security now that we have the police and Iraqi Civil Defense Corps (ICDC) standing up. You just become a target. Our fears proved correct as my platoon guarding the Samarra Bank took a keyhole shot and we couldn't regain contact. Get out of the fixed-site security. Way too dangerous. That night we worked Route RATTLER using a new technique. We split into multiple sectors with the Brads, tanks pushed out to the east covering the movement with a lot more standoff, and we hit the entire route with the platoons moving independently. No one shot at us. Amazing. I definitely advocate using that method of clearance, and sometimes you just avoid routes that limit your ability to fight.

We performed pretty much the exact same maneuver the next morning in daylight along the southern portion of the city. We found a guy burying AK—47s—their national crop—and stopped to detain him with one of the platoons. This caused us to sit on the limit of advance a bit longer than desired, and we knew it would come; but we had good standoff with the infantry in the streets pulling security. The terrorist came out and shot at Staff Sergeant Dewolf, who scanned over and shot the guy on the back of the motorcycle. He fell off, but his buddy threw him across the back prior to running the infantry gauntlet that just riddled them. The velocity of our rounds is such that they go right through the vehicles causing minimal damage and allowing them to keep rolling unless you punch up HE; but we don't do that with infantry on the ground in the city. They will come to you. Choose your positions wisely. We detained numerous individuals after that action and then moved back to the CMOC.

Donk! A classic keyhole shot on our ride back to the CMOC. All the Brads actioned immediately, and we grabbed a motorcyclist in the alleyway attempting to flee. All bikes within a square kilometer are working together to shoot at you, so you need to detain them all. Our actions couldn't have been faster, but sometimes you don't catch them red-handed; you have to relentlessly pursue and have defined battle drills and good crosstalk. During an alleyway shot, the engaged Brad continues to move out of the alleyway and calls up the contact direction. Then all elements action down different alleyways in the direction of the contact to cut off the enemy and detain anyone suspicious. They shot between the XO's track and mine (at the XO), and we actioned right north of the contact while the trail platoon moved in the alleyway of the contact and the two alleyways to the south. The tougher the shot they take, the safer you are. However, it makes it easier for them to get away.

Our final day in Samarra would involve daylight presence patrols in Zone 6. We wanted an easy day. We dropped off the infantry, and the men immediately found a huge cache of demolitions, RPGs, rounds, and small arms. We had to call for a 5-ton truck to police up all the equipment. We kept the Brads out on the open ground while the locals uploaded the equipment. I am all about local employment opportunities. The infantry caught all the shop owners as they attempted to flee and physically convinced them to work on uploading all their weapons onto the American 5-ton before we take them downtown to the intelligence teams.

We continued to clear all the shops on Albino Street and to work the area for more intelligence. The 5-tons arrived and uploaded the gear. *Donk!* We all dove into the shop and prayed the RPG didn't hit all that demolition—it's a four-foot cube of C4, blasting caps, dynamite, and det cord. We hear coax firing before the next boom, ending the RPG flight of terror. We run out to see Blue Platoon's Bradleys mowing down an alleyway where the cloud of smoke from the RPG lingers. The Civil War charge across the field starts. The XO and I get a little out front running and look back to make sure the infantry is moving. Yes, we have learned to march to the sound of the guns and quickly. All of Blue's Brads disappear into the alleyway and our Bradleys catch up to us out in the field ... I hated running the 400-meter in track. The breathless crosstalk starts, and the infantry moves to shut down the road while the Brads flush out the prey. A different dynamic than the Brads cordoning while the infantry flushes, but we adapt our tactics on the fly.

We have a destroyed car, and there are numerous blood trails at the scene. We start following those until we have contact back out on the main road with a black BMW attempting to engage our infantry. Bad choice. The M240 gunner steps into the street and fires a burst from the hip right into the car as it speeds by. The infantry squads unload on the guy, and we maintain the chase with the Brads following the gas trail. BMW makes a car that can really take a beating. My XO finishes it off with coax as it turns into a back alley. It has dead guys in the vehicle, but the driver got away ... in real bad shape from the blood trail and the bone fragments left in the car. About this time we get the secondary reports on our wounded soldier. Second Lieutenant Tumlinson took shrapnel to the calf. Sergeant First Class Tetu, the platoon sergeant, rolls a section to medevac him down to STODDARD, and I let battalion handle the aircraft while we continue the hunt.

The headquarters guys are all moving down the back alleyways on the blood trail using most of the proper techniques for urban movement. Everyone needs to know street movement. Our little squad has my dismounted radio telephone operator, Cutuca; the XO, Jimmy Bevens; fire support officer, Rick Frank; FSNCO (forward support noncommissioned officer), Staff Sergeant Kerns; Q36 radar chief, Albreche; the commander; and a random infantryman from the back of the track that came with us. We place a barrel in every orifice, soft-clear the cars, Rolling T down the alleys, high-low the corners, scroll to the road on linear danger areas ... keep moving, look deep, and watch rooftops, windows, and doors—eyes always moving. The blood trail dies. He must have gotten in a car. We clear a couple of buildings, but these guys are like the Viet Cong with policing up their wounded and dead. I know the future donk is coming, so we load up and move back to the FOB. We fought them on our terms today. You always know when they are pissed because they mortar you when you get back. They were pissed but fired only three rounds ... they must have an ammunition shortage. I hope we put a dent in things. That is the lowest incoming mortar count yet.

BULLETED LESSONS

* Apply all street-movement techniques all the time. It's exhausting work, sustainable for two hours at most, but you can't just walk through. The danger is too great.

* Work your marksmanship program hard. We have a myriad of CQM (close-quarters marksmanship) tables that require you to fire from alternate firing positions under varying circumstances while positively identifying targets: SAWs and 240s. We also have a crude shoot house with windows that requires only a 90-degree range fan, and we try to shoot three times a week. We are building stairwells and alleys to add to our marksmanship training.

* The people do not like you: they learned to respect us in the end. I don't think we intimidated them initially, and that is the best relationship we can hope for there. They viewed our attempts at cordiality as a sign of weakness.

* Fight the enemy on your terms and don't fight the plan. Don't go on Market or Elm Street without actionable intelligence. Don't go out at night unless you have a mission. I think our daylight searches and patrols made us some money, but at night we didn't find anything and just got shot at by a disappearing enemy. We won; we just have to rebuild the country. Do all your raids at night—that is when you are on the offensive.

* If you are driving around trying to get shot, you will. They will engage you on their terms if you do stupid stuff like that.

* The enemy will come to you, so ensure you have standoff with your Brads and other weapon systems and that the infantry is on the ground to seal their fate.

- Samarra needs an area where you can conduct demonstration firing, especially with the tanks down the streets blocking off alleys. The people want and need to hear that main gun go off in their city. The south side parallel to Power Line out into the trash area is a great region to do this. I regret never allowing the tankers to fire 120-mm. out into the trash dumps or working attack aviation into some demonstration fires. The locals would have loved it.

- Face camo terrifies the locals. We used it to our advantage on raids.

- The kids throw rocks at the last vehicle. Throw rocks back or throw smoke. They hate that.

- The Brads in Samarra desperately need reactive armor.

- Never get involved in fixed-site security. You must always vary your patterns and techniques. While we were there, a company involved in fixed-site security had a soldier lose an arm and another lose an eye because they are targets out there.

- They track you through the city with numerous messengers. If you don't want contact, just take the most random, haphazard route. You can see the confusion in the spotters' faces when you do this—you just can't prove they are spotters. Also use multiple axes with smaller formations moving more quickly when infantry is not on the ground.

- They hide weapons in the cemeteries and the mosques. We need to out-guerrilla the guerrilla with our police, ICDC, and interpreters.

- Start using non-tactical vehicles to spot RPG firers in front of a convoy. This requires coordination; but since my guys were the only ones in that sector, we could have pulled it off. I regret not putting a couple of spotters out in front of the convoy in man-dresses and beat-up Iraqi cars.

- We desperately need to put some bad RPGs on the market. Rockets that blow up when you fire them. We did it in Vietnam and can do it here. I know we put a large dent in their weapons trafficking—seventeen caches and six 5-tons' worth of ammunition, weapons, and demolitions. I am proud of those numbers but terrified of what else is out there. They need resupply, and we should help them with some booby-trapped rockets. Word would spread fast after the first few faulty rockets.

- Return fire at every contact. We just have to make it incredibly violent and scary to remain a terrorist in our area of operations, and the people know what is going on. They know we only shoot when shot at, but at the same time all they understand is force. For twenty-four years they lived under a brutal dictator whose previous government résumé listed torturer as his occupation. Pussyfooting around will only lead to more problems for both sides. Controlled violence.

- My next task would have been to develop immediate spider-web battle drills for contacts in each of the different zones to more effectively cordon off the area. So we could just say "Brads execute Web Zone 9 North," and everyone would know exactly where to go to establish checkpoints and block the enemy's egress routes.

- Intelligence reporting went up quite a bit while we were there. We just need to action on all of it. We did some raids with Special Forces informants and got a lot of RPG shooters and gunrunners off the streets; I think the locals appreciate that. It always feels good to go on the offensive. They don't like you, but they like the fighting even less.

- Americans should not live in Samarra, unless we plan to really invest in building the defense there. Otherwise, the force protection will handicap you. We should work civil-military activities and surge into the city for combat operations. The city is ripe for clearing entire sectors at a time with multiple battalions. It's the only way to clean it up.

- I felt the bad guys were off balance when we left, but they will regroup. We killed some guys attempting to conduct suicide car bombings against U.S. forces and must remain ever vigilant in that regard.

- Guys desperately need mortar-proof shelters to sleep in at night. We grew accustomed to the mortars falling and us piling into the Brads from a dead sleep. With all our engineer assets and CMO activities, it is criminal that we don't have everyone sleeping in mortar-proof shelters. Aren't we spending $87 billion on this place?

- Bottom line is that Samarra is an infantry battalion's fight, and you can't piecemeal forces into it. The 1-12 IN must move back in or give 1-66 AR some light infantry companies from the 101st. After all, they have one of their armor companies, and they are going to air-assault school from what I heard. The 1-8 IN gets spread way too thin when we attempt to cover Abu Hishma, Balda, Balad, Duluya, and Route 1; and my assigned sector now has Syrians moving in after our "vacation."

- Samarra changed my opinion of this place. When I went up there, I had under my belt six contacts where I personally had to fire. I had treated American wounded three times. I considered myself experienced and ready for Samarra—my cherry was popped. I knew how to fight this enemy, and we had trained military operations on urban terrain (MOUT) extensively. However, I was not prepared for the contact we had in Samarra, as it came everyday, very loudly, and much more violently. It made us all extremely aggressive and less tolerant of the win-the-hearts-and-minds campaign. We spent much more time as Mr. Hyde, and engaging and killing bad guys came instinctively and quite easily You can't walk down Market Street, listen to the RPG go off, get terrified, watch the RPG go by and explode accompanied by the AK fire, get in a firefight, kill bad guys, treat and evacuate your wounded, go home and try to fall asleep in the foot-deep moon dust, wake up to incoming, dive into your track in bare feet and boxer shorts, giggle like a school girl as the mortars get closer, worriedly get 100 percent accountability, go back to sleep in the moon dust, wake up covered in sand, and then report back that all is well. And we just need to work with the locals. It's a different fight, and we lived it every day. Operating dismounted in that city will change your point of view.

- If you want to avoid contact, you can. Just don't patrol or drive through the city real fast. They don't shoot unless they are set up, but they will fight you asymmetrically with mortars, IEDs, and ambushes elsewhere.

- The MOUT battle is a dismounted fight. You cannot fight it solely mounted. The commander has to get on the ground. I normally sifted through the initial contact mounted, reported to higher, and got things moving in the right direction before I got on the ground to get a feel for the specific street and action. It's a light infantry fight; mechanized commanders must figure out all the nuances that go with it and adapt men, weapons, and equipment to fight dismounted or mounted. I switched back and forth sometimes several times in a single fight. I knew that I would fight off the Bradley a lot, and we had a plan with radios, RTOs, security, XO controlling Brads, etc.

CONCLUSION

I started this as a military paper, but somewhere along the line it gained a novelistic quality in both style and length. My apologies, but Samarra isn't as cut and dried as you like, and you have to understand that a war still exists there. Bulleted comments don't capture what the soldier/leader goes through under *urban* contact, and I know 95 percent of the guys here haven't experienced it to the degree Samarra offers. The intensity and fear factor of our contacts skyrocketed during our tenure up there. I found my personal inclinations varying from jump off the Bradley and charge into the fray to curl up in the fetal position on the floor and hide from the donk. Fortunately, the HQ element was always right behind me when the former actions rang true, and their confidence and aggressiveness never allowed me to do the latter—but you will feel that way at times regardless of who you are. This was the first time I thought that we would take significant casualties and that we would surely have a Brad catastrophically killed. The company's aggressiveness, teamwork, and dynamic squad leaders like Reagan, Lillie, Jarrell, Robertson, Kapheim, Martinez, Guidry, Zawisa, and Blackwell made it happen and kept the men moving when they did not want to. I witnessed many an action that in a different war during a different time would have earned my men different medals than the Army Commendation Medals and Army Achievement Medals we could give them. The frontal charge into the fray proved the accepted norm for this band of brothers, and no man lagged behind.

APPENDIX C

CIVIL SAMARRA

This paper depicts the experiences of B/1-8 IN (Company B, 1st Battalion, 8th Infantry) during its tenure in Samarra from 12 December 2003–7 February 2004. We were supposed to conduct battalion-level operations for seven to ten days and return to our Forward Operating Base (FOB) by Christmas ... it went on a bit longer. Our mission was to increase the amount of infantry conducting dismounted patrols, action on all previously collected intelligence, and deny the enemy sanctuary in this unique city previously described. We learned a great deal during our time in Samarra operating under both 1-8 IN and 1-66 AR (1st Battalion, 66th Armor). This paper meanders chronologically through this second go-around and attempts to offer the changing viewpoint we had following our October experience.

THE FIRST 72 HOURS

We started our Samarra redux with the division's Operation IVY BLIZZARD that consisted of hitting every target built up in 1-66 AR's, THT's (Tactical Humint Team's), and ODA's (Operational Detachment A's) queue. Bravo Company had Zone 7, the area I specifically asked to never return to again. We gave giant Op Orders and had multiple synchronization meetings, but in the end I knew that the only platoon I would see would be the one I traveled with and that the reinforcements in the town would come from within the company. The city is platoon actions with "Company C2." If you want to understand the fight, you have to operate on the squad-leader level—that is where the true interaction and actions occur.

We dropped ramp fifty meters from the Golden Mosque, and the squads quickly moved into the alleyways in cover of darkness. They kept a good spread, and we had the textbook Rolling T going along the wide streets and in-your-face alleyways. No one had to convince us how dangerous this place could turn—22 rocket-propelled grenade (RPG) ambushes and 107 RPGs shot at the company kind of makes you paranoid. The men know every gun in every alley, door, and window and their assigned sectors—high through low, methodically soft-clearing everything with their eyes rapidly. We extensively trained military operations on urban terrain (MOUT) live on our Hogan's Alley range at LION FOB and knew how fast and furious the engagements would come.

Any amount of time spent standing still in downtown Samarra under the lights of the Golden Mosque makes me absolutely cringe. The pluggers (encrypted military global positioning systems) and Garmins took forever to pick up satellites in the multistoried downtown streets, and you need those 10-digit grids if you want to use demolition breaches. The falcon-view imagery is great but not enough when you talk of using demo. We needed to use the breaches to make the statement to Samarra that "We are stronger and can bring more force than you can imagine." They understand and respect you for *bringing it.*

At 0200 we moved down the street, got the Garmins working, and placed the charges on the outer doors. We used tent pegs filled with C4 (a very simple tamped charge that you could blow fifteen meters away using shock tube without incident)—one for the weaker doors and two for the bigger ones. The physical damage from the charges proved quite minimal, but the noise volume and psychological gains we attained proved quite robust. The 48-hour period of conducting all entries with demolitions enabled us to set the tone for the subsequent deluge of money and Civil Affairs projects ... you have two choices: cooperate and enjoy the money or we can go back to demolition entries. It's what works—big stick diplomacy.

We quickly worked through the queue in a few days but became inundated with walk-up sources. We had to rapidly turn around the intelligence gathered from these sources and prove that we would act quickly to gain the trust and confidence of the populace and encourage the great deal of cooperation we received from the locals. Most informants agreed to travel with us provided we disguised them. Since we don't use Humvees, our tactics, techniques, and procedures (TTP) with informants was to place them in the back of the Bradley with the troop hatch open. Our interpreter would give us directions on a manpack radio, guiding us to within 400 meters of the target. We would dismount at a distance to establish an infantry outer cordon while maintaining surprise and protection. This TTP evolved over time; initially we botched it a couple of times—the first raid ended with our Iraqi interpreter beating the informant with the radio hand mike. Once we got the interpreter fully integrated with what we wanted, we could work the *informant* raid flawlessly. This type of raid proved far more beneficial than the *10-digit grid* or *name/neighborhood raid*, and we learned to always request that the informant go with us. On one occasion we caught two divisional HVTs (high-value targets) driving to the objective area of another target. Having sources and trained interpreters proved key to our successes on the 75-plus raids during this 60-day period.

While the infantry continued to work off the sources, other units developed and resourced the Iraqi Civil Defense Corps (ICDC) and police and fire departments at breakneck speed. The actions of the continuous raids created a gap between the populace and the insurgency. Once we established this gap, we had to keep it open with the ICDC and police. No city wants the amount of combat power we placed in Samarra permanently, so they turned against the root cause of the problem—the insurgents. Gapping the populace is easy: you just inundate the region with combat power and lots of action. The more violent you seem and the more scared they are, the more they cooperate. Some say this smacks of a war we didn't do too well in, Vietnam, with the idea of *destroying the village in order to save it*. However, we were far from the point of wanton destruction, and the entire intent of this operation was to get the town peaceful enough to get money moving for the infrastructure and government. The psyops battle with flyers and loudspeakers proved a huge ticket to the peaceful acceptance of the overwhelming American presence, and we used that angle daily. The locals love getting flyers.

The follow-on to gapping the populace and insurgency represents the tough part and ultimately determines the path of the city. After three days of blow up your door and drag out the "accused" bad guys, known to us as "Jerry Springer" raids, we converted to a more psyops, hearts-and-minds campaign. We revisited multiple target homes and paid for damages if we assessed the accused as not deserving detention. Taking the individuals directly to their homes and turning them over to their mothers had a twofold effect. It gained us the moral high ground and positive interaction with the populace. We also drank tea and ate "repatriation" meals with each of the accused, which made those unending patrols a little more bearable. The released individuals provided us a source to the inner workings of the city, and they all had some level of unprovable dirt. At this point in the operation, it became more detective, intelligence-type work that we struggled through.

Company commanders need money. The gathering of intelligence and destruction of things happens at the company level. We hit cars, talk to shop owners, meet rock-throwers' parents, break windows, receive intelligence tips, knock down doors, run over sewage lines, cut electrical wiring, etc. The immediate payoff for hot information and minor damaged goods creates a huge network of informants and allies. We could also keep them at bay for larger claims and change awkward situations of writing notes for bureaucratic claims processes into rapid turnaround intelligence and street-side popularity. I am talking about $20 payouts' making the difference here. You have to work the streets like a cop with your series of narcs, petty criminals, and people who owe you a favor. Your ability to fix problems and bring money to bear determines the populace's attitude toward Americans in the city, and that is the fight that we will wage for the foreseeable future.

Contacts

The enemy fought us much more asymmetrically this time than last. We brought a lot more firepower, a more offensive approach, and a caged trailer that bad guys really didn't like to ride in behind a Bradley during the cold January rain. The abundance of combat power coupled with the 30 November smackdown from Red Platoon disrupted the enemy's normal fight patterns. They moved away from the RPG and mortar as the weapons of choice in favor of the mine and 107-mm. rocket. They moved a lot of the popular IED (improvised explosive device) operations out to Route 1. The city seemed completely foreign to me as the "lemming" portion of the populace waved and cheered for the Americans like the sunflowers they are … they quickly sided with us because now we were winning.

We fired 25-mm. and below on a test-fire berm across the street from the old FOB Daniels, which aided our psychological domination tactics. As the sources and information dried up, we found ourselves conducting a lot more close-quarters marksmanship (CQM) training and test-firing of our larger weapon systems. Our first contact this go-around came during one of these test-fires. The insurgents had the old FOB dialed in with 107-mm. rockets that they fired from a berm thirteen kilometers away. We heard one of the rockets launch—they are quite loud—and we just sat around joking about the random loud noises you could hear in the distance. We heard another one of these noises a couple of seconds later as proof of our humor. About thirty seconds later we got the incredibly loud boom with the accompanied shockwave from the first rocket landing across the street. Clamoring up the front slope and into the turret knowing one of those rockets is still hurtling toward you makes for a very uncool experience in self-control.

Fortunately, they fell short and all we got was the terror of the noise, vibration, and shockwave. We got the Q36 grid from battalion and destroyed two more dud rockets with 25-mm. after a goose chase and interaction with a farmer at the vicinity of the point of origin (POO). He knew the location but wouldn't tell us until we described the space shuttle bomb in great detail to him (we told him that our sensors in outer space know that a rocket fired from a field he owned and that we would destroy it unless he showed us where they fired from). He did not like this bomb and decided to show us the canyon where they basically laid these rockets on their side against a berm, fused them with time fuse, and aimed them with a compass. Truly a weapon of terror that has just as much likelihood of hitting the Golden Mosque as it has of hitting the test-fire area, but the bad guys really don't care—after all, the mosque is Shiite. Their TTP for shooting at us out there involved a spotter at the minaret traffic circle (that we identified in hindsight), a Thuraya cell phone, and then the rocket crew with cigarette lighters. They wanted to fight us on the periphery of the city since the imams had started preaching against the collateral damages caused by actions within. We did not return fire at the POO because of farmhouses. That is a huge mistake if you want to discourage them from firing. The people know and support counterfire. If there is collateral damage you work the psyops piece to get the locals on your side supporting you in rooting out the Fedayeen that fire from their fields. I know this works—I have seen my battalion commander work it magically for another unit.

The test-fire area became a contested piece of ground over the next few days as the other infantry companies ran over landmines. The insurgents watch your patterns and will get you if you use the same off-road paths. We mitigated this by creating a new route into the test-fire area with each use. However, it's still a nerve-racking experience going cross-country after the tank-destroying IEDs, and you can imagine my displeasure when our source took us to that site to dig up a weapons cache. We uncovered 137 82-mm. mortar rounds using mine detectors without incident, but it proved a little disheartening to know they were buried across the street from an FOB in our test-fire area. Our days fell into a tedious process of taking a source out, digging up someone's yard, finding a bunch of weapons, detaining some bad guys, coming home, and eating pork cutlets. We have taken enough weapons off the market that the going rate of the RPG has gone from $40 in October to $125. This threefold increase is heartening, but the fact remains that it's still less than my weekly grocery bill for two humans and two canines.

We normally drop off the infantry and move the Bradleys to the outskirts of the city while the infantry squads move independently through zones. We stage the Bradleys south of South Park Road in the trash heaps while the infantry patrols through Zone 10. Once they reach the LOA (limit of advance), we push our Bradleys forward to 50 Yard Line Road to pick them up and move onto the next mission. It was the Iraqi weekend, Thursday, 8 January, and we had been back in Samarra nearly a month without the donk of the RPG. We were just talking about how peaceful the city seemed, but we could never relax down there. First Lieutenant Higgins called that they had reached the LOA, and we bounded his Bradleys forward to pick him up. Second Lieutenant Amick called the same, and we moved to send his Brads forward with the HQ Brads in tow. I took off my Kevlar to swap out for the CVC (combat vehicle crewman) helmet on the track.

Donk! goes the RPG.

"Sh—!" goes the infantry.

Kaboom! goes the RPG.

"Contact right, we are engaging," goes Sergeant First Class Harkness, the experienced platoon sergeant. I yell for my driver to haul ass as I try to gain situational awareness, put on my CVC, and observe White Platoon's Bradleys thumping away with 25-mm. down the street. I think the insurgents shot at the wrong group of guys … Staff Sergeant Legendre is a master gunner in the BC slot and Hansen is a super-experienced gunner with several Eagle Plays of the Day under his belt for favorable contacts. As I swallow the terror lump in my throat and finally get my CVC on, Legendre spits out the target description and Hansen splits the car right down the center in low magnification—adjusting his aim point for the offset of the ISU (integrated sight unit). Yeah, you should see what he can do in high mag. They switch to high mag and smoke four of the five cars used by the shooters for travel and cover. I breathe deep and turn the corner behind the lead Brads of White Platoon. The cars and stores are smoking, and a large electrical fire is developing above a bike store.

I push their Brads down the street to seal it off and try to secure the engagement area with the two headquarters Bradleys, but we don't have any infantry with us. I start calling for the company to assemble on the giant black smoke plume moving into the air. I think everyone was a bit concerned about moving that way during the engagement, but now they come running down from all over the place. 2d Platoon's infantry moves past the Bradleys and immediately sets up far-side security and takes over rooftops for vantage points: Kapheim and Robertson move them into great urban fighting positions without anyone even hinting to do so. I run back up the street and look up to see Lillie on the rooftop directing his squad and assigning sectors of fire. Reagan's squad is doing the same at a building to the north while Jarell secures some witnesses. More Bradleys move into position as well—it makes you feel so much better when you get more guns into the fight. It's also really nice being around guys that know how to fight in the city. Once security is established, we set the medics to work on patching up guys—civilians first, shooters later. This doesn't go quite as well, and there are some pretty gruesome scenes.

The ICDC shows up and sets up an outer outer-cordon, and the police and ambulances arrive on the scene. We were all amazed to see these forces in action, but the real kicker came when the fire truck pulled up and doused the fire. I thought I was in a really bad Cheech and Chong routine. Lieutenant Colonel Sassaman and Major Wright arrived, and we got to work immediately with the psyops piece and questioning. It's great having a battalion commander and S–3 willing to fight like squad leaders, and we all breathe easier when they get there. Eagle Six wants to have an awards presentation on site, but we had to keep things moving. If you want to destroy the insurgency, this is the type of contact you need to have—an incredible display of overwhelming combat power toward the bad guys. You cannot pussyfoot around when they shoot RPGs at you because that will embolden them to shoot more. I have thought through the violence-begets-violence argument that a lot of people cling to, but the statistics and my personal experience have led me to a different conclusion about the surgical application of controlled violence. I witnessed a city that averaged three attacks per day drop to one attack per week when we took off the gloves. That represents a 95 percent drop in contacts. Trust me on this argument: I have seen both sides.

Always trust your instincts and investigate the things that don't feel right. The next Iraqi weekend, we went across the Huwaish cut en route to a mission with ODA, and we observed thirteen military-age males hanging out by the train tracks. I called it up that they looked up to no good but kept moving because we were late to the raid. We linked up with ODA and hit the first gas station objective. I knew we should put the tanks up front versus the soft-skin vehicles and kept on volunteering to do so, but it wasn't our intel and mission to run. ODA had the source up front in a Land Cruiser, and we sped off to the next objective on Power Line Road. ODA had to move more slowly because of our tanks and Bradleys, and it made for the opportune IED target. As I scanned right, I saw a guy on a black motorcycle acting totally suspect. As I passed off the target to observe, he disappeared down a back alley.

Boom! An IED goes off on the lead ODA vehicle and they speed out of the kill zone. There is dust and confusion everywhere as we attempt to regain contact with them and assess the situation. We establish security, call the medevac, and set up the helicopter landing zone (HLZ). We have one seriously wounded, a phenomenal Special Forces soldier. I watch the 18D [Special Forces medic] work miracles to keep him alive, cutting and inserting a tracheotomy and bandaging the head. My medics assist the 18D, Andy Sinden is talking to the helicopters, and Red Platoon sets up the HLZ. I know how long the bird takes to get there and I just can't sit still, so I grab the interpreter and start reducing the IED kill zone with a tank. I end up with about 100 detainees and some destroyed walls. I already know who did it, the guy on the black motorcycle, but he is long since gone—I am just hoping to get a name. The helicopter lands and leaves as do we, knowing that the wounded is not going to live. That day I knowingly violated the rules of speed and protection; the situation just didn't feel right. Our vehicles slowed the team down without offering any Chobham armor protection out front. Sassaman always stresses to us that all deaths here are preventable. This one was, and it was my fault.

We continued on with the raids that day, nabbing some bad guys, and then headed back to our FOB. As we moved through Huwaish cut, we passed Alpha 1-8 IN and gave them the situation brief via FM. *Boom!* Their Brad hits a mine and blows shrapnel everywhere. One of my tank commanders took some shrapnel to the face but luckily nothing serious. The thirteen jackasses from earlier had placed a mine in the cut. It was a day of not trusting my instincts. We should have searched the thirteen guys, put the tanks up front, and engaged the guy on the black motorcycle. We had a long discussion about following your instincts, but it cost us one killed and one wounded in action. The price of learning in Iraq is incredibly high.

The next day we searched some shops that everyone agreed looked suspect, and we all tried to follow every instinct. I had the THT with me doing a target reconnaissance while the infantry searched the shops. Bingo, we got fifteen RPGs, IED material, and a bunch of small arms. Roger, we'll blow the cache in place—a must-do in my book. We do some on-site psychological questioning and then grab three sticks of C4, clear out the populace, and place the charge internally. I blocked off the doors and tamped them with a couch and generator. We cut two minutes of time fuse and moved down the street about fifty meters. The charge is impressive, but it knocks the walls down and turns the cache shop into a causeway. Unfortunately, we ruined a small street vendor's store in the process. It's an easy psyops fix. I give them the rehearsed, emotional RPG speech in pigeon Arabic, and they give us the name of the leaser and owner, whom we pick up later. They love the American "ana mejnuun" speech (basically I let them know how crazy it makes me that they store RPGs in their shops). I then gather all the local shop owners together and we work out the value of the store. There is a ton of bargaining going on and a lot of feigned illnesses and chicken pox scars that doubled as bullet holes from the Saddam Hussein regime … proof that they are clearly on our side. We work this piece for awhile and then write out some receipts.

I got the money from higher and returned a week later. I walked up to the adjacent shop's owner and asked him the location of our guy. He goes on some big speech about "Bono" making him rich, etc. I told the guy I was Bono, and we soon had the entire mob scene going on. Our friend finally broke through the mob, and we held hands and walked over to his house where he had a huge spread of food and the whole nine yards' worth of service. All the leaders of the area came over, and we discussed Iraqi politics, Samarra, families, and America. We then rebargained and paid up following all the TTP I got from the books *The Arab Mind* and *The Hajj*. We exited the neighborhood with "porn star" popularity. They respected our martial exploits coupled with the payback and made us honorary members of the tribe. We did the "brother" kiss and promised to return once a week for dinner. We bought the loyalties and respect of a neighborhood with three sticks of C4 and $1,000. We haven't had any trouble with them since, and they have reported multiple "Ali Babbas" and turned in extra weapons.

The insurgents continued to fire rockets and rocket-assisted mortars at the FOB, but in general the city proved far more peaceful than the incredibly violent month of Ramadan. They did start utilizing car bombs both at the Tribal Council next to the CMOC (Civil-Military Operations Center) and out on Route 1 as an IED. I don't have any conclusive after-action comments from those contacts other than car bombs are really loud. The ability to place them anywhere creates an incredible amount of paranoia for all those who perform the thankless job of walking the streets on patrol for hours on end. Just ensure that you always stay spread out and keep good standoff at your living areas.

The day before we left we got the call from the police to investigate a possible IED at a grid that didn't make any sense. My Blue Platoon attached to "Aggressor" went down to link up with the police and investigate the IED. When they got to the grid, they found no police and no IED. They moved to pack it up when the police called and told them to stay in place and that someone was coming to show them. *Donk!* RPG contact north. The infantry returned fire and the Bradleys fought through some of the initial confusion to join in the fray. They got the report of a red vehicle and found one shortly thereafter ... with a police truck. As the Brads moved in, both vehicles fled in a "as high a speed as the Bradley can get" chase. The gunner disabled the car with coax while traveling at forty-five mph and proved the validity of the stabilization system that allows the Bradley to shoot while moving.

ICDC confirmed the car and its driver as one of their targets. Ten minutes later the police reported a cache of RPGs at their headquarters ... could you please come pick them up? We are not dealing with a very smart enemy, just a tenacious and corrupt one. I was of the mind to arrest the entire police force and lock them in their own jails under ICDC control; but cooler heads prevailed and they decided to work through the police leadership to find the bad apples. I don't think they will have to look very far in that organization to find bad apples. ICDC later reported that they believed it was a police setup but could not confirm it. I wish the ICDC could train the police.

Infrastructure

The Samarra hospital sucks. Samarra is used to a higher standard of living due to its enormous historical fame, hydroelectric dam, and position within Iraq. The ICDC, police, fire station, and road network are far better than anywhere else because the Samarrans had these things before and understand organization and technology. Their hospital is far worse. The drugs have run dry despite the State Drug Industry (SDI) in town, and they have no equipment. If I had money, it would go into the hospital. The locals at every level concur.

The ICDC is America's jewel in Samarra. Their camp with all the Soviet weaponry, uniforms, plethora of animals, and rank cooking fires reminds me of a bad seventies movie set in Colombia. We started working with them a lot more, and they proved eager to learn and train as well as share their animals and food. With the CB radio system and the standing up of the Joint Operations Center (JOC), our interaction with them and performance improved greatly. The connection and friendships we developed aided greatly in the sharing of information, and they began actioning on targets independently from us. They provided outer cordon on numerous raids, but we learned to trust and use them much more inside the buildings as they spoke the language and could identify the targets far easier then we could. Their lieutenant colonel is a class act, replete with "Bogota" shades and a Colt .357 that he normally carries at the ready surrounded by his posse of ICDC toting AK–47s. The joint raids resembled a classic movie—quality funny. Although some of the joint actions were JV, the strides we made in empowering the locals will ultimately be our ticket home.

The police in Samarra are the most corrupt collection of humanity assembled in one city. They represent an internal affairs wet dream. The difference between the ICDC and police stems from their creation. We stood up, selected, and trained the ICDC. The police came from local mob-type hire and represent all the problems we are currently facing. They set us up for RPG ambushes, ambushed us with IEDs, and generally did a poor job working cases and bringing forth information. Whenever I visited them, they were asleep and requested more bedding to better accomplish their missions. I am not sure how blankets and more beds will help a police force perform better, but that is probably why I aligned myself with the ICDC. They have more personality too.

The electricity in Samarra functions very well, probably a byproduct of living right next to a major hydroelectric site. Few people complained about a lack of electricity compared to other areas I have operated in. We destroyed the roads in town with our vehicles, and I have watched them slowly deteriorate with each subsequent visit. Many of the streets turned into packed gravel roads from so many tracks driving on them. The fire department is fully functional, but you must drive to the station and get them as we discovered during one of our rather large blazes. The firemen proved eager and brought water with them, a task some of the other fire trucks failed at in the past— with quite disastrous consequences for the building they wished to save. Many of the civil issues continue to improve, but the next unit will have to fight the phone system and cabling issue that has come to the forefront of Samarra's agenda.

CONCLUSION/VIEWPOINT

We worked out a lot of the kinks in our street movement and perfected our methodology of fighting each of the different Samarra zones with battle plays. Although our focus remained the direct firefight, we found the endeavor tending more and more toward the civil service side: empowering ICDC and police through spontaneous joint patrolling and urban operations training. It seemed like we were winning the hearts and minds through our engagements, sometimes with dialogue and sometimes with 25-mm.—both proving equally effective. Some accuse me of not understanding the larger psyops fight, and that may be true. However, I am an honorary member of five of the twelve major Samarra tribes, and I have had countless offers to help me convert to Islam so I can marry into their bloodline. While this was a very generous and humorous proposition that reminded me of Colonel Kurtz from *Apocalypse Now,* I explained to the sheiks that I was very happy with my wife in particular and Catholicism in general. They appreciated this, and we drank more tea—"in shaa' Allaah."

The nature of the fight in Iraq has many faces depending on the area you operate. Samarra is not Balad, which is not Tikrit, which is not Kirkuk, etc. Each area requires a different approach and an on-the-ground understanding that you can't get from books or reports … although they do definitely help, as does learning a bit of the language. The hearts-and-minds campaign will decide our success in Iraq, but don't in a million years think that they will love you, respect you, and cooperate with you because you rebuild the hospital and schools and fully equip the ICDC and police force. You are smoking crack if you think that money and projects can buy you these things. You have to interact with the people daily and convincingly demonstrate your ability to destroy the bad guys' opposing stability. They respect this kind of action. Iraq is moving from a brutal dictator that used the movie series *The Godfather* as a methodology to run the country.

B/1-8 IN continues to fight organizations that resemble mafias and organized crime versus a Ho Chi Minh–flavored guerrilla war with a hierarchal construction. If we were faced with that kind of organization, the attacks would have stopped after we knocked off the various high-ranking members of the local organizations. However, we haven't seen the attacks stop. A lot of people compare our efforts here to the Philippine Insurrection; however, I compare it to taking on the well-armed Gotti, Capone, Malone, Gambini, and Escobar families all at the same time in a very foreign language—the problem being that these families have numerous connections to pick up the slack and a penchant for revenge. Note: I speak only for my microcosm called B/1-8 IN; making macro assessments of the nature of violence like this gets you into a lot of trouble.

Saddam ruled the people of Iraq with fear, intimidation, and torture. His regime survived for thirty years through unadulterated physical abuse. We are attempting to fill the power vacuum left by the Ba'ath Party with a Western-style democracy based on freedoms and liberties that most of the individuals I deal with simply do not understand. You don't wake up after thirty years of that kind of rule and immediately assimilate all the values and mores that we grew up with. I deal daily with a culture that I desperately attempt to understand and help. At times, I realized I accomplished far more for the Iraqis and the soldiers using the psychological intimidation tactics of a mob boss than I could ever accomplish through some "good ol' boy from North Carolina" routine. You have to adapt your leadership style according to the populace—sometimes you are the overbearing drill sergeant, and other days you are the ambassador of diplomacy and good tidings. The trick remains knowing when to play these different roles, and playing the wrong role will set your area back. At this point in the fight, you should err on the side of the drill sergeant—it's been *my experience* that people respect and cooperate with authoritarian figures much more. Respect and cooperation enable you to root out bad guys, eliminate attacks, and create stability, which enables the NGOs (nongovernmental organizations) and Civil Affairs to operate—eventually leading to our victory. Bottom line: you have to understand and play within the mob psychology if you want to win. Otherwise, just stay at home.

If you have read this far in the monologue, you are either really interested in the fighting going on in Iraq or a really close relative. As I look back on the things I wrote, I realize that I have become a far more aggressive person over the past year in ways that my mother would not necessarily approve. A year over here will change you. A year ago seven of my close friends, Ranger squad members, and classmates were still alive and 15 percent of my company didn't have Purple Hearts. I had never seen a dead or dying American soldier in uniform or had American soldiers' blood physically on my hands. While you block all those things out and continue your mission, it still changes who you are, directly affecting your motivation and ability to deal with the daily vagaries of rebuilding this country. As new people flow in, I realize that they look much fresher and cleaner than I do and they will be the ones to truly rebuild Iraq and watch it reach its potential. It's much like the changing of the American guard in Nazi Germany following the war; time and interaction will bridge the gap. Iraq is getting better, and you are set up to make great strides.

APPENDIX D

A t the time of writing, I had intermittent responsibility for the most mortared area in Iraq for seven months, so take all my comments with a grain of salt.

Countermortar operations begin with intelligence preparation of the battlefield (IPB). The dense vegetation, twisting Tigris River, multiple zigzag canals, small villages, and different access routes to Logistics Support Area ANACONDA make it the ideal target for enemy mortars and rockets. With over 15,000 soldiers and airmen stationed at the LSA (most living in tin-can huts and not wearing proper gear), the insurgents have a huge, juicy target that many travel for miles to try to hit. The enemy's accuracy is not a condition for success; he simply needs to get rounds in the air. Breaking down the potential firing points for mortars numerically demonstrates the daunting task of preventing them from firing. Mathematically speaking, an 82-mm. mortarman has 84.9 square kilometers to set up within. A 120-mm. mortarman has 200.96 square kilometers. You cannot cover this huge swath of land, so your MCOO (modified combined obstacle overlay) and spider-web battle drills must be right on. In this paper I will examine the offensive approach to the mortar battle, the defensive approach, and our TTP (tactics, techniques, and procedures) progression in this fight over time. The mortar battle is very specific to the target you are attempting to protect, and the LSA has physical and emotional dynamics that set it apart.

The countermortar fight starts with where you live and works its way out. If you live in mortar-proof bunkers and wear all your gear, you make a very poor target; the enemy knows and understands this. With the number of people and flow of personnel on the LSA, most soldiers live in tents or beer-can-thin trailers. Couple this with the thousands of local nationals that roam the LSA, and you have a great soft target replete with on-site reconnaissance. To mitigate these conditions, you must establish a battle drill to react to mortars and rockets. You must have a battle plan for accountability and a place to go when the mortars start falling. You must gain accountability and rapidly move to your assigned blocking positions and the point of origin (POO) from multiple directions. We developed several TTP for the firing from the farm fields, but the harder problem you face is the enemy's ability to fire from the farm field and walk over to the local coffee shop, melting back into the society.

The enemy's greatest threat is identification. If we identify him firing, we kill him. If a local identifies him and reports him, we cart him off in a nighttime raid. He works and learns as we do. Although I still believe the tribe outside the LSA is the dumbest in all Iraq, they have learned to use mortars and rockets to their advantage. The dumb insurgents are all gone, deselected according the rules laid forth by Darwin with the assistance of 120-mm. and attack aviation. The people attacking are trained and very patient. They use mortars and rockets to avoid detection, and they fire when they won't be seen. If you lay out the time period for the vast majority of the attacks, they occur when the farmers are not in the fields, namely early morning, early evening, or just prior to a storm.

OFFENSIVE

Knowing the primary time for firing enables you to saturate the areas they fire from with active patrolling and infantry squads in ambush locations. They never fired when we had a large presence in the surrounding villages. The active patrolling (with mine detectors) enables you to discover caches and mortar tubes that proved finite despite what we thought during the 140-degree dog days of August. Active patrolling during peak mortar-firing times enabled us to find countless caches and effectively shut down the insurgents' ability to use their established firing points. We had immense success with this technique and captured the vast majority of their mortar systems. We integrated helicopters into the search, which proved a huge deterrent to the mortarmen. The insurgents fired once that I know of while we had helicopters in the air, and that was that group's last action.

During the month of September we moved into a more aerial approach. We had two UH–60s with a rifle platoon stationed at our FOB ready to interdict the firers on call. The attack helicopters served as an aerial platform for observation and destruction if they could identify the target in the thick orchards. The AH–64s would also pass on grids for helicopter landing zones for the infantry near the POO. The infantry would move in and clear the orchard area for BDA (battle damage assessment), mortars, and insurgents. This proved the fastest means for getting infantry to the POO, but we never executed this particular TTP at an actual firing point. We did conduct numerous rehearsals with Bradleys reinforcing, and it was our most effective means of getting to the firing point. Unfortunately, we lost the helicopters to other missions; but if the asset is available, it works. Most of the enemy firing points in our area were along dirt trails that we could not effectively isolate before they ran into a town unless we had aerial coverage. We could shut down the MSRs (main supply routes), which works for the drive-by mortar but not the trail networks. If you don't have the aerial platform, you must counterfire. You should counterfire regardless.

It took us a long time to figure out the whole counterfire issue. We seemed to take it in bite-size pieces as our frustration grew with our inability to cover the entire 84.9 square kilometers and the lack of cooperation we received from the populace. They feared and respected the mortarmen more than us. We grew wise to this dilemma and started firing demonstration illumination artillery after curfew. We eventually started firing HE. I can remember sitting on top of the Yethrib water tower at 0100 in the pitch black trying to adjust fire on the riverbank three kilometers north of anything in order to intimidate the mortarmen. I don't think the action intimidated anybody, and I tore a muscle in my shoulder climbing down with all the gear.

Over the next few weeks we nominated counterfire targets in response to Q36 hits. We had a series of ten targets in the area, and we would fire at the closest ones if they shot at us. We would also fire some harassing and interdicting illumination at the POO; I am not sure how illumination harasses and interdicts, but it provided a great opportunity to train specialists in calling for fire. It also demonstrated our ability to reach out and touch them, but we could never close with them with infantry. If you don't witness the mortar fire, you have lost the contest. The insurgents move out way too fast. Counterfire represents your most likely option of destroying the enemy, distantly followed by aircraft, still more distantly followed by infantry. Egress options are just too great. It took us a long time and several Purple Hearts to start firing back at the POO. A good technique is to let the unit getting shot at return fire because they will be quite pissed off—that's what you need.

You have to fire back at the POO with a massive amount of rounds for two reasons. One, it denies the enemy the ability to use that point and you might destroy him. The second is purely psychological. If you explain to the sheiks the reason behind the counterfire, they agree with it and that serves as a huge deterrent within the community. It causes the locals to respect your firepower and proves to the insurgents the dangers of the bravado attacks on the Americans. This increases the locals' cooperation and enables you to police up many of the bad actors in nighttime raids. Using white phosphorus and other incendiaries to destroy the field or orchard that the firers used also makes a huge statement to the insurgents and the populace—there are consequences. If they fire mortars or rockets at you and you don't return fire, just chalk that one up in the loss column. You have to shoot back every time; don't allow yourself to get sucker punched. Otherwise, your loss column will grow, and the populace will view you as the big loser wearing the jersey complete with giant "L." We were all raised with Western-style Judeo-Christian values. Shooting at unknown targets sucks and is sometimes cruel, but it definitely works. It is war, and more Americans will suffer and die if we fail to act.

DEFENSIVE

The defensive approach works. It is not my personally preferred technique, and it violates several of the rules I advocate; but it works to maintain the status quo on the LSA. The basic concept of LSA defense is to man observation points 24/7. The time coverage is comforting, and you can prevent the insurgents from firing within the vicinity of the OPs. It also intimidates would-be firers and makes the locals believe you are everywhere. However, the 24-hour shift work shuts off your interaction with the populace and limits your flexibility and ability to actively patrol and cover ground. A good mortar-firing point requires a five-foot square of generally flat ground, so choosing the proper OP is quite difficult. You won't see them fire, but you can scare them from firing on the LSA.

As any graduate of any counterterrorism class will tell you, you must vary your routine. We found it very difficult to vary our routine when on the defense. There are only so many access roads on the canals and good observation points for a named area of interest. The first time we went defensive, we shut down all firing on ANACONDA, namely because we became the targets. They fired 60-mm. and 82-mm. mortars at our OPs and started mining all the access trails. We also experienced direct-fire RPG ambushes as our *varied routine* became better known. The whole survivability move only goes so far. We tried to vary it as much as possible, but you can be only so creative in the defense. It limits your ability to conduct raids. Leaders must constantly fight complacency, especially after about two weeks of the twelve-hour shift inside the same square kilometer. It's brutal on both the men and the machines.

The defense does provide a continuous unadulterated presence that seems to break the enemy's ability to fight ANACONDA. You just have to react to the new target—you. The Iraqi Army teaches its soldiers that "nothing is impossible," so they will continue to improvise asymmetric means to fight you, including homemade rockets and time-delayed initiation systems. The attackers evolved as we did. We are dealing with trained ex-artillerymen who continually upgrade their tactics. They are using 107-mm. rockets hooked to alarm clocks to fire long after they have left the area. They are incredibly difficult to capture, but the rockets are incredibly inaccurate. The only real way to fight the rockets is to cover as much firing ground as possible.

CHRONOLOGY

Our actions in the beginning seem quite "Junior Varsity," after looking back through the kaleidoscope of violence in Samarra and comparing our actions in Samarra with our actions around the LSA in July. We didn't have a functioning Q36 at the LSA early on, and all the firing points we got were four-digit grids based on crater analysis, which proved completely inaccurate despite what the crater analysis "experts" would tell you. We would sit out on the bluffs until 0300 in soft-skin Humvees overlooking Abu Hishma just waiting for them to fire. When we finally got the Q36 up and running, we were able to find the mortar points and, after countless searches, the tubes and ammunition. After six hours of beating brush in 130-degree heat, we would rejoice at finding the firing tube ... not knowing we still had thirty-nine more to go based on intelligence we found later. We moved into a daily routine of patrols during the daylight and counterambushes at night. We experienced relative success with this technique by eliminating the tubes when they fired and by denying them peak times to fire.

Success in this area enabled us to go up to Samarra—to the real gun show. When we returned, our TTP proved much more aggressive. We immediately responded to a Q36-confirmed firing with 155-mm. If the 155 couldn't shoot, we fired the battalion mortars; and, if they couldn't range, we fired M203 before we searched the POO. I believe this technique works well. The company has not been here for a mortar attack on the LSA since early September—nearly five months. They have fired on the LSA, but it was most likely due to a decreased American presence in the area because of operations elsewhere. The most effective means to fight the mortar fight is through counterfire, an aerial Quick Reaction Force, and attack aviation.

Short of those TTP, we could buy the land around the area, relocate the populace, and shut off their ability to fire at the LSA (they would represent the first refugees from this war). It is not a really feasible operation, but they have done it before in America.

APPENDIX E

The Bradley's main mission is to deliver seven infantrymen to the fight. The squad of infantry rides in the back and enters and exits from the rear ramp. It carries a number of different weapon systems including AT–4 antitank missiles, Javelin antitank missiles, M240 7.62-mm. machine guns, M249 5.56-mm. machine guns, and M4 rifles. Each infantryman also has a pair of night vision goggles (NVGs), either the passive vision sight (PVS)–14 or PVS–7. This allowed us to operate in the infrared spectrum, enabling the use of infrared lasers (invisible to the naked eye) on weapons to identify and destroy targets. The night vision devices make chemical lights (small glow sticks that illuminate from a chemical reaction) look like large spotlights, and the NVGs diminish the necessity to use flashlights mounted on the rifles.

While you can seat seven soldiers in the back of a Bradley, it becomes quite crowded when you consider all the additional equipment. We strapped much of this to the outside of the vehicles, which caused them to look somewhat like gypsy wagons early on. Initially, we had to carry all of our water and MREs (meals ready to eat, basic camping meals that have improved significantly over time with regard to quality, taste, and variety but can still stop movement in even the most aggressive digestive tracts). As time went on, we reevaluated and adjusted our load plans. We were able to store the personal gear and most of the chemical detection equipment and suits, freeing up a significant amount of space. Bradley commanders (BCs) had a vested interest in keeping the clutter down to a minimum since the long bench seat in the back served as their bed while the short one belonged to the gunner, according to Bradley etiquette. The infantry squad slept outside.

The Bradley is armed with a 25-mm. chain gun that fires both high-explosive (HE) and armor-penetrating rounds. We favored the HE round for its burst radius, and we always used it for reconnaissance by fire in the thick orchard areas and trash heaps. After being ambushed, we conducted reconnaissance by fire to force the enemy to react. This normally caused the enemy to hide or do something incredibly stupid that we would often cite as having won the Darwin award. The HE round proved quite effective both physically and psychologically due to its burst radius and associated noise. The Bradley is also armed with a 7.62-mm. coaxial machine gun mounted to the right of the main gun, which we used in most of our engagements in urban areas. The gunner has the option of "punching up" sabot, HE, or coax for a given engagement. He can also select one of the two TOW antitank missiles for long-distance tank engagements or to knock down walls and disable fleeing vehicles.

The crew of a Bradley consists of a driver, gunner, and Bradley commander. The driver sits in the front left of the Bradley, next to the engine compartment. He is normally a new soldier and has the responsibility of maintaining the track, road wheels, and suspension system, as well as basic engine repairs. He has the dubious honor of sitting isolated in the hottest portion of the Bradley. We always made the drivers drive with their hatches closed outside the forward operating bases because they were very susceptible to small-arms fire with the hatches open. This, of course, created a convection oven up front for the driver and the repetitive question, "Sir, can I open my hatch?" It proved a very unenviable job until the weather cooled off.

The gunner is a more experienced soldier, and he resides in the turret with the BC. He is responsible for the turret, gun, and radios. He controls the turret from his hand station. The gunner has a multitude of buttons and switches that allow him to select ammunition, rate of fire, and type of sight and to control lasers to determine both distances and target grids. He has a good deal of high-tech equipment to ensure he hits the target the first time he fires.

The Bradley commander is in overall charge. He normally rides with his head sticking out of the hatch to identify targets, maneuver the Bradley, and coordinate with adjacent Bradleys during movement. He also has a hand station to override the gunner's, and it enables him to engage targets from his position. While the crew talks on an internal commo net, the BC is responsible for external communications through a radio system. Some of the newer Bradleys have digital systems and computers (Blue Force Tracker or Force XXI Battle Command, Brigade and Below [FBCB2]) that connect them digitally to one another, providing a myriad of additional capabilities. These capabilities, while extremely useful at times, also take up much needed space in the vehicle, leading to a substantial amount of complaining and scars affectionately called Bradley Bites—small cuts and bruises sustained by crew members while working on various pieces of equipment in very confined spaces.

The Bradley Fighting Vehicle represents the combinations of a multitude of capabilities and plans to design an all-purpose delivery system for mechanized infantry. The plethora of add-on capabilities and designs led to the satirical comedy *Pentagon Wars*. While there is certainly truth in our humor, the Bradley continues to represent the vehicle of choice in the Iraqi theater.

The Bradley's ability to sustain hits from rocket-propelled grenades, improvised explosive devices, mortars, and small arms saved many lives. It also shocked all of us on the number of miles we were able to cover with the limited amount of maintenance we were able to perform. When coupled with infantry on the ground, the Bradley's performance in street fighting proved unparalleled, and it continues as the weapon system of choice in the Sunni Triangle.

GLOSSARY

A2C2	Air Assault Command and Control
AAM	Army Achievement Medal
AAR	after-action review
ABN	Airborne
ACR	Armored Cavalry Regiment
ADC-S	assistant division commander for support
ALOC	Administrative and Logistical Operations Center
AO	area of operations
APC	armored personnel carrier
ARCOM	Army Commendation Medal
Ba'athist Party	pan-Arab socialist party that Saddam Hussein had espoused
Badr Corps	armed Islamic organization
BC	battalion commander
BCT	Brigade Combat Team
BDA	battle damage assessment
BDU	battle dress uniform
BFT	Blue Force Tracker
BRT	Brigade Reconnaissance Team
BSA	Brigade Support Area
BUB	battle update briefing
CAR	combined arms rehearsal
CASH	Corps Area Support Hospital
CG	commanding general
CI	counter intelligence
CJCS	Chairman of the Joint Chiefs of Staff
CJTF	Coalition Joint Task Force
CKP	Communist Kurdish Party
CLS	Combat Life Saver
CMOC	Civil-Military Operations Center
Coax (có·ax)	coaxially mounted machine gun
COC	change of command
COSCOM	Corps Support Command
CP	command post
CPA	Coalition Provisional Authority
CQB	close-quarters battle

CQM	close-quarters marksmanship
CSC	Corps Support Command
CVC	combat vehicle crewman's helmet
DCU	desert combat uniform
DIVARTY	Division Artillery
D-Main	Division Main Headquarters
EMT	emergency medical treatment
EPW	enemy prisoner of war
ETS	end term of service
FAS	Forward Aid Station
FBCB2	Force XXI Battle Command, Brigade and Below
FOB	Forward Operating Base
Frago	fragmentary order
FSB	Forward Support Battalion
FSNCO	forward support noncommissioned officer
FSO	fire support officer
FTCP	Field Trains Command Post
H&I	harassing and interdicting fires
HE	high-explosive munitions
HET	heavy equipment transporter
HHC	Headquarters and Headquarters Company
HLZ	helicopter landing zone
HMMWV	high mobility, multipurpose wheeled vehicle (Humvee)
HUMINT	human intelligence
HVT	high-value target
ICDC	Iraqi Civil Defense Corps
IED	improvised explosive device
IGC	Iraqi Governing Council
IMT	individual movement techniques
IO	information operations
IPB	intelligence preparation of the battlefield
ISB	Intermediate Support Base
ISU	integrated sight unit
JAG	Judge Advocate General
JOC	Joint Operations Center
JRTC	Joint Readiness Training Center, Fort Polk, Louisiana
KDP	Kurdish Democratic Party
LD	line of departure
LOA	limit of advance
LOGPAC	logistical package

MEK	Mujahedin-e Khalq, an anticlerical organization exiled from Iran
MKT	mobile kitchen trailer
MOUT	military operations on urban terrain
MRE	meal, ready to eat
MSR	Main Supply Route
MTOE	modified table of organization and equipment
MWR	morale, welfare, and recreation
9 Line	standard medical evacuation request
NCO	noncommissioned officer
NGO	nongovernmental organization
NOD	night observation device
Noise-ex	noise generated by firing at unknown targets to suppress or intimidate the enemy
NTC	National Training Center, Fort Irwin, Calif.
NVGs	night vision goggles
ODA	Operational Detachment A
Op Order	operations order
OPD	officer professional development
OPLAN	operations plan
ORHA	Office of Reconstruction and Humanitarian Assistance
PCC	precombat checks
PCI	precombat inspections
Peshmerga	Kurdish fighters, literally "those who face death"
PIR	Parachute Infantry Regiment
POO	point of origin
Psyops	psychological operations
PT	physical training
PUK	Patriotic Union of Kurdistan
PVS	passive vision sight
PX	post exchange
QRF	Quick Reaction Force
RBA	Ranger body armor
ROE	rules of engagement
RPG	rocket-propelled grenade
RTO	radio telephone operator
S–1	personnel officer
S–2	intelligence officer
S–3	operations officer
S–4	supply officer
SAMS	School of Advanced Military Studies

SAW	squad automatic weapon
SCIRI	Supreme Council of the Islamic Revolution in Iraq
SEN	small extension node
SF	Special Forces
SINCGARS	Single-Channel Ground and Airborne Radio System
SIPR	Secure Internet Protocol Router
SOP	standard operating procedure
TAA	Tactical Assembly Area
TAC	Tactical Actions Center
TACSAT	tactical satellite
TACSOPs	tactical standard operating procedures
TAT	to accompany troops
THT	tactical HUMINT team
TOC	Tactical Operations Center
T-rats	tray rations
TTP	tactics, techniques, and procedures
UAV	unmanned aerial vehicle
UMCP	Unit Maintenance Collection Point
Wahabi	member of a strict Sunni Muslim sect
WMDs	weapons of mass destruction
XO	executive officer

INDEX